STUDY GUIDE

for use with

STATISTICAL TECHNIQUES IN BUSINESS AND ECONOMICS

Ninth Edition

Robert D. Mason
Douglas A. Lind
Both of the University of Toledo

IRWIN

Chicago • Bogotá • Boston • Buenos Aires • Caracas
London • Madrid • Mexico City • Sydney • Toronto

W9-APJ-008

© Richard D. Irwin, a Times Mirror Higher Education Group, Inc. company, 1967, 1970, 1974, 1978, 1982, 1986, 1990, 1993, and 1996

All rights reserved. No part of this publication may be reproduced, stored in a retrieval system, or transmitted, in any form or by any means, electronic, mechanical, photocopying, recording, or otherwise, without the prior written permission of the publisher.

Printed in the United States of America.

ISBN 0–256–17371–0

1 2 3 4 5 6 7 8 9 0 EB 2 1 0 9 8 7 6 5

Preface

This study guide is especially designed to accompany the Ninth Edition of *Statistical Techniques in Business and Economics* by Robert D. Mason and Douglas A. Lind. It can also be used alone, or as a companion to most other introductory statistics texts. It provides a valuable source of reinforcement for the material in the text. The chapters in the text and the study guide are parallel in topics, notation, and the numbering of formulas. The major features of the study guide include:

- **Chapter goals** are listed first. They stress the main concepts covered and the tasks students should be able to perform after having studied the chapter. It is recommended that students refer to the goals before reading the chapter to get an overview of the material to be studied and again after completing the chapter to confirm mastery of the material.

- Starting with Chapter 2, a brief Introduction follows the goals. In capsule form the material covered in previous chapters is tied with that covered in the current chapter, thus maintaining continuity throughout the book.

- Next there is a discussion of the relevant **statistical tools** described in the chapter.

- A **glossary** follows the chapter discussion. The glossary provides definitions of the key terms used in the chapter.

- **Chapter problems,** including solutions, come next. In this section the step-by-step method of solution is presented along with an interpretation of the results. The values are kept small to emphasize the concept.

- Following each chapter problem is an **exercise.** The student completes the exercise and checks the answer in the answer section at the end of the guide. Thus the student can check their comprehension of the material as they progress through the chapter.

- Finally, starting with Chapter 2, **chapter assignments** cover the entire chapter and are intended to be completed outside the classroom. Part I of the assignment consists of multiple-choice questions, Part II is fill-in the blank, and Part III is problems, with space for students to show essential work. The pages are perforated, so that assignments can be torn out and handed in to the instructor for grading.

Students will attain the most benefit if they study the textbook first, and then read the corresponding chapter in the study guide. We wish to thank Raymond Pohlman for checking the solutions to the problems, and Wendy McGuire of Santa Fe Community College for her careful review of the manuscript.

Douglas A. Lind
Robert D. Mason

CONTENTS

1

WHAT IS STATISTICS?

CHAPTER GOALS

After completing this chapter, you will be able to:

1. Define what is meant by statistics.
2. Cite some uses of statistics in business and other areas.
3. Explain what is meant by descriptive and inferential statistics.
4. Cite some of the sources of business data.
5. Explain the purpose of a questionnaire.
6. Cite the differences between nominal, ordinal, interval, and ratio levels of measurement.

Introduction

No doubt you have noticed the large number of facts and figures, often referred to as *statistics*, that appear in the newspaper and magazines you read, the television you watch (especially sporting events), and in the grocery stores where you shop.

A single figure is called a **statistic**. The largest paid circulation for a consumer magazine is Readers Digest, with an annual paid circulation of 17,900,000. That figure is a **statistic**. If we cite the collection of circulation figures, such as *Ebony* (1,250,000), *Business Week* (845,000), and *Newsweek* (2,950,000) the collection is called **statistics** (plural). Citing a few other examples: 455 out of every 100,000 Americans are in prison. The number 455 is a statistic. There are 20,000 men who are members of Bald-Headed Men of America, headquarters in Moorehead, North Carolina. That one statistic might be a percent—such as 2.2 percent of our labor force are employed in farming. Finally, only 19 percent of the person's who responded to a questionnaire thought that members of congress have good moral and ethical standards.

As a result, you may think of statistics simply as a collection of numerical information. However, statistics has a much broader meaning. We shall define **statistics** as *the science of collecting, organizing, presenting, analyzing, and interpreting numerical data for the purpose of making better decisions.*

Note in this definition of statistics cited above that the initial step is the collection of pertinent information. This information may come from newspapers or magazines, the company's human relations director, the local, state, or federal government, universities,

nonprofit organizations, the United Nations, and so on. A few publications of the federal government and others are:

- *Statistical Abstract of the United States,* published annually by the U.S. Department of Commerce.
- *Monthly Labor Review*, published monthly by the U.S. Department of Labor.
- *Survey of Current Business*, published monthly by the U.S. Department of Commerce.
- *Social Security Bulletin*, published annually by the U.S. Social Security Administration.
- *Crime in the United States*, published annually by the U.S. Federal Bureau of Investigation.
- *Vital Statistics of the United States*, published annually by the National Center for Health Statistics.

If the information is not available from company records or public sources, it may be necessary to conduct a **survey**. For example, the A.C. Nielsen Company surveys about 1,200 homes on an ongoing basis to determine which TV programs are being watched, and Gallup surveys registered voters before an election to estimate the percent that will vote for a certain candidate. These firms also sample the population regarding food preference, what features in automobiles are desirable, and what appliances consumers will most likely purchase next year. *Fortune* surveyed 8,000 senior executives, outside directors, and financial analysts in 307 companies to find the ten most admired firms, and the least admired firms. Each executive was asked to rate a list of firms on eight attributes, namely quality of management; quality of products or services; long-term investment value; financial soundness; ability to attract, develop and keep talented people; responsibility to the community and the environment; and wise use of corporate assets. Each attribute was rated on a scale of zero (poor) to ten (excellent). The ten most admired companies are:

RANK	LAST YEAR	COMPANY	SCORE
1	1	**Merck** Pharmaceuticals	9.02
2	2	**Rubbermaid** Rubber and plastic products	8.66
3	4	**Wal-Mart Stores** Retailing	8.58
4	10	**Liz Claiborne** Apparel	8.43
5	20	**Levi Strauss Associates** Apparel	8.26
6	8	**Johnson & Johnson** Pharmaceuticals	8.22
7	6	**Coca-Cola** Beverages	8.13
8	6	**3M** Scientific and photo equip.	8.12
9	5	**PepsiCo** Beverages	8.00
9	3	**Procter & Gamble** Soaps, cosmetics	8.00

Questionnaires are used to gather information in many different areas. For examples, here is a summary of the 1995 Office Ethics Survey cited in the Sarasota (Florida) Herald-Tribune.

Ethics Survey

Here are highlights of the Nan DeMars 1995 Office Ethics Survey, sponsored by Professional Secretaries International. Survey results were based on 2,000 responses from throughout the United States and Canada:

■ **Misdeeds:** More than 17 percent of secretaries said they had notarized something without witnessing the signature. Thirty percent said they had seen others do that. Nearly 11 percent said they had removed or destroyed damaging information. Nearly 20 percent said they had observed that behavior in others.

■ **Harassment:** Nearly a third said they had experienced sexual harassment. More than 37 percent said they had seen others being harassed. More than 55 percent said they had experienced verbal abuse, and 64.3 percent said they had seen others verbally abused.

■ **Sharing confidential information:** More than 27 percent said they had shared information about hiring, firing and layoffs. Nearly two-thirds said they had

observed others sharing such information. Only 7 percent said they had shared company or business trade secrets, but nearly a quarter of those surveyed said they had observed others sharing such information.

Descriptive and Inferential Statistics

The definition of statistics referred to "collecting, organizing, and presenting numerical information." Data stored in a computer's memory or in a filing cabinet are of little value. Techniques are available that organize this information in a more meaningful form. Such aids are called **descriptive statistics**. A statistical tool designed to describe the movement of a series of numbers over a long period of time—such as production, imports, wages, and stock market trends—is called a *line chart*. The line chart at the top of page 3, for example, depicts the upward movement of the Dow Jones average of 30 industries since 1987.

Notice how easy it is to describe the trend of common stock prices. The prices of the 30 industrials, as represented by the Dow-Jones Industrial Average, increased steadily from about 1500 in 1987 to over 4660 in July of 1995.

Another descriptive measure is an average. Some examples of averages include:

- The average savings yield on 3-year certificates of deposit at the 18 Toledo-area banks and savings and loans was 5.71 percent in July 1995.
- The average price per barrel of West Texas intermediate crude oil was $18.52 in June 1995. This is down from $19.05 in June 1993.
- The median (an average) age for men at the time of their first marriage is 26.1 years, and 23.9 years for women, according to the Bureau of the Census.
- The average length of a hospital stay for someone over 65 years of age is 8.9 days.
- The team batting average of the Cleveland Indians is .294 after the first 65 games of the 1995 Major League Baseball season.

A second aspect of statistics is called **inferential statistics**. This branch of statistics deals with problems requiring the use of a sample to infer something about the population. A population might consist of all 3,336,000 people in Puerto Rico, or all 453,588 people in Wyoming. Or, a population might consist of all the teams in the Canadian Football League, the PE ratios for all chemical stocks, or all the banks in the United States. A **population** is the total collection of individuals, objects, or things under consideration. A population does not have to be large. For example, the population might consist of the six radio stations in the Chicago market with a hard rock format, the

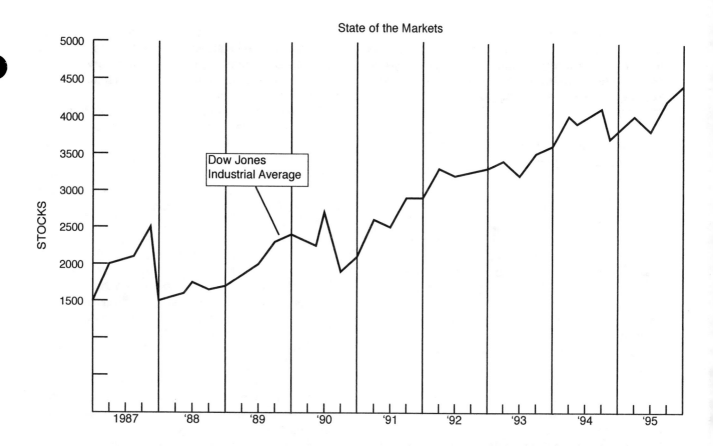

State of the Markets

Dow Jones
Industrial Average

nine fast food restaurants in Warren, PA, or the six oil paintings owned by a particular art collector.

A **sample** is that part, or portion, of a population that is actually being studied. A sample might consist of 5,290 persons out of the 3,336,000 persons in Puerto Rico, 12 headlights selected for a life test, or the three scoops of grain selected at random to be tested for moisture content from a 15 ton truckload of grain. If we found that the three scoops of grain consisted of 1.50 percent moisture, we would infer that all the grain in the 15-ton load had 1.50 percent moisture. We start our discussion of inferential statistics in Chapter 5.

Levels of Measurement

Data may be classified into four categories or levels of measurement. These categories are nominal, ordinal, interval, and ratio.

Nominal Level

When data can only be classified into categories, we refer to it as being **nominal** level of measurement. At this level the categories have no particular order or rank and are **mutually exclusive,** meaning that the characteristic of interest can be tallied into only one category. For example, the Office of Special Educa-

tion, U.S. Department of Education gave these counts of the major type of handicap for children 3 to 21 years old who were in special educational programs.

Type of Handicapped	Numbers Served
Visual impairments	23,000
Serious emotional impairment	382,000
Speech impairments	974,000
Deaf-blindness	2,000
Learning disabilities	2,060,000
Mental retardation	565,000
Hearing impairments	58,000
Orthopedic impairments	48,000
All others	140,000
Total	4,252,000

The above data is nominal level of measurement because it can only be classified into categories and it is immaterial what order the type of handicap is listed. Mental retardation could be listed first, serious emotional impairment second, and so on. The categories are mutually exclusive meaning that the most severe type of handicap a child has can be counted into only one category. And such categories are said to be **exhaustive,** meaning that a handicapped child enrolled in the program must appear in one of the categories. Chapter 14 on Chi-Square introduces a statistical technique that can be applied to nominal level data.

Ordinal Level

Ordinal level of measurement implies some sort of ranking. The Department of the Army gave these counts of females on active duty.

	Number
Commissioned officers	11,959
Warrant officers	505
Enlisted personnel	71,119

It is implied that female warrant officers are "higher" in rank than female enlisted personnel. And, commissioned officers are ranked higher than warrant officers. Further, the categories are mutually exclusive meaning that a female on active duty can only be counted in one category. She cannot be a commissioned officer and an enlisted personnel at the same time. Also, the categories are exhaustive meaning that a female *must* appear in one of the categories. Chapter 15 deals with ordinal level of measurement.

Interval and Ratio Level

If we are concerned with data that has some sort of physical unit of measurement, such as length in terms of meters or feet; time in years, months, or seconds; money in dollars or cents; weight in pounds; temperature in degrees Fahrenheit; and so on, the data is said to be on an **interval scale.** Note for interval level of measurement the exact difference between numbers such as 6 inches and 7 inches is 1 inch. And, the exact difference between 7 inches and 8 inches is also 1 inch. Likewise, the difference in years between the first grade and the third grade is the same as the difference between the 10th grade and the 12th grade.

If our data is on an interval level scale, we can legitimately use operations of arithmetic such as addition, subtraction, and square roots. We will encounter these operations starting in Chapter 2 which require interval level of measurement.

For data having an absolute zero point it is said that the measurement is on a **ratio scale.** Some statisticians claim that any differences between interval and ratio level of measurement are purely academic. To circumvent these arguments, we will say something like this: "the level of measurement is at least on an interval scale."

In summary of the four levels of measurement, it is essential that we know what level our data is so that the correct statistical tools can be applied. Nominal level data is the simplest level. Data is tallied into the categories such as Democrat, Republican, or Independent. The categories have no particular order and are mutually exclusive. This means that an observation can only be put in on category. The categories are exhaustive signifying that each observation must go in one category.

Measures of central tendency and dispersion, covered in Chapters 3 and 4, cannot be computed for the nominal level of measurement. However, the sign test and chi-square (Chapter 14 and 15) can be applied to this level of measurement. Ordinal level of measurement possess all the characteristics of nominal level but the data can be ranked. Interval and ratio level measurement is the next higher level possessing the characteristics of nominal and ordinal level measurement. In addition, these levels are concerned with measurable characteristics such as time, length, speed, age, and weight. If we have this level we can compute measures of central tendency and dispersion in the data, develop confidence intervals and tests of hypotheses and do regression and correlation studies, as described in Chapters 12 and 13.

GLOSSARY

Statistics—Techniques used to facilitate the collection, organization, presentation, analysis, and interpretation of numerical data to make better decisions.

Descriptive statistics—Techniques used to describe data that has been collected.

Inferential statistics—An estimation or generalization about a population based on sample information.

Population—The total collection of individuals, objects, or things under consideration.

Sample—A portion or subset of the population.

Nominal scale—Data that are organized into categories the order of which is not important.

Ordinal scale—Data or categories that can be ranked, that is, one category is higher than another.

Interval scale—The distance between numbers is a known and constant size, but the zero point is arbitrary.

Ratio scale—The data has a natural zero point and the differences between values are meaningful.

Mutually exclusive—If an object, individual, or item is classified into one category it is excluded from all others.

Exhaustive—Each object, individual, or item must be classified into one of the categories.

CHAPTER ASSIGNMENT 1
What is Statistics?

Name _____ Section _____ Score _____

Part I Select the correct answer and write the appropriate letter in the space provided.

___ 1. The collection of all possible individuals, objects, or measurements is called
    a. a sample.
    b. a ratio measurement.
    c. a population.
    d. an inference.

___ 2. Techniques used to describe the data that have been collected are called
    a. populations.
    b. samples.
    c. inferential statistics.
    d. descriptive statistics.

___ 3. An individual, measurement, or object that can appear in only one category is said to be
    a. mutually exclusive.
    b. exhaustive.
    c. inferential.
    d. descriptive.

___ 4. Techniques used to determine something about a population, based on a sample, are called
    a. descriptive statistics.
    b. inferential statistics.
    c. populations.
    d. samples.

___ 5. The Equal Employment Opportunity Act requires that employees be classified by national origin. What level of measurement is this classification?
    a. nominal.
    b. ordinal.
    c. interval.
    d. ratio.

___ 6. In your history course last semester you received the following scores (out of 100) on three tests: 88, 96, 82, and 85. This is an example of which level of measurement?
    a. nominal.
    b. ordinal.
    c. interval.
    d. ratio.

___ 7. The faculty at most universities are classified as Professor, Associate Professor, Assistant Professor, and Instructor. What level of measurement is this classification?
    a. nominal.
    b. ordinal.
    c. interval.
    d. ratio.

___ 8. Which level of measurement has a meaningful zero point?
    a. nominal.
    b. ordinal.
    c. interval.
    d. ratio.

___ 9. The nominal level of data requires the categories to
    a. not include numbers.
    b. be exhaustive.
    c. include zero.
    d. be ranked.

___ 10. A difference between the interval scale and the ratio scale is
    a. the interval scale cannot be ranked.
    b. the zero point on the interval scale is arbitrary.
    c. the ratio scale does not meet the exhaustive criteria.
    d. the interval scale does not meet the mutually exclusive criteria.

Part II Fill in the blanks with the correct answer.

11. List the four levels of measurement.
    a. _____
    b. _____
    c. _____
    d. _____

12. The categories are _____ if each, item or individual must fit into one of the categories.

13. The categories are _____ when each object, item, or individual is classified into one category it is excluded from all others.

14. _____ is a body of techniques used to collect, organize, analyze, present and interpret data to make better decisions.

15. Techniques used to describe the data that has been collected are called _____.

2

SUMMARIZING DATA: FREQUENCY DISTRIBUTIONS AND GRAPHIC PRESENTATION

CHAPTER GOALS

After completing this chapter, you will be able to:

1. Organize raw data into a frequency distribution.
2. Draw a histogram, a frequency polygon, and cumulative frequency polygon.
3. Develop a stem-and-leaf chart.
4. Summarize the numerical information using charts, such as line charts, bar charts, and pie charts.

Introduction

This chapter begins our study of **descriptive statistics**. Recall from Chapter 1 that when using descriptive statistics we merely describe a set of data. For example, suppose we want to describe the entry level salary for a select group of professions. We find that the entry level salary for accountants is $28,000, for systems analysts $30,000, for infectious disease specialists $70,000, and so on. This unorganized data provides little insight into the pattern of entry salaries making conclusions difficult.

This chapter presents a technique that is used to organize raw data into some meaningful form. It is called a **frequency distribution**. Then the frequency distribution will be portrayed in the form of a frequency polygon, a histogram, or a cumulative frequency polygon.

Frequency Distributions

A **frequency distribution** is a grouping of data into categories, showing the number of observations in each category. As noted, a frequency distribution is used to summarize large amounts of data into some meaningful form.

The steps to follow in developing a frequency distribution are:

1. Decide on the number of classes or the class interval.
2. Tally the observations into the appropriate classes.

3. Count the number of tallies in each class.

As a sample example, suppose the lengths of service, in years, of a sample of nine employees are:

4	3	2	6	6
5	8	4	4	

The nine observations are referred to as **raw data.** To organize the lengths of service into a frequency distribution we first set up groups called **classes.** We decided to use classes 1 up to 3, 3 up to 5, and so on. Then we **tally** the lengths of service into the appropriate classes. We count the number of tallies in each class as follows:

Lengths of service	Tallies	Number of employees
1 up to 3 years	/	1
3 up to 5 years	////	4
5 up to 7 years	///	3
7 up to 9 years	/	1
Total		9

How many classes should there be? A common guideline is from 5 to 15. Having too few or too many classes gives little insight into the data. The size of the class interval may be a value such as 3, 5, 10, 15, 20, 50, 100, 1,000, and so on. The size, or width, of the **class interval** can be approximated by the formula:

$$\text{Class interval} = \frac{\text{highest value} - \text{lowest value}}{\text{number of classes}}$$

Each class has a lower class limit and an upper class limit. The lower limit of the first class is usually slightly below the smallest value.

In the previous example, the smallest number of years of service is 2. Therefore, we selected 1, which is slightly below 2, as the lower limit of the first class. The lower limit of the second class is 3 years, and so on.

The number of tallies that occurs in each class is called the **class frequency**. The class frequency of the lowest class is 1. For the next higher class it is 4.

The **class midpoint** divides a class into two equal parts. In the example, the class midpoint of the 5 up to 7 class is 6 found by (5 + 7)/2. The **class interval** is the distance between the lower limit of two consecutive classes. It is 2 found by subtracting 1 (the lower limit of the first class) from 3 (the lower limit of the second class).

When constructing frequency distributions follow these guidelines:

1. Whenever possible, the width of the class intervals should be equal.
2. Avoid classes that overlap, such as 4–6 and 6–8. We would not be able to determine in which class to tally 6.
3. Avoid open-ended classes, such as "over 6."

Stem-and-Leaf Displays

This technique is a combination of sorting and graphing. It is an alternative to the frequency distribution for highlighting the pattern in the data. The first step is to locate the largest value and the smallest value. This will provide the range of the stem values. The **stem** is the leading digit or digits of the number, and the **leaf** is the trailing digit. For example, the number 15 has a stem value of 1 and a leaf value of 5. For another problem the number 231 has a stem value of 23 and a leaf value of 1.

The following are the amounts spent (in dollars) in the grocery store by a sample of 12 people.

12 28 32 24 17 06
34 18 22 42 36 26

The range of values is from $6 to $42. The first digit of each number is the stem and the second digit is the leaf. The first customer (upper left) spent $12. Hence, the stem value is 1 and the leaf value is 2. The completed display after each trailing digit is arranged from low to high follows.

Leading Digit	Trailing Digit
0	6
1	278
2	2468
3	246
4	2

Graphically Portraying a Frequency Distribution

To get reader attention a frequency distribution is often portrayed graphically in a histogram or some other type of chart.

Histogram

The simplest type of a statistical chart is called a **histogram**. A histogram employs bars, whose heights correspond to the number of frequencies in each class. For the length of service for the sample of nine employees a histogram would appear as:

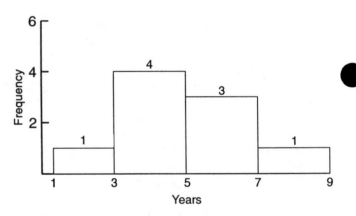

Note that to plot the bar for the 5 up to 7 years, for example, we drew lines vertically from 5 and from 7 years to 3 employees on the Y-axis and then connected the end points by a straight line.

Frequency Polygon

A second type of chart used to portray a frequency distribution is the **frequency polygon**. For the frequency polygon, the assumption is that the observations in any class interval are represented by the class midpoint. A dot is placed at the class midpoint opposite the number of frequencies in that class. For the distribution of years of service, the first plot is made

10

by going to 2 years on the *X*-axis (the midpoint) and then going vertically on the *Y*-axis to 1 and placing a dot. This process is continued for all classes. Then the dots are connected in order.

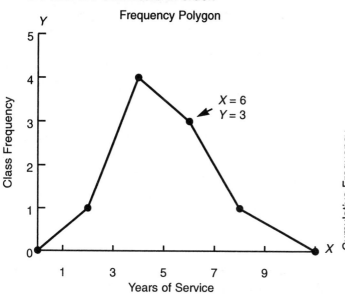

Normal practice is to anchor the frequency polygon to the *X*-axis. This is accomplished by extending the lines to the midpoint of the class below the lowest class (0) and to the midpoint of the class above the highest class (10).

Cumulative Frequency Polygon

A **less-than-cumulative frequency polygon** reports the number and percent of observations that occur less than a given value. Before we can draw a cumulative frequency polygon we must convert the frequency distribution to a cumulative frequency distribution. To construct a less-than-cumulative frequency distribution we add the frequencies from the lowest class to the highest class.

Number of Years of Service	Class Frequency		Cumulative Frequency
1 up to 3 years	1		1
3 up to 5 years	4	ADD	5
	↓	DOWN	
5 up to 7 years	3		8
7 up to 9 years	1		9

The cumulative frequencies are plotted on the vertical axis (*Y*-axis) and the lengths of service on the *Y*-axis.

It may be helpful to plot the cumulative frequencies on the left side of the vertical axis and the percent of the total on the right side as shown in the following polygon.

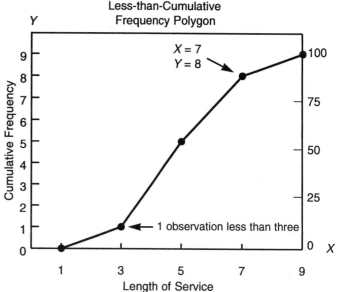

Note that the years of service are scaled on the *X*-axis and the cumulative frequencies on the *Y*-axis. Thus, 8 employees had less than 7 years of service.

A **more-than-cumulative polygon** is plotted in a similar fashion—except we "add up" the frequencies and plot the cumulative frequencies on the *Y*-axis and the lower limit of each class on the *X*-axis. There is an example of more-than-cumulative frequency polygon in the **Chapter Problem** section.

Other Graphical Techniques

Several other charts are discussed in this section. Each is designed to emphasize certain characteristics in the data. The **simple line chart** displays information over a period of time. The **bar chart** is more often used to display categories. In the line chart the values for various periods are connected by a line. For a bar chart, the data for each period are represented by bars. As an example, shown below is the recurring profit (in billions of yen) of the Matsushita Electric Industrial Co., Ltd. since 1992.

Simple Line Chart

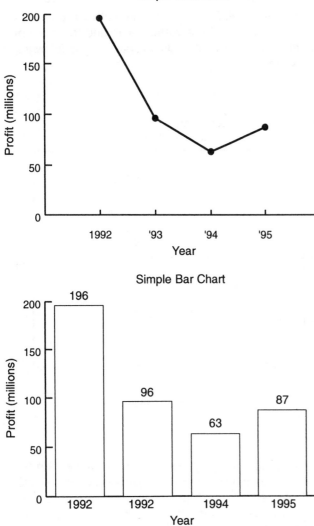

Simple Bar Chart

The increases are plotted in the form of bars to the right of the origin (0) and the decreases to the left of 0.

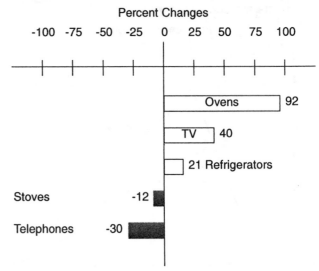

Another popular chart is a **pie chart**. Its purpose is to show the relative comparison between parts of a total. Suppose we want to show where our tax dollar goes.

Percent
20	for roads
40	for education
15	for welfare
18	for salaries
7	for miscellaneous (travel, etc.)

After drawing a circle (pie) we put 0 on the top and go around the circle in increments of 5.

As the name implies, a **two-directional bar chart** presents such changes as profit or loss over a period of time. As an illustration, here are the percent increases and decreases in sales for selected electronic items from 1987 to 1995.

Item	Percent change
TV sets	+40
Stoves	−12
Microwave ovens	+92
Telephones	−30
Refrigerators	+21

We organize the increases from high to low

	% Increase
Microwave ovens	92
TV sets	40
Refrigerators	21

Then we rank the decreases from low to high

	% Decrease
Stoves	−12
Telephones	−30

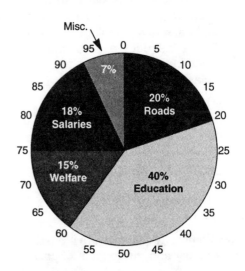

To plot the percent going for roads we draw a line from 0 to the center of the circle and another line from the center to 20. Then 20 + 40 = 60 and this area represents the amount going for education. This process is continued for the remaining items.

GLOSSARY

Frequency distribution—A grouping of numerical data into categories showing the number of observations in each category.

Histogram—The frequency of each class is represented by a rectangle or bar. The values of each variable are scaled along the horizontal axis and the frequency of occurrence in each class along the vertical axis.

Frequency polygon—The frequency of each class is represented by a dot above the class midpoint. The dots are then connected by line segments. The values of each variable are scaled along the horizontal axis and the frequency of occurrence in each class along the vertical axis.

Chart—A pictorial presentation of numerical information.

Cumulative frequency polygon—A chart to portray the cumulative frequency distribution. There are two forms—a "less-than" and a "more-than" cumulative frequency polygon. They are often referred to as "ogives."

Stem-and-leaf display—A method for organizing data that divides each numerical value into a "stem" and a "leaf" for ease of sorting.

Note that on the first page of this chapter there was a listing of the chapter goals. These goals were followed by a brief discussion of the chapter highlights, and a glossary of terms. Now comes several problems and the solution of each of the problems. They are intended to show you how to construct a frequency distribution, how to draw a histogram, and so on. The following problem and solution concentrates on how to construct a frequency distribution.

CHAPTER PROBLEMS

Problem 1

A sample of 30 homes sold during the past year by Gomminger Realty Company was selected for study. (Selling price is reported in thousands of dollars.)

$76	$94	$71	Low ————	$67	$80	High ———→	$78
80	82	67		88	72		99
85	76		84	82	98		80
72	82		90	95	94		78
91	70	82		86	78		77

Organize these data into a frequency distribution and interpret your results.

Solution

First, observe that the home with the lowest selling price was $67 thousand and the highest was $99 thousand. We decided to let $65 be the lower limit of the first class and the class interval to be $5. Thus, the first class will be $65 up to $70 and the second class $70 up to $75, and so on.

Next, the selling prices are tallied into each of the classes. The first home sold for $76 thousand, therefore the price is tallied into the $75 thousand up to $80 thousand class. The procedure is continued, resulting in the following frequency distribution.

Selling Price ($000)	Tallies	Number of Homes
$65 up to $70	//	2
$70 up to $75	////	4
$75 up to $80	//// /	6
$80 up to $85	//// ///	8
$85 up to $90	///	3
$90 up to $95	////	4
$95 up to $100	///	3
		30

Observe that the largest concentration of the data is in the $80 up to $85 thousand class. As noted before, the class frequencies are the number of observations in each class. For the $65 up to $70 class the class frequency is 2, and for the $70 up to $75 class the class frequency is 4. This indicates that two homes sold in the $65 up to $70 thousand price range and four in the $70 up to $75 thousand range.

It is also clear that the interval between the lowest and highest selling price in each category is $5 thousand. How would we classify a home selling for $70 thousand? It would fall in the second class. Homes selling for $65,000 up through $69,999.99 go in the first class, but a home selling for more than this amount goes in the next class. So the $70,000 selling prices puts the home in the second class.

The class midpoint is determined by going halfway between the lower limit and the upper limit of the class. Halfway between $65 and $70 is $67.5, the class midpoint

---

Exercise 1

Check your answers against those in the ANSWER section.

This is the first in a series of exercises designed to check your comprehension of the material just presented. It is suggested that you work all parts of the exercise. Then check your answers against those given in the answer section of this study guide.

The Jansen Motor Company has developed a new engine designed to further reduce gasoline consumption. The new engine was put in 20 mid-sized cars and the number of miles per gallon recorded (to the nearest mile per gallon).

29	32	19	30	40
27	28	21	36	20
27	18	32	37	29
30	23	25	19	30

Develop a frequency distribution. (Use a class interval of 10, with 15 as the lower limit of the first class.

Problem 2

Based on the information from Gomminger Realty in Problem 1, develop a histogram.

Solution

The class frequencies are scaled on the vertical axis (Y-axis) and the selling price on the horizontal (X-axis). A vertical line is drawn from the two class limits of a class to a height corresponding to the number of frequencies. The tops of the lines are then connected.

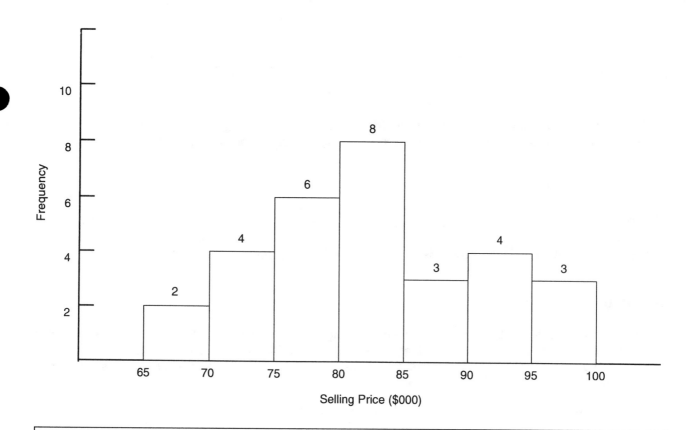

Selling Price ($000)

Exercise 2

Check your answers against those in the ANSWER section.
Use the Jansen Motor Company data in Exercise 1 to construct a histogram.

Problem 3

Based on the information from Problems 1 and 2, construct a frequency polygon.

Solution

The class frequencies are scaled on the vertical axis (Y-axis) and the class midpoints along the horizontal axis (X-axis). The first plot is at the point 67.5 on the X-axis and 2 on the Y-axis. To complete the frequency polygon, the midpoint of the class below the first class and above the last class are added. This allows the graph to be anchored to the X-axis at zero frequencies.

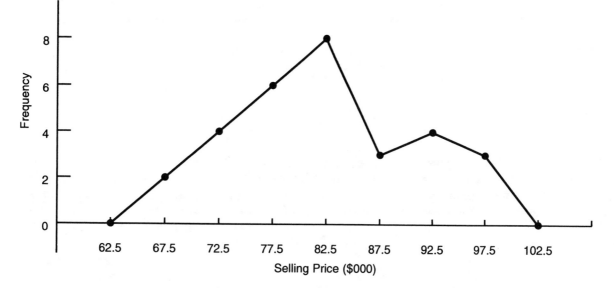

Selling Price ($000)

┌───┐

Exercise 3

Check your answers against those in the ANSWER section.
Use the Jansen Motor Company data in Exercise 1 to construct a frequency polygon.

Problem 4

Based on the information in the Problems 1, 2, and 3, develop a stem-and-leaf chart.

Solution

As noted, an observation is broken down into a leading digit and a trailing digit. The leading digit is called the **stem**, and the trailing digit the **leaf.** The first home sold for $76,000. The $000 were dropped, so the stem value is 7 and the leaf value is 6. The actual data ranges from $67 up to $99 so the stem values range from 6 to 9 using an increment of 10.

Stem	Leaf
6	77
7	0122667888
8	00022224568
9	0144589

The display shows that there is a concentration of data in the $70 up to $80 and the $80 up to $90 groups.

Exercise 4

Check your answers against those in the ANSWER section.
Use the Jansen Motor Company data in Exercise 1 to construct a stem-and-leaf chart.

Problem 5

Based on the information in Problem 1, construct a less-than-cumulative frequency polygon.

a. Estimate the price below which 75 percent of the homes were sold.
b. Estimate the number of homes sold for less than $72,000.

Solution

A less-than-cumulative frequency distribution is constructed by using the class limits. The first step is to determine the number of observations "less than" the upper limit of each class. Two homes were sold for less than $70 and six were sold for between $65 and $75 thousand. The six is found by adding the two that sold for $65 to $70 thousand and the four that sold for between $70 and $75 thousand. The cumulative frequency for the fourth class is obtained by adding the frequencies of the first four classes. The total is 20, found by 2 + 4 + 6 + 8. The less-than-cumulative frequency distribution would appear as:

Class limits ($000)	Class frequency	Cumulative frequency
$65 up to $70	2	2
$70 up to $75	4	6
$75 up to $80	6	12
$80 up to $85	8	20
$85 up to $90	3	23
$90 up to $95	4	27
$95 up to $100	3	30

To construct a less-than-cumulative frequency polygon the upper limits are scaled on the X-axis and the cumulative frequencies on the Y-axis. The cumulative percents are placed along the right-hand scale (vertical) scale. The first plot is $X = 70$ and $Y = 2$. The next plot is 75 and 6. As shown, the points are connected with straight lines (See the following chart.)

Less-Than-Cumulative Polygon

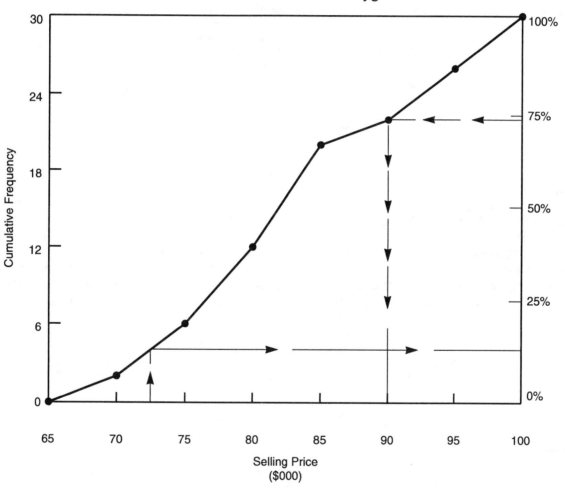

To estimate the amount for which less than 75 percent of the homes were sold, a horizontal line is drawn from the cumulative percent (75) over to the cumulative frequency polygon. At the intersection, a line is drawn down to the X-axis giving the approximate selling price. It is about $88 thousand. Thus, about 75 percent of the homes sold for $88,000 or less.

To estimate the percent of the homes that sold for more than $72,000 first locate the value of $72 on the X-axis. Next, draw a vertical line from the X-axis at 72 up to the graph. Draw a line horizontally to the cumulative percent axis and read the cumulative percent. It is about 12%. Hence, we conclude that about 12 percent of the homes were sold for less than $72,000.

●

Exercise 5

Check your answers against those in the ANSWER section.

Use the Jansen Motor Company data in Exercise 1 to construct a less-than-cumulative frequency polygon. (a) Estimate the percent of the automobiles getting less than 30 miles per gallon. (b) Twenty percent of the automobiles obtain how many miles per gallon or less?

Problem 6

The percentage of disposable income (disposable income is the amount of income left after taxes) spent for groceries for the period from 1975 to 1995 is shown below. Draw a line chart to depict the trend.

Year	Percent of disposable income spent on groceries
1975	13.0
1980	12.3
1985	11.2
1990	10.1
1995	9.5

●

Solution

Time (five year intervals in this problem) is scaled on the horizontal axis, and the percent of disposable income spent for groceries on the vertical axis. Note that the vertical axis is broken. That is, some of the values are omitted. In this case the first value reported is 13.0%. The first plot therefore, is at 1975 and 13.0%. To plot move vertically from 1975 to 13.0% and place a dot. The next plot is 1980 and 12.3%. Continue this process for the remaining three periods. The dots are then connected with straight lines. What information does the chart convey? It appears we are spending a smaller percent of disposable income for groceries.

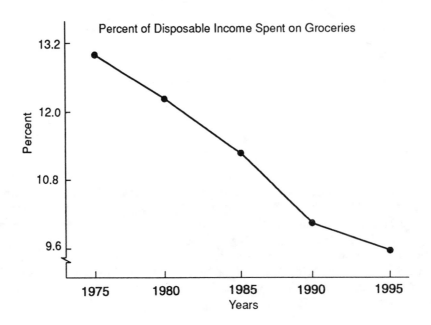

Exercise 6

Check your answers against those in the ANSWER section.

The expenditures on research and development for the Hennen Manufacturing Company are given below. Construct a simple line chart. (It is suggested the Y-axis be broken from $0 to $80.)

Year	Expenditure ($000)
1989	94
1990	103
1991	115
1992	145
1993	175
1994	203
1995	190

Problem 7

Refer to Problem 6. Develop a simple bar chart for the percent of disposable income spent for groceries.

Solution

The usual practice is to scale time along the horizontal axis. The height of the bars corresponds to percent of disposable income spent for groceries. To form the first bar, draw parallel vertical lines from 1975 up to 13.0%. Draw a line parallel to the X-axis at 13.0% to connect the lines. This process is continued for the other periods. The interpretation of the chart is the same as **Problem 6**, we are spending a smaller and smaller proportion of disposable income for groceries. Note that there is a small space between the bars. For a histogram there is no space between the bars.

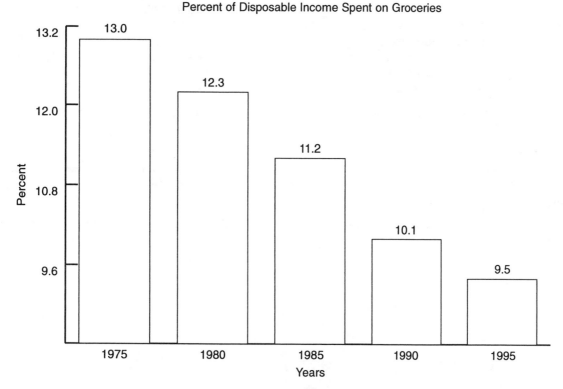

Percent of Disposable Income Spent on Groceries

Exercise 7

Check your answers against those in the ANSWER section.

Use the Hennen Manufacturing data of Exercise 6 to construct a simple bar chart.

Problem 8

A comparison of selected earnings for the first quarters of 1988 and 1996 of the Moon Petroleum Corporation is to be made. The amounts are:

Earnings	First Quarter Ended March 31	
	1996	1988
Selling, and other operating costs (millions)	$220.7	$165.3
Income before taxes (millions)	$789.0	$938.6
Interest and other income (millions)	$ 40.7	$ 15.9
Dividends per share	$0.55	$0.375
Net income per share	$3.05	$3.37

There is interest only in portraying the percent changes from 1988 to 1996.

Depict the percent changes for each of the selected items in the form of a two-directional bar chart.

Solution

The percent change from 1988 to 1996 for each of the items is shown in the following table. The percent change for selling and other operating costs is +33.5%, found by ($220.7 − $165.3)/$165.3.

	Percent Change from 1988 to 1992
Selling and other operating costs	+ 33.5%
Income before taxes	− 15.9%
Interest and other income	+156.0%
Dividends per share	+ 46.7%
Net income per share	− 9.5%

As noted previously, the usual practice is to arrange the increases in descending order and the decreases in ascending order.

Increases		Decreases	
Interest and other income	156.0%	Net income per share	− 9.5%
Dividends per share	46.7%	Income before taxes	−15.9%
Selling costs	33.5%		

The percent increases from 1988 to 1996 are plotted first to the right of the centerline of 0. The percent decreases are plotted to the left of the centerline.

20

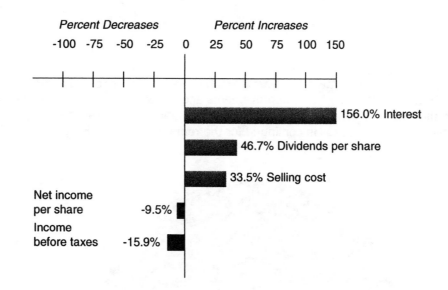

Percent Decreases   Percent Increases

-100 -75 -50 -25   0   25   50   75   100 150

156.0% Interest

46.7% Dividends per share

33.5% Selling cost

Net income
per share   -9.5%

Income
before taxes   -15.9%

Exercise 8

Check your answers against those in the ANSWER section.

A real estate company is studying the changes in the type of living quarters in a large city. A sample of 800 family units in 1984 and 1996 yielded the following results:

Type of Living Quarters	Frequency 1996	1984
High rise apartments	210	200
Multiple family house	260	240
Single family house	270	320
Mobile home	60	40
Total	800	800

Depict the percent changes from 1984 to 1996 for the four types of living quarters in the form of a two-directional bar chart.

Problem 9

The purpose of home equity loans by the Home Bank and the percent of each type of loan relative to the total is shown below:

Loan Purpose	Percent of Total	Cumulative Percent
Home improvement	32%	32%
Debt Consolidation	30	62
Car Purchase	11	73
Education	10	83
Other	9	92
Investments	8	100

Portray the home equity loans information in the form of a pie chart.

Solution

The first step is to draw a circle. Next draw a line from 0 to the center of the circle and another from the center of the circle to 32%. Adding the 32% for home improvements and the 30% for debt consolidation gives 62%. A line is drawn from the center to 62%. The area between 32% and 62% represents the percent of equity loans for debt consolidation. The process is continued for the remaining cumulative percents.

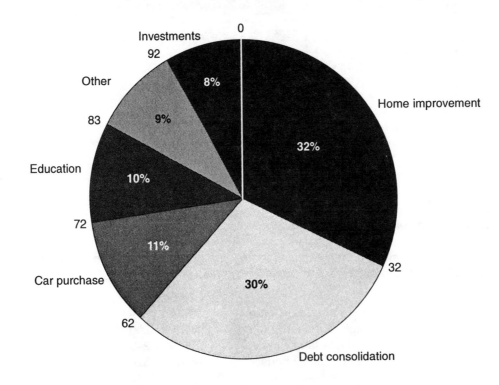

Exercise 9

Check your answers against those in the ANSWER section.

New cars sold in the United States during the year are classified by manufacturer.

Manufacturer	Cars sold (Millions)
General Motors	3.2
Ford	1.8
Chrysler	2.5
Foreign	2.5

Portray these data in the form of a pie chart.

CHAPTER ASSIGNMENT 2
Summarizing Data: Frequency Distributions and Graphic Presentation

Name _____ Section _____ Score _____

Part I Select the correct answer and write the appropriate letter in the space provided.

___ 1. A grouping of data into categories giving the number of observations in each category is called a(an)
    a. bar chart.
    b. frequency distribution.
    c. pie chart.
    d. cumulative frequency distribution.

___ 2. The distance between the largest and the smallest value in a class is called the
    a. class interval
    b. frequency distribution.
    c. class midpoint
    d. class frequency

___ 3. The class midpoint is
    a. equal to the number of observations.
    b. found by adding the upper and the lower class limit and dividing by 2.
    c. equal to the class interval.
    d. all of the above.

___ 4. The number of observations in a particular class is called the
    a. class interval.
    b. class frequency.
    c. frequency distribution.
    d. none of the above.

___ 5. It is usually good practice to
    a. use open-ended classes.
    b. have 20 or more classes.
    c. have fewer than 5 classes.
    d. none of the above.

___ 6. In a *less-than-cumulative* frequency distribution
    a. all the classes have the same number of observations.
    b. the class frequencies are added from the first to the last class.
    c. the clases are added from the largest frequency to the smallest.
    d. there should be at least 20 classes.

___ 7. In a *relative frequency* distribution
    a. the class frequencies are divided by 100.
    b. there should not be more than 5 classes.
    c. the class frequency is divided by the total number of observations.
    d. there should be at least 30 observations.

___ 8. For a line chart the horizontal or *X*-axis always represents
    a. the dependent variable.
    b. time.
    c. dollars.
    d. the class frequency.

___ 9. A pie chart requires at least what level of data?
   a. nominal
   b. ordinal
   c. interval
   d. ratio

___ 10. A graphic representation of a frequency distribution constructed by connecting the class midpoints with lines is called a
   a. histogram.
   b. line chart.
   c. pie chart.
   d. frequency polygon.

Part II Fill in the blanks with the correct answer.

11. What is the main use of a two-directional chart? _____

_____

12. How is a relative frequency determined? _____

13. What is the difference between a line chart and a frequency polygon? _____

_____

14. What is the main use of a pie chart? _____

_____

15. What is the difference between a stem-and-leaf chart and frequency distribution? _____

_____

Part III Show all your work. Write the answer in the space provided.

16. The Isaac Development Corporation is considering building a new shopping mall in the Spring Meadows area. Of concern is the number of times adults in the area visit a mall, For a sample of 30 adults, the following data reports the number of times each adult visited a mall last month.

8	4	7	3	1	13	3	12	4	3	13	5
5	2	12	6	5	13	5	6	8	5	6	4
5	4	10	9	11	10						

a. Organize the data into a frequency distribution. Use an interval of 3 visits and 0 as the lower limit of the first class.

b. Using the frequency distribution in part a, organize the data into a less-than-cumulative frequency distribution.

c. Using the frequency distribution constructed in part a, construct a histogram. Be sure to label the axes.

17. The following is a breakdown of the marital status of residents, over the age of 18, in the city of Sugar Grove. Develop a pie chart to portray the data. Interpret the results.

Marital Status	Residents
Married	210
Single	70
Widowed	13
Divorced	55

18. The following stem-and-leaf display is number of miles per week driven by a sample of students.

Stem	Leaf
6	138
7	34589
8	122469
9	001224559
10	113488

a. How many students were studied? _____
b. What was the longest distance?_____ What was the shortest distance? _____
c. How many students traveled less than 70 miles? _____
d. List the number of miles traveled by each student who travel between 60 and 69 miles.

3

DESCRIBING DATA—MEASURES OF CENTRAL TENDENCY

CHAPTER GOALS

After completing this chapter, you will be able to:

1. Compute the mean, median, and mode for grouped and ungrouped data.
2. Describe the characteristics uses, advantages, and disadvantages of the mean, median, and mode.
3. Compute and understand the geometric mean.
4. Compute and understand the weighted mean.

Introduction

A measure of **central tendency** is a single value used to describe a set of data. Example of measures of central tendency are:

• The average stock on the New York Stock Exchange (NYSE) gained $0.23 yesterday.
• The average discount rate for the $10.6 billion in three month treasury bills sold by the Treasury Department last week was 5.19 percent.
• Michael Jordan averaged 32.6 points per game, after he retired from baseball and returned to the National Basketball Association in 1995.
• The median age of those incarcerated for rape in Oregon is 32 years.

There are several measures of central tendency. We will consider five: the **arithmetic mean,** the **median**, the **mode**, the **weighted mean**, and the **geometric mean.**

Mean, Median, and Mode

The most widely used measure of central tendency is the **arithmetic mean** or more simply the **mean**. It is calculated by summing the observations and dividing the total by the number of observations. As an example, last year the dividends paid for three stocks were: $0.45, $0.75, and $1.11 per share. The sum of these three values is $2.31. The mean dividend is $0.77, found by ($0.45 + $0.75 + $1.11)/3. The dividend data is referred to as **raw data** or **ungrouped data.**

The raw data may consist of all the persons or items being considered. A listing of all the scores of the students in your section of Statistics 101 is an example of raw data. The medical benefits paid to all General Electric employees is another example.

The mean of a population is computed as follows:

$$\text{Population mean} = \frac{\text{Sum of all the values in the population}}{\text{Number of values in the population}}$$

In terms of symbols, the formula for the arithmetic mean of a population is:

$$\mu = \frac{\Sigma X}{N} \qquad 3\text{–}1$$

where μ stands for the population mean, N for the number of items in the population, X for the particular value, and Σ for the operation of summing all the values. Therefore, the symbols ΣX indicates that the values in the population should be summed. Note that the number 3–1 is to the right of the equation. This is the formula number and is used to identify the particular formula. So if we need to identify the formula for the population mean, we will refer to it as 3–1. The same formula numbers are used in the Study Guide as in the text.

If we have a sample taken from a population the formula for the sample mean is:

$$\bar{X} = \frac{\Sigma X}{n} \qquad 3\text{–}2$$

In some situations the arithmetic mean may not be representative of the data. For example, the mean annual income of a group of five executives is $94,800. Their salaries were: $40,000, $42,000, $44,000, $48,000, and $300,000. Notice how the one extreme value ($300,000) pulled the mean upward. Four of the five executives earned less than the mean, raising a question whether the value of $98,000 really a typical value.

The **median** is a useful measure when a problem with an extreme value is encountered. To determine the median, the values are ordered from low to high, or high to low, and the middle value selected. Hence, half the observations are above the median and half are below it. For the executive incomes, the middle value is $44,000, the median. Obviously, it is a more representative value in this problem then the mean of $94,800.

Note that there were an odd number of executive incomes (5). For an odd number of ungrouped values we just order them and select the middle value. To determine the median of an even number of ungrouped values, the first step is to arrange them from low to high as usual, and then determine the value half way between the two middle values.

As an example, the final grades of the six students in Mathematics 126 were: 87, 62, 91, 58, 99, and 85. Ordering these from low to high: 58, 62, 85, 87, 91, and 99. The median grade is halfway between the two middle values of 85 and 87. The median grade is 86. Thus we note that the median (86) may not be one of the values in a set of data.

A third measure of central tendency is the **mode**. The mode is the value that occurs most often in a set of raw data. The dividends per share declared on five stocks were: $3, $2, $4, $5, and $4. Since $4 occurred twice, which was the most frequent, the mode is $4.

The mean, median, and mode of a set of data are usually not all equal. However, if they are identical the distribution is **symmetrical**. That is, a symmetric is distribution is the same shape on both sides of the median. The following bell-shaped distribution is symmetrical.

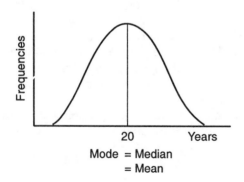

Mode = Median
= Mean

If the distribution is not symmetrical it is said to be **skewed** and the relationship between the mean, median, and mode changes. For a **positively skewed distribution** the mean is the largest of the three measures of central tendency, followed by the median and the mode. The mode is at the apex of the curve. (See the following chart.)

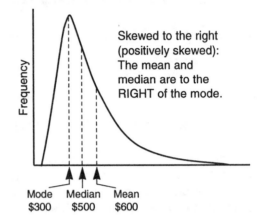

Skewed to the right (positively skewed): The mean and median are to the RIGHT of the mode.

Mode	Median	Mean
$300	$500	$600

For a **negatively skewed** distribution the mean is the smallest value (because it is being pulled down by the small observation). The mode is the highest of the three measures of central tendency.

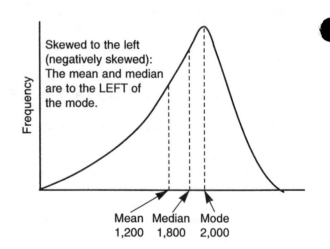

Skewed to the left (negatively skewed): The mean and median are to the LEFT of the mode.

Mean	Median	Mode
1,200	1,800	2,000

GLOSSARY

Measure of central tendency—A value that is typical or representative of the data.

Arithmetic Mean—The sum of the observations divided by the total number of observations.

Median—The value of the observation in the center after all observations have been arranged from the smallest to the largest, or vice versa.

Mode—The value that appears most frequently in a set of data.

Symmetrical—A distribution that has the same shape on either side of the median.

Positively skewed—The distribution is not symmetrical. The long tail is to the right, that is, in the positive direction. The mean is larger than the median or mode. The mode occurs at the apex of the curve.

Negatively skewed—The distribution is not symmetrical. The long tail is to the left, or in the negative direction. The mean is smaller than the median or mode. The mode occurs at the apex of the curve.

Geometric mean—The nth root of the product of n values.

Weighted mean—The value of each observation is multiplied by the number of times it occurs. The sum of these products is divided by the total number of observations to give the weighted mean.

CHAPTER PROBLEMS

Problem 1

A comparison shopper employed by a large grocery chain recorded these prices for a 340-gram jar of Kraft blackberry preserves at a sample of six supermarkets selected at random.

Supermarket	Price X
1	$1.31
2	1.35
3	1.26
4	1.42
5	1.31
6	1.33
Total	$7.98

Compute the mean, median, and mode.

Solution

The mean price of this raw data is determined by summing the prices for the six jars and dividing the total by six. Recall the formula for the mean of a sample was given previously. (See Formula 3–2.)

$$\bar{X} = \frac{\sum X}{n} = \frac{\$7.98}{6} = \$1.33$$

As noted above the *median* is defined as the middle value of a set of data, after the data is arranged from smallest to largest. The prices for the six jars of blackberry preserves have been ordered from a low of $1.26 up to $1.42. Because this is an even number of prices the median price is halfway between the third and the fourth price. The median is $1.32.

Prices arranged from
low to high
$1.26
1.31
1.31   median is $1.32
1.33
1.35
1.42

Suppose there were an *odd* number of blackberry preserve prices, such as $1.31, $1.31, $1.33, $1.35, and $1.42. The median is the middle value ($1.33). Of course, to find the median the values must first be ordered from low to high.

The mode is the price that occurs most often. The price of $1.31 occurs twice in the original data, and is the mode.

Exercise 1

Check your answers against those in the ANSWER section.

The number of semester credit hours for seven part-time college students is: 8, 5, 4, 10, 8, 3, and 4. Compute the mean, median, and modal number of hours.

Problem 2

The hourly wages for a sample of plumbers were grouped into the following frequency distribution. Since the wages have been grouped into classes, we refer to the following distribution as being *grouped* data.

	Number
Hourly Wages	f
$ 8 up to $10	3
$10 up to $12	6
$12 up to $14	12
$14 up to $16	10
$16 up to $18	7
$18 up to $20	2
	40

Compute the arithmetic mean, the median, and the mode.

Solution

The arithmetic mean of this sample data, grouped into a frequency distribution, is computed by formula 3–7.

$$\bar{X} = \frac{\Sigma fX}{n} \qquad\qquad 3\text{–}7$$

where X is the class midpoint, f is the frequency of occurrence, and n is the total number of observations.

It is assumed that the observations in each class are represented by the midpoint of the class. The midpoint of the first class is $9.00 found by ($8.00 + $10.00)/2. For the next higher class, the midpoint is $11.00. Using formula 3–3, the arithmetic mean hourly wage is $13.90.

	Frequency	Class Midpoint	
Wage Rate	f	X	fX
$ 8 up to $10	3	$ 9.00	$ 27.00
$10 up to $12	6	11.00	66.00
$12 up to $14	12	13.00	156.00
$14 up to $16	10	15.00	150.00
$16 up to $18	7	17.00	119.00
$18 up to $20	2	19.00	38.00
Total	40		$556.00

Determining the arithmetic mean hourly wage:

$$\bar{X} = \frac{\Sigma fX}{n} = \frac{\$556.00}{40} = \$13.90$$

The median of data grouped into a frequency distribution is found by applying formula 3–8 as follows:

$$\text{Median} = L + \frac{\frac{n}{2} - CF}{f} \text{ (i)} \qquad\qquad 3\text{–}8$$

where L is the lower limit of the class containing the median, n is the total number of frequencies, CF is the cumulative number of frequencies in the class immediately preceding the class containing the median, and i is the width of the class containing the median.

The hourly wage distribution of a sample of plumbers is repeated and a column giving the cumulative frequencies added.

	Hourly Wages	Frequency f	Cumulative Frequency CF
	$ 8 up to $10	3	3
	10 up to 12	6	9
Median Class	12 up to 14	12	21
	14 up to 16	10	31
	16 up to 18	7	38
	18 up to 20	2	40

The median class is located by dividing the total number of observations by 2. Thus 40/2 = 20. The class containing the 20th plumber can be located by referring to the cumulative frequency column in the above table. Notice that 9 plumbers earn less than $12. And, 21 plumbers earn less than $14. Thus, the 20th plumber earns some amount between $12 and $14, the lower limit (L) of that class is $12. This class in the middle of the distribution is designated as the *median class*.

The cumulative number of frequencies (CF) in the class preceding the median class is 9. The number of frequencies (f) in the median class is 12. The width of the median class (i) is $2.00. Solving for the median:

$$\text{Median} = L + \frac{\frac{n}{2} - CF}{f} \text{ (i)} = \$12 + \frac{\frac{40}{2} - 9}{12} (\$2.00) = \$13.83$$

The **mode** is the value that occurs most often. For data grouped into a frequency distribution, the mode is the midpoint of the class containing the most observations. There are more observations (12) in the $12 up to $14 class than in any other class. The midpoint of the class is $13 which is the mode.

We computed three measures of central tendency for the hourly wage data. Observe that the mean ($13.90), the median ($13.80), and the model ($13.00) are all different. Generally, this is the case. What measure of central tendency to select to represent the data will be discussed shortly.

Exercise 2

Check your answers against those in the ANSWER section.

The annual exports of 50 medium-sized manufacturers were organized into a frequency distribution. (Exports are in $ millions.)

Exports	Frequency
$ 6 up to $ 9	2
9 up to 12	8
12 up to 15	20
15 up to 18	14
18 up to 21	6

Compute the mean, median, and mode.

Problem 3

At Sarasota College there are 10 instructors, 12 assistant professors, 20 associate professors, and 5 professors. Their average annual salaries are $32,000, $35,000, $38,000, and $44,000 respectively. What is the weighted mean salary?

Solution

The number of faculty for each rank is not equal. Therefore, it is not appropriate simply to add the average salaries of the four ranks and divide by 4. We have a better method for weighting the averages. In this problem the salaries for each rank are multiplied by the number of faculty in that rank, the products totaled, then divided by the number of faculty. The result is the weighted mean.

The calculation for the weighted mean using formula 3–4 are:

$$\bar{X}_w = \frac{w_1X_1 + w_2X_2 + w_3X_3 + w_4X_4}{w_1 + w_2 + w_3 + w_4}$$ **3–4**

$$= \frac{10(\$32,000) + 12(\$35,000) + 20(\$38,000) + 5(\$44,000)}{10 + 12 + 20 + 5}$$

$$= \frac{\$1,720,000}{47}$$

$$= \$36,596$$

Problem 4

From 1982 to 1996 the number of croquet clubs in the United States increased from 5 to 300. Compute the mean annual percent increase in the number of croquet clubs.

Solution

The geometric mean (GM) annual percent increase from one time period to another is determined using formula 3–6.

$$GM = \sqrt[n-1]{\frac{\text{Value at the end of the period}}{\text{Value at the start of the period}}} - 1 \qquad \text{3–6}$$

Note that there are 15 years involved. However, there are only 14 annual rates of change. The annual changes are from 1982 to 1983, from 1983 to 1984, and so forth, So, n is 15 and $n - 1 = 15 - 1 = 14$ annual percent increases.

$$GM = \sqrt[15-1]{\frac{300}{5}} - 1 = \sqrt[14]{60.0} - 1$$

The 14th root of 60 is 1.33971, found by

$$\sqrt[14]{60} = \frac{\log \text{ of } 60}{14} = \frac{1.77815125}{14} = 0.127010803$$

The antilog of 0.127010803 is 1.33971. The value 1 is subtracted, according to formula 3–6, so the rate of increase is .33971, or 33.971% per year. Croquet clubs are increasing at a rate of almost 34% per year.

For those with a $\sqrt[x]{y}$ or y^x key on their calculator, the geometric mean can be solved quickly by:

$$GM = \sqrt[n-1]{\frac{300}{5}} - 1 = \sqrt[14]{60.0} - 1$$

Then using the calculator:

	Display
$300 \div 5 =$	60
Depress $\sqrt[x]{y}$ or y^x key*	
Depress 14**	1.33971
Depress $- 1 =$	.3371, or about 34%

* On some calculators you must depress the 2nd function mode before depressing y^x
** If y^x key is on the calculator use the reciprocal of 14, or $1/14 = .0714286$.

Exercise 3

Check your answers against those in the ANSWER section.

In 1950 there were 51 countries with membership in the United Nations. By 1995 there were 159. What was the geometric mean annual percent increase in membership?

CHAPTER ASSIGNMENT 3

Describing Data—Measures of Central Tendency

Name _____ Section _____ Score _____

Part I Select the correct answer and write the appropriate letter in the space provided.

___ 1. The arithmetic mean is computed by
   a. summing the values and dividing by the number of values.
   b. finding the middle observation and dividing by 2.
   c. finding the value that occurs most often.
   d. selecting the value in the middle of the data set.

___ 2. To compute the arithmetic mean at least the
   a. nominal level of measurement is required.
   b. ordinal level of measurement is required.
   c. interval level of measurement is required.
   d. ratio level of measurement is required.

___ 3. The value that occurs most often in a set of data is called the
   a. mean.
   b. median.
   c. mode.
   d. geometric mean.

___ 4. What level of measurement is required for the median?
   a. nominal.
   b. ordinal.
   c. interval.
   d. ratio.

___ 5. What level of measurement is required to determine the mode?
   a. nominal.
   b. ordinal.
   c. interval.
   d. ratio.

___ 6. For a symmetric distribution
   a. the mean is larger than the median.
   b. the mean, median, and the mode are equal.
   c. the mean is smaller than the median.
   d. the mode is the largest value.

___ 7. Which of the following is **not** true about the arithmetic mean.
   a. all the values are used in its calculation.
   b. half of the observations are always larger than the mean
   c. it is influenced by a large value.
   d. it is found by summing all the values and dividing by the number of observations.

___ 8. In a *negatively* skewed distribution
   a. the mean and median are equal.
   b. the mean is larger than the median.

c. the mean is smaller than the median.

d. the median and the mode are equal.

___ 9. The Dow Jones Industrial Average increased from 961 in 1980 to 4500 in July 1995. The annual rate of increase is best described by the

a. geometric mean.

b. weighted mean.

c. median

d. mode.

___ 10. What is the shape of a frequency distribution with an arithmetic mean of 12,000 pounds, a median of 12,000 pounds, and a mode of 12,000 pounds?

a. flat

b. symmetric

c. geometrically skewed.

d. positively skewed

Part II Fill in the blank with the correct answer.

11. When the deviations from the mean are summed the result is always what value? _____

12. An open-ended class might appear as ''$25,000 and over'' or ''under $15.'' Why can't the arithmetic mean be computed from a frequency distribution with an open-ended class? _____
_____

13. How is the mode of grouped data determined? _____

14. Write and describe the symbols for the mean of a sample and the mean of a population. _____
_____
_____

15. How is the median of raw data determined if there is an even number of observations? _____
_____
_____

Part III Record your answer in the space provided. Where necessary show the essential calculations.

16. The weights of a sample of seven FedEx shipments, to the nearest pound, are:

10   7   11   10   13   5   4

a. Give the formula for the mean weight of this sample.

b. Compute the sample mean.

c. What is the median?

d. What is the modal weight?

Answer

Answer

Answer

Answer

36

17. The Jimmy's Old Rustic Fence Company sells three type of fencing to residential customers. Grade A costs $6.00 per running foot to install, grade B costs $4.00, and grade C $3.00. Yesterday, Jimmy's installed 300 feet of grade A, 450 feet of grade B, and 225 feet of grade C. What was yesterday's average installation cost per foot?

a. Give the formula to compute the average installation cost.

b. Determine the average installation cost per foot of the fencing.

Answer

18. In 1990, 28 billion dollars was spent on weight-loss and diet food in the United States. By 1996 it is estimated that $50 billion will be spent. What is the geometric mean rate of increase per year?

Answer

19. The Ohio Bureau of Employment gathered the following sample information on the number of hours unemployed workers spent looking for work last week.

Hours spent searching	Number unemployed
0 up to 10	3
10 up to 20	7
20 up to 30	15
30 up to 40	10
40 up to 50	5
Total	40

a. What is the mean length of time?

Answer

b. What is the median length of time?

Answer

c. What is the mode length of time?

Answer

4

MEASURES OF DISPERSION AND SKEWNESS

CHAPTER GOALS

After completing this chapter, you will be able to:

1. Compute various measures of dispersion for both grouped and ungrouped data.
2. Discuss the uses, characteristics, advantages and disadvantages of the range, interquartile range, quartile deviation, mean deviation, variance, and standard deviation.
3. Discuss the Empirical Rule and Chebyshev's Theorem.
4. Compute and interpret the coefficient of variation and the coefficient of skewness.

Introduction

In Chapter 2 we discussed methods of organizing data into a frequency distribution and presented various graphical techniques. In Chapter 3 measures of central tendency were examined. A direct comparison of two sets of data based only on two measures of central tendency can be misleading. For example, suppose a statistics instructor had two classes, one in the morning and one in the evening; each with six students. In the morning class the students' ages are; 18, 20, 21, 21, 23 and 23 years. In the evening class the ages are 17, 17, 18, 20, 25, and 29 years. Note that for both classes the mean age is 21 years but there is more variation or dispersion in the ages of the evening students. This chapter considers several measures of dispersion, namely, the **range**, the **mean deviation**, the **variance**, the **standard deviation**, the **interquartile range**, and **quartile deviation**.

Range

Perhaps the simplest measure of dispersion is the range. The **range** is the difference between the largest and the smallest observation. In the statistics class example cited above, the range for the morning class is 5 years, found by 23 − 18. For the evening class it is 12 years, found by 29 − 17. Thus we can say that there is more spread in the ages of the students enrolled in the evening class compared with the day class (because 12 years is greater than 5 years). The advantages of the range are that it is easy to compute and easy to understand. It is computed by Range =

Highest value − lowest value

The range has two disadvantages. It can be distorted by a single extreme value. Suppose the same statistics instructor has a third class of five students. The ages of these students are 20, 20, 21, 22, and 60 years. The range of ages is 40 years, yet four of the five students' ages are within two years of each other. The 60-year-old student has distorted the spread. Another disadvantage is that only two values, the largest and the smallest, are used in its calculation.

Mean Deviation

In contrast to the range, the **mean deviation** considers all the data. It is computed by first determining the difference between each observation and the mean. These differences are then averaged without regard to their signs. For the evening statistics class the mean deviation is 4.0 years found by (| 17 − 21| + | 17 − 21| + | 18 − 21| + | 20 − 21| + | 25 − 21| + | 29 − 21|)/6. The parallel lines | | indicate absolute values. To interpret, 4.0 years is the mean amount by which the ages differ from the arithmetic mean age of 21.0 years. In terms of symbols:

$$MD = \frac{\Sigma |X - \bar{X}|}{n} \qquad \text{4-2}$$

Variance of Standard Deviation

The disadvantage of the mean deviation is that the absolute values are difficult to manipulate mathemati-

39

cally. The problem of absolute values is eliminated by squaring the differences from each value and the mean. These squared differences are used both in the computation of the **variance** and the **standard deviation**.

Squaring units of measurement, such as dollars or years, makes the variance cumbersome to use since it yields units like "dollars squared" or "years squared." However, by calculating the standard deviation, which is the positive square root of the variance, we can return to the original units, such as years or dollars. Because the standard deviation is easier to interpret, it is more widely used than is the mean deviation or the variance. The standard deviation is used in both Chebyshev's Theorem and the Empirical rule which follows. The formula for the standard deviation of a sample is:

$$s = \sqrt{\frac{\Sigma(X - \bar{X})^2}{n - 1}} \qquad 4\text{-}8$$

Chebyshev's Theorem and The Empirical Rule

The standard deviation is used to estimate the proportion of the observations that lie within a specified number of standard deviations from the mean. **Chebyshev's Theorem** states that, regardless of the shape of the distribution, at least $1 - 1/k^2$ of the observations lie within $\pm k$ standard deviations of the mean. k must be greater than 1.

If the distribution is approximately symmetrical and bell shaped then the **Empirical rule**, or **Normal Rule** as it is sometimes called, is applied. This rule states that the mean, plus and minus one standard deviation will include about 68 percent of the observations. The mean plus and minus two standard deviations include about 95 percent of the observations. Virtually all (99.7%) of the observations will lie within three standard deviations of the mean.

The Interquartile Range and the Quartile Deviation

Two other measures of dispersion are the **interquartile range** and the **quartile deviation**. Both are concerned with the middle 50 percent of the observations. How are they computed? First, we order the data from smallest to largest. Recall that the median divides these ordered values so that half are below it and half are above it. The lower half of the values can be further subdivided so that one-fourth are less

than a particular value. This value is called the **first quartile**, designed Q_1. Similarly, the upper half of the observations is divided in half at the **third quartile**, Q_3.

The interquartile range is the distance between the first and the third quartiles. The quartile deviation is half that distance. What are the advantages of these measures? Both are easy to compute and not affected by extremely large or extremely small values. Also, they partition the frequency distribution curve into several parts. The disadvantage is that not all observations are used in their calculation.

Relative Dispersion and Skewness

Suppose we want to compare the variability of two sets of data that are measured in different units—one in dollars and the other in years, for example. How can this be done? The **coefficient of variation** is used. It is a measure of relative dispersion. To compute the coefficient of variation, the standard deviation is divided by the mean and the result is multiplied by 100. This measure reports the standard deviation as a percent of the mean. In terms of a formula:

$$CV = \frac{s}{\bar{X}} (100) \qquad 4\text{-}17$$

If, for example, in a study of executives the coefficient of variation for incomes is 29 percent and for their ages is 12 percent, we would conclude that there is more relative dispersion in the incomes of the executives than in their ages.

The measures of central tendency described in Chapter 3 and the measures of dispersion described in Chapter 4 are both descriptive characteristics of a set of data. A third characteristic of a distribution is its **skewness**. As noted in Chapter 3, a **symmetric distribution** has the same shape on either side of the median and it has no skewness. For a **positively skewed** distribution the long tail is to the right, the mean is larger than the median or the mode, and the mode appears at the highest point on the curve. For a **negatively skewed** distribution the mode is the largest value and is at the highest point of the curve, while the mean is the smallest.

The **coefficient of skewness**, designated sk, measures the amount of skewness and may range from -3.0 to $+3.0$. It is computed by subtracting the median from the mean, multiplying the result by 3, and dividing by the standard deviation. In terms of a formula:

$$sk = \frac{3(\bar{X} - \text{median})}{s} \qquad 4\text{-}18$$

GLOSSARY

Dispersion—The amount of variation in the data.

Range—The difference between the largest and the smallest value in a set of data.

Mean Deviation—The mean of the absolute values of the deviations from the arithmetic mean.

Variance—The mean of the squared deviations between each observation and the mean.

Standard deviation—The positive square root of the variance. A measure of dispersion reported in the same units as the original data.

Interquartile range—The difference between the values of the first and third quartile, indicating the range of the middle fifty percent of the observations.

Quartile deviation—Half of the interquartile range.

Percentile—Divides a distribution into one hundred equal parts.

Percentile range—The distance between any two percentiles.

Chebyshev's Theorem—The proportion of observation in any data set that occurs within k standard deviations of the mean. It is equal to $[1 - (1/k^2)]$, where k is greater than 1.0.

Empirical or Normal Rule—About 68 percent of the observations will lie within one standard deviation of the mean; about 95 percent of the observations will lie within two standard deviations of the mean; and virtually all (99.7%) will lie within three standard deviations of the mean.

Coefficient of variation—A measure of relative dispersion, which expresses the standard deviation as a percent of the mean. It is useful for comparing distributions in different units.

Coefficient of skewness—A measure of the lack of symmetry of a distribution. It relates the difference between the mean and the median to the standard deviation.

CHAPTER PROBLEMS

Problem 1

A sample of the amounts spent in November to heat all-electric homes of similar sizes in Scarsdale revealed these amounts (to the nearest dollar):

$191, $212, $176, $129, $106, $92, $108, $109, $103, $121, $175, $194

What is the range? Interpret your results.

Solution

Recall that the range is the difference between the largest value and the smallest value.

$$\text{Range} = \text{Highest value} - \text{Lowest value}$$
$$\$212 - \$92 = \$120$$

This indicates that there is a difference of $120 between the largest and the smallest heating cost.

Problem 2

Using the heating cost data in Problem 1, compute the mean deviation.

Solution

The mean deviation is the mean of the absolute deviations from the arithmetic mean. For raw, or ungrouped data, it is first computed by determining the arithmetic mean. Next, the difference between each value and the arithmetic mean is determined. Finally, these differences are totaled and the total divided by the number of observations. We ignore the sign of each difference. The formula for sample mean (3–1) and for the mean deviation formula (4–2) are shown below.

Sample Mean   **Mean Deviation**

$$\bar{X} = \frac{\Sigma X}{n} \qquad MD = \frac{\Sigma |X - \bar{X}|}{n}$$

where X is the value of each observation, $\bar{X}$ is the arithmetic mean of the values, n is the number of observations, and $| \, |$ indicates the absolute value. In other words, the signs of the deviations from the mean are disregarded.

Payment X	$X - \bar{X}$		Absolute Deviations
$ 191	|$+48|	=	$ 48
212	| +69|	=	69
176	| +33|	=	33
129	| −14|	=	14
106	| −37|	=	37
92	| −51|	=	51
108	| −35|	=	35
109	| −34|	=	34
103	| −40|	=	40
121	| −22|	=	22
175	| +32|	=	32
194	| +51|	=	51
$1,716			$466

$$\bar{X} = \frac{\Sigma X}{n} = \frac{\$1,716}{12} = \$143.00$$

$$MD = \frac{\Sigma |X - \bar{X}|}{n} = \frac{\$466}{12} = \$38.83$$

This indicates that the typical electric bill deviates $38.83 from the mean of $143.00.

Problem 3

Using the same heating cost data in Problem 1, compute the variance and the standard deviation.

Solution

The sample variance, designated s^2, is based on squared deviations from the mean. For ungrouped (raw) data it is computed using formula 4–6 or 4–7.

			Formula 4–6			Formula 4–7	

$$s^2 = \frac{\Sigma(X - \bar{X})^2}{n - 1}$$

$$s^2 = \frac{\Sigma X^2 - \frac{(\Sigma X)^2}{n}}{n - 1}$$

Computing the sample variance both ways:

X	X − X̄	(X − X̄²)	X²		
$ 191	$ 48	2,304	36,481	$s^2 = \dfrac{\Sigma(X - \bar{X})^2}{n - 1} = \dfrac{20,410}{12 - 1} = 1,855.45$	
212	69	4,761	44,944		
176	33	1,089	30,976	or	
129	− 14	196	16,641		
106	− 37	1,369	11,236	$s^2 = \dfrac{\Sigma X^2 - \dfrac{(\Sigma X)^2}{n}}{n - 1}$	
92	− 51	2,601	8,464		
108	− 35	1,225	11,664		
109	− 34	1,156	11,881		
103	− 40	1,600	10,609	$= \dfrac{265,798 - \dfrac{(\$1,716)^2}{12}}{12 - 1} = 1,855.45$	
121	− 22	484	14,641		
175	32	1,024	30,625		
194	51	2,601	37,636		
$1,716	0	20,410	265,798		

The standard deviation of the sample, designated by s, is the square root of the variance. The square root of 1,855.45 is $43.07. Note that the standard deviation is in the same terms as the original data, that is, dollars.

Exercise 1

Check your answers against those in the ANSWER section.

The manager of a fast-food restaurant selected several checks at random. The amounts spent by customers were $12, $15, $16, $10, and $30. Compute the range, the mean deviation, the sample variance, and the sample standard deviation.

Problem 4

The office manger of the Mallard Glass Company is investigating the ages in months of the company's word processing equipment currently in use. The ages of 30 units selected at random were organized into a frequency distribution. Determine the range:

Age to the Nearest Month	Number of Word Processors
20 up to 25	3
25 up to 30	5
30 up to 35	10
35 up to 40	7
40 up to 45	4
45 up to 50	1

Solution

The range is the difference between the lower class limit of the lowest class and the upper class limit of the highest class.

$$\text{Range} = 50 - 20 = 30 \text{ months}$$

Problem 5

Using the ages of the word processing equipment in Problem 4, compute the variance and the standard deviation.

Solution

Formula 4–10 is used to compute the standard deviation of grouped data.

$$s = \sqrt{\frac{\Sigma fX^2 - \frac{(\Sigma fX)^2}{n}}{n - 1}}$$

where X is the midpoint of a class, f is the class frequency, and n is the total number of sample observations.

Applying this formula to the distribution of the ages of the word processing equipment in Problem 4, the standard deviation is 6.39 months.

Age	f	Class Midpoint X	fX	fX²
20 up to 25	3	22.5	67.5	1,518.75
25 up to 30	5	27.5	137.5	3,781,25
30 up to 35	10	32.5	325.0	10,562.05
35 up to 40	7	37.5	262.5	9,843.75
40 up to 45	4	42.5	170.0	7,225.00
45 up to 50	1	47.5	47.5	2,256.25
	30		1010.0	35,187.50

$$s = \sqrt{\frac{\Sigma fX^2 - \frac{(\Sigma fX)^2}{n}}{n - 1}}$$

$$= \sqrt{\frac{35,187.50 - \frac{(1010)^2}{30}}{30 - 1}}$$

$$= 6.39 \text{ months}$$

The variance is the square of the standard deviation.

$$s^2 = (6.39)^2 = 40.83$$

Problem 6

Use the age of the Mallard Glass word processing equipment (Problem 5) to compute the interquartile range and the quartile deviation.

Solution

The interquartile range and the quartile deviation are computed by:

Formula 4–11   *Formula 4–14*

$$\text{Interquartile range} = Q_3 - Q_1 \qquad \text{Quartile deviation, Q.D.} = \frac{Q_3 - Q_1}{2}$$

where Q_3 is the third quartile and Q_1 is the first quartile.

The formula for the first and third quartiles are:

Formula 4–12

$$Q_1 = L + \frac{\frac{n}{4} - CF}{f} \text{ (i)}$$

Formula 4–13

$$Q_3 = L + \frac{\frac{3n}{4} - CF}{f} \text{ (i)}$$

where:
  L is the lower limit of the class containing the first (or third) quartile.
  n is the total number in the sample.
CF is the cumulative number of frequencies occurring before the class containing the first (or third) quartile.
  f is the number of frequencies in the class containing the first (or third) quartile.
  i is the width of the class interval containing the first (or third) quartile.

The calculations for Q_1 and Q_3 are similar to those for the median (Q_2) discussed in Chapter 3. To find Q_1: The first step is to search for the class in which Q_1 is located. Note there are 30 word processors. One-fourth of 30 is 7.5. Refer to the following table. Count down in the class frequency column. The first cumulative frequency is 3, the next 8, found by 3 + 5, the next is 18, found by 3 + 5 + 10, and so on.

Note in the cumulative frequency column that 3 word processors have been in use less than 25 months. Eight processors have been in use less than 30 months. The 7.5 processors must be in the 25 up to 30 age class.

Age (Stated Limits)	True Limits	Class Frequency		Cumulative Frequency
20 up to 25		3	COUNT	3
25 up to 30		5	DOWN	8
30 up to 35		10		18
35 up to 40		7		25
40 up to 45		4		29
45 up to 50		1		30
		30		

Using the formula (4–12) the values to find first quartile (Q_1) are:
$L = 25$, the lower limit of the class containing the first quartile.
$n = 30$, the total number of word processors in the sample.
$CF = 3$, the cumulative number of frequencies occurring prior to the class containing the first quartile.
$f = 5$, the number of frequencies in the class containing the first quartile.
$i = 5$, the width of the 25 up to 30 class.

Computing the first and third quartile.

$$Q_1 = L + \frac{\frac{n}{4} - CF}{f} \text{ (i)}$$

$$= 25 + \frac{\frac{30}{4} - 3}{5} \text{ (5)}$$

$$= 29.5$$

$$Q_3 = L + \frac{\frac{3n}{4} - CF}{f} \text{ (i)}$$

$$= 35 + \frac{\frac{3(30)}{4} - 18}{7} \text{ (5)}$$

$$= 38.21$$

Fifty percent of the word processors have been in use more than 29.5 months but less than 38.21 months. The interquartile range is 8.71, found by $Q_3 - Q_1 - .29 = 8.71$ months. The quartile deviation is:

$$Q.D. = \frac{Q_3 - Q_1}{2} = \frac{38.21 - 29.5}{2} = \frac{8.71}{2} = 4.355 \text{ months}$$

Exercise 2

Check your answers against those in the ANSWER section.

The weekly income of a sample of 60 part-time employees of a fast-food restaurant chain were organized into the following frequency distribution.

Weekly Incomes	Number of Employees
$100 up to $150	5
150 up to 200	9
200 up to 250	20
250 up to 300	18
300 up to 350	5
350 up to 400	3

Compute the (a) standard deviation and (b) the quartile deviation.

Problem 7

A sample of the business faculty at state supported institutions in Ohio revealed the mean income to be $52,000 for 9 months with a standard deviation of $3,000. Use Chebyshev's Theorem and the Empirical Rule to estimate the proportion of faculty that earn more than $46,000 but less than $58,000.

Solution

To find the proportion of faculty who earn between $46,000 and $58,000 we must first determine k; k is the number of standard deviations above or below the mean.

$$k = \frac{X - \bar{X}}{s} = \frac{\$46,000 - \$52,000}{\$3,000} = -2.00$$

$$k = \frac{X - \bar{X}}{s} = \frac{\$58,000 - \$52,000}{\$3,000} = 2.00$$

Applying Chebyshev's Theorem: $1 - \frac{1}{k^2} = 1 - \frac{1}{2^2} = 0.75$

This means that at least 75 percent of the faculty earn between $46,000 and $58,000.

The Empirical rule states that about 68 percent of the observations fall within one standard deviation of the mean, 95 percent are within plus and minus two standard deviations of the mean, and virtually all (99.7%) will lie within three standard deviations from the mean. Hence, about 95 percent of the observations fall between $46,000 and $58,000, found by $\bar{X} \pm 2s = \$52,000 \pm 2(\$3,000)$. Compare these results with those obtained from Chebyshev's Theorem.

Problem 8

Recall from Problem 7 that the study of business faculty at state supported institutions in Ohio revealed that the arithmetic mean salary for nine months is $52,000 and the standard deviation of the sample is $3,000. The study also showed that the faculty had been employed a mean of 15 years with a standard deviation of 4 years. How does the relative dispersion in the distribution of salaries compare with that of the lengths of service?

Solution

The coefficient of variation measures the relative dispersion in a distribution. In this problem it allows for a comparison of two distributions expressed in different units (dollars and years). Formula 4–17 is used:

$$CV = \frac{s}{\bar{X}} (100)$$

For the salaries:

$$CV = \frac{\$3,000}{\$52,000} (100)$$

$$= 5.8\%$$

For the length of service:

$$CV = \frac{4 \text{ years}}{15 \text{ years}} (100)$$

$$= 26.7\%$$

The coefficient of variation is larger for length of service than for salary. This indicates that there is more dispersion in the distribution of the lengths of service relative to the mean than for the distribution of salaries.

Problem 9

The research director of a large oil company conducted a study of the buying habits of consumers with respect to the amount of gasoline purchased at full-service pumps. The arithmetic mean amount is 11.50 gallons, and the median amount is 11.95 gallons. The standard deviation of the sample is 4.5 gallons. Determine the coefficient of skewness. Comment on the shape of the distribution.

Solution

The coefficient of skewness measures the general shape of the distribution. A distribution that is symmetrical has no skewness and the coefficient of skewness is 0. Skewness ranges from -3 to $+3$. The direction of the long tail of the distribution points in the direction of the skewness. If the mean is larger than the median, the skewness is positive. If the median is larger than the mean, the skewness is negative. The coefficient of skewness is found by formula 4–18:

$$sk = \frac{3(\bar{X} - \text{median})}{s}$$

For this problem:

$$= \frac{3(11.50 - 11.95)}{4.5}$$

$$= -0.30$$

This indicates that there is a slight negative skewness in the distribution of gasoline purchases from full-service pumps.

Exercise 3

Check your answers against those in the ANSWER section.

An automobile dealership pays its salespersons a salary plus a commission on sales. The mean monthly commission is $990, the median $950, and the standard deviation $70. Is the distribution of commissions positively skewed, negatively skewed, or symmetrical? To verify your answer compute the coefficient of skewness.

CHAPTER ASSIGNMENT 4

Measures of Dispersion and Skewness

Name _____ Section _____ Score _____

Part I Select the correct answer and write the appropriate letter in the space provided.

____ 1. Which of the following is a disadvantage of the range?
    a. It is in squared units.
    b. It is always equal to the mean.
    c. A set of data can have more than one range.
    d. It is based on only two observations.

____ 2. The mean deviation
    a. is in the same units as the original values.
    b. is based on the deviations from the mean.
    c. uses absolute values in its calculation.
    d. all of the above are correct

____ 3. The sum of the deviations from the mean is
    a. equal to the mean.
    b. equal to 0.
    c. always positive.
    d. equal to the median.

____ 4. The square of the standard deviation is equal to
    a. the mean.
    b. the variance.
    c. the median.
    d. the mean deviation.

____ 5. The quartile deviation and the interquartile range
    a. are both based on the median.
    b. are both based on the mean deviation.
    c. are related in that the square of the former is equal to the latter.
    d. are both based on the middle 50 percent of the observations.

____ 6. Suppose the coefficient of skewness was computed and was found to equal -2.50.
    a. A mistake was made because it cannot be negative.
    b. The distribution is positively skewed.
    c. Fifty percent of the observations are less than -2.50.
    d. The mean is smaller than the median.

____ 7. The coefficient of skewness
    a. is always positive.
    b. may range from -3.00 up to 3.00.
    c. is a measure of relative dispersion.
    d. is equal to the range.

____ 8. The coefficient of variation
    a. is found by dividing the standard deviation by the mean and multiplying the result by 100.
    b. is a measure of relative dispersion.

    c. is reported in percent.

    d. all of the above are correct.

___ 9. The range of a sample of 10 values is 5 and the largest observation is 50. The lowest value is

    a. 40.

    b. 45.

    c. 55.

    d. cannot be computed from the data given.

___ 10. A study by the Wood County Tax Assessor showed that among delinquent tax payers, the mean number of days delinquent was 25 and that the variance was 36. The units associated with the variance is

    a. hours.

    b. days.

    c. no units are involved.

    d. days squared.

Part II Fill in the blank with the correct answer.

11. The second quartile is also called the _____

12. According to Chebyshev's Theorem, at least _____ percent of the observations are within 1.8 standard deviations of the mean.

13. Under what conditions could the standard deviation assume a negative value? _____
_____

14. According to the Empirical Rule, about what percent of the observations will be within 2 standard deviations of the mean? _____

15. The distribution of hours worked last week by the sales staff at Ed Schmidt Pontiac is symmetrical, with a mean and a mode of 50 and quartile deviation of 5. The middle 50 percent of the sales staff worked between what two values? _____

Part III Record your answers in the space provided. Show all essential calculations.

16. The following is the number of shares traded (in 100's) for a sample of eight stocks listed on the New York Stock Exchange.

        62 41 60 49 39 45 26 38

  a. Compute the range.

                                                    Answer

  b. Compute the mean deviation.

                                                    Answer

  c. Compute the standard deviation.

                                                    Answer

17. The Community Transit Company is studying the number of passengers riding the bus from Rocky River, Ohio to downtown Cleveland during the morning rush hour. A sample of 50 buses revealed the following number of passengers.

Number of Passengers	Frequencies
15 up to 20	3
20 up to 25	8
25 up to 30	12
30 up to 35	15
35 up to 40	7
40 up to 45	5
Total	50

a. What is the range?

Answer

b. Determine the standard deviation.

Answer

c. Determine the first and third quartiles.

Q_1

Answer

Q_1

Answer

d. Determine the quartile deviation.

Answer

51

18. The mean number of gallons of gasoline pumped per customer at Ray's Marathon Station is 9.5 gallons with a standard deviation of 0.75 gallons. The median number of gallons pumped is 10.0 gallons. The arithmetic mean amount of time spent by a customer in the station is 6.5 minutes with a standard deviation of 2 minutes.

a. According to Chebyshev's Theorem, what proportion of the customers spend between 3.30 minutes and 9.70 minutes at the station?

a [   ]
Answer

b. According to the Empirical Rule, what proportion of the customers pump between 8.00 gallons and 11.00 gallons?

b [   ]
Answer

c. Compute coefficient of variation for both the time spent at Ray's Marathon and the gasoline pumped. Comment on the relative dispersion of the two distributions.

c [   ]
Answer

d. Compute the coefficient of skewness for the number of gallons pumped. Interpret it.

d [   ]
Answer

5

A SURVEY OF PROBABILITY CONCEPTS

CHAPTER GOALS

After completing this chapter, you will be able to:

1. Define the term probability.
2. Explain the three classifications of probability.
3. Understand the terms event, experiment, and outcome.
4. Define the terms conditional probability and joint probability.
5. Calculate probabilities using the rules of addition and multiplication.
6. Calculate a probability using Bayes' Theorem.
7. Determine the number of possible outcomes of an experiment using the rules for permutations and combinations.

Introduction

Chapters 2 through 4 emphasized **descriptive statistics.** In those chapters we described methods used to collect, organize, and present data, as well as measures of central tendency, dispersion, and skewness used to summarize data. In this chapter, we begin our study of **inferential statistics.**

An inference is defined as a *generalization about a population based on information obtained from a sample.* Probability plays a key role in inferential statistics. It is used to measure the reasonableness that a particular sample could have come from a particular population. Probability also allows us to measure effectively the risks in selecting one alternative over the others.

Probability Defined

A **probability** is a measure of the likelihood that a particular event will happen. It is expressed either as a percent or as a decimal. The likelihood that any particular event will happen may assume values between 0 and 1.0. A value close to 0 indicates the event is unlikely to occur, whereas a value close to 1.0 indicates that the event is quite likely to occur. To illustrate, a value of .60 might express your degree of belief that tuition will be increased at your college, and .05 the likelihood that your first marriage will end in divorce.

In our study of probability we will make extensive use of several key words. They are: *experiment, outcome,* and *event.* An **experiment** is an observation of some activity, or the act of obtaining some type of mea-

surement. For example, you roll a die and observe the number of spots that appear face up. The experiment is the act of rolling the die. Your survey company might be hired by Ford to find out how many consumers plan to buy a new American-made car this year. You contact 5,000 consumers. The act of counting the consumers who indicated they would purchase an American-made car is the experiment. The particular result of an experiment is called an **outcome.**

One outcome of the die-rolling experiment is the appearance of a 6. In the experiment of counting the number of consumers who plan to buy a new American-made car this year, one possibility is that 2,258 plan to buy one, another outcome is that 142 plan to buy one. A collection of one or more outcomes is called an **event.** Thus, the event that the number appearing face up in the die-rolling experiment is even is the collection of the outcomes 2, 4, or 6. Similarly the event that more than half of those surveyed plan to buy a new American-made car is the collection of the outcomes 2,501, 2,502, 2,503, and so on all the way up to 5,000.

Types of Probability

There are three types or classifications of probability: *classical, relative frequency,* and *subjective.* The **classical** type is based on the assumption that there are several equally likely outcomes for an experiment. To find the probability of a particular outcome we divide the number of favorable outcomes by the total number of possible outcomes. For example, suppose you take a multiple-choice examination and have no idea which one of the choices is correct. In desperation you decide to guess the answer to each question. The four choices for each question are the outcomes. They are equally likely, but only one is correct. Thus the probability that you guess a particular answer correctly is .25 found by 1/4.

To find a probability using the **relative frequency** approach we divide the number of times the event has occurred in the past by the total number of observations. Suppose the Civil Aeronautics Board maintained records on the number of times planes arrived late at the Newark International Airport. If 54 flights in a sample of 500 were late, then, according to the relative frequency definition, the probability a particular flight will be late is .108, found by 54/500.

Subjective probability is based on whatever information is available—personal judgment, intuition, or "hunches." The likelihood that the horse Sir Homer will win the race at Perry Downs today is based on the subjective view of the racetrack oddsmaker.

Probability Rules

In the study of probability it is often necessary to combine the probabilities of events. This is accomplished through both *rules of addition* and *rules of multiplication*. There are two rules for addition, the *special rule of addition* and the *general rule of addition*.

Special Rule of Addition

The **special rule of addition** states that the probability of the event A or the event B occurring is equal to the probability of event A plus the probability of event B. The rule is expressed by:

$$P(A \text{ or } B) = P(A) + P(B) \qquad 5\text{--}2$$

To apply the special rule of addition the events must be **mutually exclusive.** This means that when one of the events occurs, none of the others can occur at the same time. When a single die is rolled once, for example, a 2 and a 6 cannot both appear at the same time.

Venn Diagram

Venn diagrams, developed by English logician J. Venn, are useful for portraying events and their relationship to one another. They are constructed by enclosing a space, usually in a form of a rectangle which represents the possible events. Two mutually

exclusive events such as A and B can then be portrayed—as in the following diagram—by enclosing regions that do not overlap (that is, that have no common area).

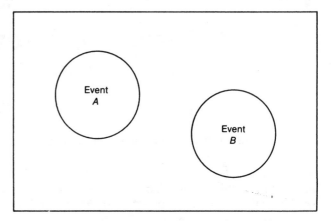

The **complement rule** states that the probability of the event A not occurring, written $P(\tilde{A})$, is equal to one minus the probability of the event A occurring. This is written $P(\tilde{A}) = 1 - P(A)$ or it could be written $P(A) = 1 - P(\tilde{A})$.

General Rule of Addition

What if the events are *not* mutually exclusive? In that case the **general rule of addition** is used. The probability is computed using the text formula 5–4.

$$P(A \text{ or } B) = P(A) + P(B) - P(A \text{ and } B) \qquad 5\text{--}4$$

where $P(A)$ is the probability of the event A, $P(B)$ the probability of the event B, and $P(A \text{ and } B)$ the probability that both events A and B occur. For example, a study showed 15 percent of the work force to be unemployed, 20 percent of the work force to be minorities, and 5 percent to be both unemployed and minorities. What percent of the work force are either minorities or unemployed? Note that if P (unemployed) and P (minority) are totalled, the 5 percent who are both minorities and unemployed are counted in both groups—that is, they are double-counted. They must be subtracted to avoid this double counting. Hence,

P (unemployed or minority)
 $= P$ (unemployed) $+ P$ (minority)
  $- P$ (unemployed and minority)
 $= .15 + .20 - .05$
 $= .30$

These two events are not mutually exclusive and would appear as follows in a Venn diagram:

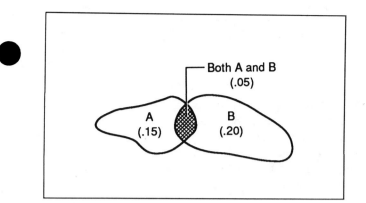

Both A and B
(.05)

A
(.15)

B
(.20)

Special Rule of Multiplication

The **special rule of multiplication** is used to combine events where the probability of the second event does not depend on the outcome of the first event. Two events are **independent** if the occurrence of one event does not affect the probability that the other event will occur. The probability of two independent events A and B occurring is found by multiplying the two probabilities. It is written as shown in text formula 5–5.

$$P(A \text{ and } B) = P(A) \times P(B) \qquad 5\text{–}5$$

As an example, a nuclear power plant has two independent safety systems. The probability the first will not operate properly in an emergency $P(A)$ is .01, and the probability the second will not operate $P(B)$ in an emergency is .02. What is the probability that in an emergency both of the plants will not operate? The probability both will not operate is:

$$
\begin{aligned}
P(A \text{ and } B) &= P(A) \times P(B) \\
&= (.01)(.02) \\
&= .0002
\end{aligned}
$$

The probability .0002 is called a **joint probability**, which is the simultaneous occurrence of two events. It measures the likelihood that two (or more) events will happen together (jointly).

General Rule of Multiplication

The **general rule of multiplication** is used to combine events that are *not* independent—that is, they are dependent on each other. For two events, the probability of the second event is affected by the outcome of the first event. Under these conditions, the probability of both A and B occurring is given in formula 5–6, where $P(B/A)$ is the probability of B occurring given that A has already occurred.

$$P(A \text{ and } B) = P(A) \times P(B/A) \qquad 5\text{–}6$$

where $P(B/A)$ is a **conditional probability**. A conditional probability is the likelihood of a second event occurring, given that the first has already happened.

For example, among a group of twelve prisoners, four had been convicted of murder. If two of the twelve are selected for a special rehabilitation program, what is the probability that both of those selected are convicted murderers? Let A_1 be the first selection (a convicted murderer) and A_2 the second selection (also a convicted murderer). Then $P(A_1) = 4/12$. After the first selection, there are 11 prisoners, 3 of whom are convicted of murder, hence $P(A_2|A_1) = 3/11$. The probability of both A_1 and A_2 happening is:

$$
\begin{aligned}
P(A_1 \text{ and } A_2) &= P(A_1) \times P(A_2|A_1) \\
&= 4/12 \times 3/11 \\
&= .0909
\end{aligned}
$$

Bayes' Theorem

Bayes' Theorem is used to revise the probability of a particular event happening based on the fact that some other event had already happened. For example, we have three machines each producing the same items. Machine A produces 10 percent defective and Machines B and C each 5 percent defective. Suppose each machine produces one-third of the total production. Since Machine A produces one-third of all the parts we naturally expect that prior to any experiment the probability of a defective being produced by Machine A is .33. Logically, the .33 is called a **prior** probability.

A part is selected at random. It was found to be defective. The question is: what is the probability that it was produced by Machine A? As noted above, Machine A produces twice as many defective parts as Machines B and C. (A produces 10%, B and C 5% each). Since we discovered that the part selected was defective, the probability it was manufactured by Machine A is now greater than .33. Bayes' Theorem will give us this revised probability. The formula is: (See formula 5–7)

$$P(A_1|B) = \frac{P(A_1) \times P(B|A_1)}{P(A_1) \times P(B|A_1) + P(A_2) \times P(B|A_2) + P(A_3) \times P(B|A_3)}$$

The probabilities to be inserted in the formula are:

P (A_1) = Probability the part was produced by Machine A = .33
P (A_2) = Probability the part was produced by Machine B = .33
P (A_3) = Probability the part was produced by Machine C = .33
P $(B|A_1)$ = Probability of a defect being produced by Machine A = .10
P $(B|A_2)$ = Probability of a defect being produced by Machine B = .05
P $(B|A_3)$ = Probability of a defect being produced by Machine C = .05

Solving:

$$P(A_1|B) = \frac{.33\ (.10)}{.33\ (.10) + .33\ (.05) + .33\ (.05)} = .50$$

Hence, the probability that the defective part was manufactured by Machine A is increased from 0.33 to 0.50. We revised upward the probability that the part was produced by Machine A, because we obtained the additional information that the part selected was defective.

Counting Rules

In previous examples it was not difficult to count the possible outcomes. However, sometimes the number of possible outcomes is quite large, and listing all the possibilities would be time consuming, tedious, and error prone. Three formulas are very useful for determining the number of possible outcomes in an experiment. They are: the *multiplication formula*, the *permutation formula*, and the *combination formula*. The **multiplication formula** states that if there are m ways of accomplishing one thing, and n ways of accomplishing another, there are m times n ways of doing both. The formula is $m \times n$.

A **permutation** is an arrangement of objects or things wherein order is important. That is, each time the objects or things are placed in a different order,

a new permutation results. The formula for the number of permutations is:

$$_nP_r = \frac{n!}{(n - r)!} \qquad 5\text{–}9$$

where P is the number of ways the objects can be arranged, n the total number of objects, and r the number of objects used at one time.

The above formula does not allow for repetitions such as a,a,b, or a,b,b, when selecting three letters from the group a, b, and c. If repetitions are permitted the formula is:

$$_nP_r = n^r$$

One particular arrangement of the objects without regard to order is called a **combination**. If, for example a, b, and c is the came as c, a, b the combination formula would be used. It is computed:

$$_nC_r = \frac{n!}{r!\ (n - r)!} \qquad 5\text{–}10$$

where C is the number of different combinations, n the total number of objects, and r the number of objects used at one time.

GLOSSARY

Probability—A measure of the degree of belief that a particular outcome will happen. Probabilities may range from 0 to 1.0, inclusive where 0 indicates that the event will not happen and 1.0 indicates it will definitely happen.

Experiment—The observation of some activity, or the act of taking some type of measurement.

Outcome—A particular result of an experiment.

Event—A collection of one or more outcomes of an experiment.

Classical probability—Each of the possible outcomes is equally likely. If there are n outcomes, the probability of a particular outcome is 1/n.

Relative frequency—The total number of times the event has occurred in the past, divided by the total number of observations.

Subjective probability—The assignment of probabilites based on whatever information is available—personal opinion, hunches, etc.

Mutually exclusive—If one of the outcomes of an experiment occurs, then none of the others can occur at the same time.

Venn diagram—A diagram useful for portraying the relationship of events.

Special rule of addition—If two events are mutually exclusive, the probability that one or the other will happen is $P(A \text{ or } B) = P(A) + P(B)$.

General rule of addition—If the two events are *not* mutually exclusive: $P(A \text{ or } B) = P(A) + P(B) - P(A \text{ and } B)$ where $P(A \text{ and } B)$ is the joint probability of the occurrence of the events A and B.

Independent events—The occurrence of one event does not affect the probability the other events will occur.

Complement Rule—The probability of an event not happening can be determined by subtracting the probability of it happening from 1. That is, $P(\sim A) = 1 - P(A)$.

Conditional probability—The probability of the occurrence of a second event given the first event has occurred.

Joint probability—The simultaneous occurrence of two events.

Special rule of multiplication—A rule for combining two or more independent events. The probability of events A and B occurring is $P(A \text{ and } B) = P(A) \times P(B)$.

General rule of multiplication—A rule for combining two dependent events. The probability of the event A and B occuring is the probability of the event A times the probability of the event B, given that the event A occurred. $P(A \text{ and } B) = P(A) \times P(B \mid A)$.

Permutations—The number of ways a group of objects can be arranged when the order is important.

Combinations—A particular arrangement of the objects without regard to order.

Bayes' Theorem—A method for revising a probability based on obtaining additional information.

Prior probability—The original or initial probability determined prior to conducting the experiment.

CHAPTER PROBLEMS

Problem 1

Dunn Pontiac has compiled the following sales data regarding the number of cars sold over the past 60 selling days.

Number of Cars sold	Number of Days
0	5
1	5
2	10
3	20
4	15
5 or more	5
Total	60

Answer the following questions:

What is the probability that two cars are sold during a particular day?
What is the probability of selling 3 or more cars during a particular day?
What is the probability of selling at least one car during a particular day?

Solution

This problem is an example of the relative frequency type of probability, because the probability of an event happening is based on the number of times the particular event happened in the past relative to the total number of observations.

The events are mutually exclusive. That is, if a total of two cars are sold on a particular day, four cannot be sold. The probability that exactly two cars are sold is:

$$P(2 \text{ cars}) = \frac{\text{Number of days two cars were sold}}{\text{Total number of days}} = \frac{10}{60} = .1667$$

The probability of selling three or more cars is obtained by using a special rule of addition given in formula 5–2. Let X represent the number of cars sold ($[\geq$ is read "greater than or equal to." The notation $>$ would be just greater than), then

$$P(X \geq 3) = P(3) + P(4) + P(5 \text{ or more})$$

$$= \frac{20}{60} + \frac{15}{60} + \frac{5}{60} = \frac{40}{60} = .67$$

Interpreting, three cars or more are sold 67 percent of the days.

The probability of selling *at least one* car is determined by adding the probabilities of selling one, two, three, four, and five or more cars. Again let X be the number of cars sold, then

$$P(X \geq 1) = P(1) + P(2) + P(3) + P(4) + P(5 \text{ or more})$$

$$= \frac{5}{60} + \frac{10}{60} + \frac{20}{60} + \frac{15}{60} + \frac{5}{60} = \frac{55}{60} = .92$$

The same result can also be obtained by using the complement rule. The probability of the occurrence of a particular event is obtained by computing the probability it did not occur and then subtracting that value from 1.0. In this example, the probability of not selling any cars is $5/60 = .08$, $1 - .08 = .92$.

$$P(X \geq 1) = 1.0 - P(0)$$

$$= 1.0 - \frac{5}{60} = 1 - .08 = .92$$

58

Exercise 1

Check your answers against those in the ANSWER section.

A study was made to investigate the number of times adult males over 30 visit a physician each year. The results for a sample of 300 were:

Number of Visits	Number of Adult Males
0	30
1	60
2	90
3 or more	120
Total	300

a. What is the probability of selecting someone who visits a physician twice a year?

b. What is the probability of selecting someone who visits a physician?

Problem 2

A local community has two newspapers. The *Morning Times* is read by 45 percent of the households. The *Evening Dispatch* is read by 60 percent of the households. Twenty percent of the households read both papers. What is the probability that a particular household in the city reads at least one paper?

Solution

If we combine the three probabilities (.45, .60, and .20), they exceed 1.00. The group that reads both papers, of course, is being counted twice and must be subtracted to arrive at the answer. Letting T represent the *Morning Times*, and D the *Evening Dispatch*, and using the general rule of addition, formula 5–4:

$$
\begin{aligned}
P(T \text{ or } D) &= P(T) + P(D) - P(T \text{ and } D) \\
&= .45 + .60 - .20 \\
&= .85
\end{aligned}
$$

Thus, 85 percent of the households in the community read at least one paper.

Exercise 2

Check your answers against those in the ANSWER section.

The proportion of students at Pemberville University who own an automobile is .60. The proportion who live in a dormitory is .20. The proportion who both own an automobile and live in a dormitory is .12. What proportion of the students either own an auto or live in a dorm?

Problem 3

The probability that a bomber hits a target on a bombing mission is .70. Three bombers are sent to bomb a particular target. What is the probability that they all hit the target? What is the probability that at least one hits the target?

Solution

These events are independent since the probability that one bomber hits the target does not depend on whether the other hits it. The special rule of multiplication, formula 5–5, is used to find the joint probability. B_1 represents the first bomber, B_2 the second bomber, and B_3 the third bomber.

$$
\begin{aligned}
P(\text{all 3 hit target}) &= P(B_1)P(B_2)P(B_3) \\
&= (.70)\,(.70)\,(.70) \\
&= .343
\end{aligned}
$$

Hence the probability that all three complete the mission is .343.

The probability that at least one bomber hits the target is found by combining the complement rule and the multiplication rule. To explain: The probability of a miss with the first bomber is .30, found by $P(M_1) = 1 - .70$. The probability for M_2 and M_3 is also .30. The multiplication rule is used to obtain the probability that all three miss. Let X be the number of hits.

$$
\begin{aligned}
P(X > 0) &= 1 - P(0) \\
&= 1 - [P(M_1)]\,[P(M_2)]\,[P(M_3)] \\
&= 1 - [(.30)\,(.30)\,(.30)] \\
&= 1 - .027 = .973
\end{aligned}
$$

Exercise 3

Check your answers against those in the ANSWER section.

A side effect of a certain anesthetic used in surgery is the hiccups, which occurs in about 10 percent of the cases. If three patients are scheduled for surgery today, and are to be administered this anesthetic, compute the probability that all three get hiccups, that none get hiccups, and that at least one gets hiccups.

Problem 4

Yesterday, the Bunte Auto Repair Shop received a shipment of four carburetors. One is known to be defective. If two are selected at random and tested: (a) What is the probability that neither one is defective? (b) What is the probability that the defective carburetor is located by testing two carburetors?

Solution

(a) The selections of the two carburetors are not independent events because the selection of the first affects the second outcome. Let G_1 represent the first "good" carburetor and G_2 the second "good" one.

$$P(G_1 \text{ and } G_2) = P(G_1) \times P(G_2|G_1)$$

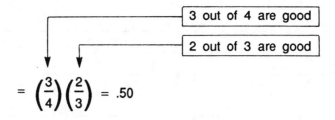

$$= \left(\frac{3}{4}\right)\left(\frac{2}{3}\right) = .50$$

Hence, the probability that neither of the two selected carburetors is defective is .50.

(b) The probability that the defective carburetor is found requires the general rule of multiplication and the general rule of addition.

In this case the defect may be detected either in the first test or in the second one. The general rule of multiplication is used. Let D_1 represent a defect on the first test and D_2 on the second test. The probability is:

$$P(\text{find the defect}) = P(G_1) \times P(D_2|G_1) + P(D_1) \times P(G_2|D_1)$$

$$= \left(\frac{3}{4}\right)\left(\frac{1}{3}\right) + \left(\frac{1}{4}\right)\left(\frac{3}{3}\right) = .50$$

To explain further, the probability that the first carburetor tested is good is $P(G_1) = 3/4$. If the first one selected is good, then to meet the requirements of the problem the second one sampled must be defective. This conditional probability is $P(D_2/G_1) = 1/3$. The joint probability of these two events is 3/12 or 1/4. The defective part could be found on the first test $[P(D_1)]$. Since there is one defect among the four carburetors the probability that it will be found on the first test is 1/4. If the defect is found on the first test then the three remaining parts are good. Hence the conditional probability of selecting a good carburetor on the second trial is 1.0 $[P(G_2|D_1)]$. The joint probability of a defective part being followed by a good part is 1/4, found by $P(D_1) \times P(G_2|D_1) = (1/4)(3/3) = 1/4$. The sum of these two outcomes is .50.

Exercise 4

Check your answers against those in the ANSWER section.

Ten students are being interviewed for a class office. Six of them are female and four are male. Their names are all placed in a box and two are selected to be interviewed tomorrow. (a) What is the probability that both of those selected are female? (b) What is the probability that at least one is male?

Problem 5

A large department store is analyzing the per-customer amount of purchase and the method of payment. For a sample of 140 customers the following cross-classified table presents the findings.

Payment Method	Amount of Purchase			Total
	B_1: Less than $20	B_2: $20 up to $50	B_3: $50 or more	
A_1: Cash	15	10	5	30
A_2: Check	10	30	20	60
A_3: Charge	10	20	20	50
Total	35	60	45	140

(a) What is the probability of selecting someone who paid by cash or made a purchase of less than $20?

(b) What is the probability of selecting someone who paid by check and made a purchase of more than $50?

Solution

(a) If we combine the events "Less than $20" ($B_1$) and "Cash payment" ($A_1$), then those who paid cash for purchase of less than $20 are counted twice. That is, these two events are not mutually exclusive. Therefore the general rule of addition formula 5–4 is used:

$$P(A_1 \text{ or } B_1) = P(A_1) + P(B_1) - P(A_1 \text{ and } B_1)$$

$$= \frac{30}{140} + \frac{35}{140} - \frac{15}{140} = \frac{50}{140} = .36$$

The probability of selecting a customer who made a cash payment or purchased an item for less than $20 is .36.

(b) Conditional probability is used to find the probability of selecting someone who paid by check (A_2) and who made a purchase of over $50 ($B_3$).

There are two qualifications: "paid by check" and "made a purchase of over $50." Referring to the table, 20 out of 140 customers meet both qualifications, therefore $20/140 = 0.14$.

This probability could also be computed in a three-step process:

1. The probability of selecting those who paid by check (A_2) is $60/140 = .43$.
2. Of the 60 persons who paid by check, 20 made a purchase of over $50. Therefore $P(B_3/A_2) = 20/60 = .33$.
3. These two events are then combined using the general rule of multiplication formula 5–6:

$$P(A_2 \text{ and } B_3) = P(A_2) \, P(B_3/A_2)$$
$$= (.43)(.33) = .14$$

Exercise 5

Check your answers against those in the ANSWER section.

Five hundred adults over 50 years of age were classified according to whether they smoked or not, and if they smoked were they a moderate or heavy smoker. Also, each one was asked whether he or she had ever had a heart attack. The results were:

	Heart Attack		Total
	Yes	No	
Do not smoke	30	220	250
Moderate smoker	60	65	125
Heavy smoker	90	35	125
Totals	180	320	500

a. What is the probability of selecting a person who either has had a heart attack, or who is a heavy smoker?

b. What is the probability of selecting a heavy smoker who did not have a heart attack?

Problem 6

The probability that a person has "BLEEBS," a rare disease that occurs in young baseball players, is .02. If a person has BLEEBS, the probability that the individual is diagnosed as having it is .80. On the other hand, if an individual does not have BLEEBS, the probability of being diagnosed as having it is .05. Given that a person is diagnosed as having BLEEBS, what is the probability that the person really does *not* have it?

Solution

This problem is solved using Bayes' Theorem. The various parts of the problem are as follows:

$P(B)$ is the probability of having BLEEBS. It is .02.
$P(NB)$ is the probability of not having BLEEBS. It is .98
$P(D|B)$ is the probability of being diagnosed as having BLEEBS, given that the person has the disease. It is .80.
$P(D|NB)$ is the probability of being diagnosed as having BLEEBS, given that the person does not have the disease. It is .05.
P($NB|D$) is the revised probability of not having BLEEBS, given that diagnosis is that of having BLEEBS.

A useful device for displaying conditional and joint probabilities is called a tree diagram. The tree diagram will be used to solve the above problem. The initial relationships are as follows:

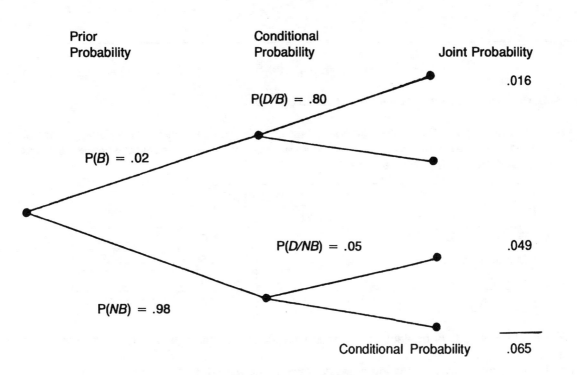

The computational form of Bayes' Theorem formula 5–7 is repeated below.

$$P(NB/D) = \frac{P(NB)\ P(D|NB)}{P(B)\ P(D/B) + P(NB)\ P(D|NB)}$$

$$= \frac{(.98)\ (.05)}{(.02)\ (.80) + (.98)\ (.05)} = .754$$

Interpreting, this means that even though a person is diagnosed as having BLEEBS, the probability of not actually having it is .754.

To explain this problem further, everyone falls into one of two categories, they have BLEEBS or they don't. Only two percent of the population actually have the condition [P(B) = .02] and 98 percent do not [P(NB) = .98]. Of those having BLEEBS, 80 percent are correctly diagnosed [P(D|B) = .80], but some people are diagnosed as having BLEEBS, when they actually do not [P(D|NB) = .05]. These are actually false positive readings.

The denominator of Bayes' Theorem computes the fraction of the population that are diagnosed as having BLEEBS. That fraction is obtained by combining the two joint probabilities as follows:

$$P(B) = P(B) \times (D|B) + P(NB) \times P(D|NB) = (.02)\ (.80) + (.98)\ (.05)$$

$$= .065$$

The .065 is the fraction of the population that will be diagnosed as having BLEEBS. However, some of those diagnosed actually have the condition [P(B) × P(D|B) = (.02) (.80) = .016] and some while diagnosed as having BLEEBS actually do not [P(NB) × P(D|NB) = (.98) (.05) = .049]. We are interested in the fraction that are diagnosed as having the condition but really don't [(.049/.065) = .754]. This result may seem rather startling, because more than 75 percent of the time the test results are actually incorrect. This indicates that the test for BLEEBS is not very discriminating.

Exercise 6

Check your answers against those in the ANSWER section.

A test on probability is to be given next week. Suppose 75 percent of the students study for the test and 25 percent do not. If a student studies for the exam the probability that he or she will pass is .90. If the student does not study, the probability that he or she will pass is 20 percent. Given that the student passed the test what is the probability he or she studied?

Problem 7

A deli bar offers a special sandwich, for which there is a choice of five different cheeses, four different meat selections, and three different rolls. How many different sandwich combinations are possible?

Solution

Using the multiplication formula, there are five cheeses (*c*), four meats (*m*), and three rolls (*r*). The total number of possible sandwiches is 60 found by:

$$cmr = (5)\,(4)\,(3) = 60$$

Exercise 7

Check your answers against those in the ANSWER section.

The Swansons are planning to fly to Hawaii from Toronto with a stopover in Los Angeles. There are five flights they can take between Toronto and Los Angeles and ten flights between Los Angeles and Hawaii. How many different flights are possible between Toronto and Hawaii?

Problem 8

Three scholarships are available for needy students. Their values are: $1,000, $1,200, and $1,500. Twelve students have applied and no student may receive more than one scholarship. Assuming all twelve students are in need of funds, how many different ways could the scholarships be awarded?

Solution

This is an example of a permutation because a different assignment of the scholarships means another arrangement. Jones could be awarded the $1,000 scholarship, Sinski the $1,200 scholarship, and Peters the $1,500 scholarship. Or, Sinski could be awarded the $1,000, Seiple the $1,200 one, and Orts the $1,500 scholarship, and so on.

$$_nP_r = \frac{n!}{(n-r)!} = \frac{12!}{(12-3)!} = \frac{12 \times 11 \times 10 \times 9!}{9!} = 1{,}320$$

where n is the total number of applicants and r is number of scholarships.

Exercise 8

Check your answers against those in the ANSWER section.

A company has four plumbers. If there are repairs to be done at eight households, in how many different ways can the households be assigned to the plumbers?

Problem 9

The basketball coach of Dalton University is quite concerned about their 40 straight losses. He is so frustrated that he decided to select the starting lineup for the DU-UCLA game by drawing five names from the 12 available players at random. (Assume that a player can play any position.) How many different starting lineups are possible?

Solution

This is an example of a combination because the order in which the players are selected is not important. Jocko, Camden, Urfer, Smith, and Marchal is the same starting lineup as Smith, Camden, Marchal, Jocko, and Urfer, and so on.

$$_nC_r = \frac{n!}{r!\,(n-r)!} = \frac{12!}{5!\,(12-5)!} = \frac{12 \times 11 \times 10 \times 9 \times 8 \times 7!}{5 \times 4 \times 3 \times 2 \times 1 \times 7!} = \frac{95{,}040}{120} = 792$$

where n is the total number of available players and r is the number in the starting lineup.

Exercise 9

Check your answers against those in the ANSWER section.

A major corporation has branch offices in eight major cities in the United States and Canada. The company president wants to visit five of these offices. How many different trip combinations are possible?

CHAPTER ASSIGNMENT 5

A Survey of Probability Concepts

Name _____ Section _____ Score _____

Part I Select the correct answer and write the appropriate letter in the space provided.

___ 1. Which of the following statements regarding probability is always correct?
    a. A probability can range from 0 to 1.
    b. A probability close to 0 means the event is not likely to happen.
    c. A probability close to I means the event is likely to happen.
    d. all of the above are correct

___ 2. A probability is
    a. never greater than 1.
    b. never less than 0.
    c. a measure of the likelihood an event will happen.
    d. all of the above

___ 3. According to the classical definition of probability
    a. all the events are equally likely.
    b. the probability is based on hunches.
    c. the number of successes is divided by the total number of outcomes.
    d. one outcome is exactly twice the other.

___ 4. The observation of some activity or the act of taking some measurement is called
    a. an outcome.
    b. an event.
    c. a probability.
    d. an experiment.

___ 5. The particular result of an experiment is called
    a. an outcome.
    b. an event.
    c. a probability.
    d. an experiment.

___ 6. An event is the collection of one or more
    a. outcomes.
    b. combinations.
    c. probabilities.
    d. experiments.

___ 7. For the special rule of addition the events must be
    a. continuous.
    b. discrete.
    c. mutually exclusive.
    d. independent.

___ 8. To apply the special rule of multiplication the events must be
    a. continuous.
    b. discrete
    c. mutually exclusive.
    d. independent.

___ 9. The complement rule states that the probability of an event happening is
   a. equal to 1 minus the probability of the event not happening.
   b. mutually exclusive.
   c. not independent.
   d. twice the probability of the event happening.

___ 10. The simultaneous occurrence of two events is called the
   a. prior probability.
   b. special rule of addition.
   c. conditional probability.
   d. joint probability.

Part II Fill in the blank with the correct answer.

11. When are two events independent?_____

_____

12. When are two events mutually exclusive?_____

_____

13. List and describe the three types of probability.
   a. _____
   b. _____
   c. _____

14. Briefly explain the difference between a permutation and a combination._____

_____

15. The probability of the occurrence of a second event given that the first event has occurred is called the _____ probability.

Part III Record your answers in the space provided. Show all your work.

16. A recent study of young executives showed that 30 percent jogged, 20 percent swam, and 12 percent did both. What is the percent of young executives who jog or swim?

```
┌──────────────┐
│              │
└──────────────┘
   Answer
```

17. A survey of construction jobs indicates that 70 percent are completed on time. If three jobs are selected for study
   a. What is the probability they are all completed on time?

```
┌──────────────┐
│              │
└──────────────┘
   Answer
```

b. What is the probability that at least one was not completed on time?

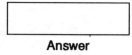

Answer

18. Today's local newspaper lists 20 stocks "of local interest." Of these stocks, ten increased, five decreased, and five remained unchanged yesterday. If we decide to buy two of these stocks, what is the likelihood that both increased yesterday?

Answer

19. A manager just bought four suits, six shirts, and ten ties. If all the suits, shirts, and ties coordinate with each other, how many outfits are possible?

Answer

20. The United Way Campaign of Greater Toledo had fifteen applications for funding this year. If eight of these applications can be funded, how many different lists of successful applications are there?

Answer

21. Rob Yelton, a management trainee at Vatter Trucking, Inc., drives to work 60 percent of the time and takes the bus the rest of the time. When he drives himself, he is late 5 percent of the time and when he takes the bus he is late 20 percent of the time. Rob was late for work this morning. What is the likelihood that he took the bus?

Answer

22. The Levinson Brothers, a large department store located in many shopping malls, is studying the relationship between the gender of customers and whether they pay by check, cash, or credit card. The following table is a two-way classification of 500 purchases last month.

	Method of payment			
	Cash	Check	Credit card	Total
Male	50	100	50	200
Female	100	50	150	300
Total	150	150	200	500

a. What is the likelihood of selecting a customer who paid cash?

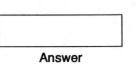

Answer

b. What is the likelihood of selecting a customer who paid cash or was female?

Answer

c. What is the likelihood of selecting a customer who paid cash and was female?

Answer

d. What is the likelihood of selecting a customer who paid cash, given that the customer was female?

Answer

6

DISCRETE PROBABILITY DISTRIBUTIONS

CHAPTER GOALS

After completing this chapter, you will be able to:

1. Define the terms probability distribution and random variable.
2. Distinguish between a discrete and a continuous probability distribution.
3. Calculate the mean, variance, and standard deviation of a discrete probability distribution.
4. List the characteristics of a binomial distribution and compute probabilities.
5. List the characteristics of the hypergeometric distribution and compute probabilities.
6. List the characteristics of a Poisson distribution and compute probabilities.

Introduction

In the previous chapter we discussed the basic concepts of probability and described how the rules of addition and multiplication were used to compute probabilities. In this chapter we expand the study of probability to include the concepts of a **random variable** and a **probability distribution**.

Random Variable

A **random variable** is a value determined by the outcome of an experiment. A random variable may have two forms: discrete or continuous. A **discrete random variable** may assume only distinct values and is usually the result of counting. For example, the number of highway deaths in Arkansas on Memorial Day weekend may be 0, 1, 2,. . . . Another example is the number of students earning a grade of B in your statistics class. In both instances the number of occurrences result from counting. Note that there can be 12 deaths or 15 B's but there cannot be 12.63 deaths or 15.27 B grades. Does this rule out the possibility that a discrete random variable may assume fractional values? No. A study of stock prices might reveal that 20 stocks increased by one-eighth of a point ($0.125) and that 12 increased by one-fourth of a point ($0.25). Note that the random variable itself may assume fractional values, but there is some distance between these values. In the stock example the result is still a count—that is, 12 stocks increased by $0.25.

A **continuous random variable** may assume an infinite number of values within a given range. For example, in a high school track meet, the winning time of the mile run may be reported as 4 minutes 20 seconds, 4 minutes 20.2 seconds, or 4 minutes 20.2416 seconds, and so on, depending on the accuracy of the timing device. We will examine the continuous random variable and the continuous probability distribution in Chapter 7.

Discrete Probability Distributions

What is a *probability distribution*? It is a listing of all the possible outcomes of an experiment, and the corresponding probability associated with each outcome. As an example, the possible outcomes on the

roll of a single die are 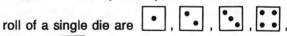. Each face should appear on about one-sixth of the rolls. Listed below are the possible outcomes and corresponding probabilities for this experiment. It is a discrete distribution because only certain outcomes are possible and the distribution is a result of counting the various outcomes.

Number of Spots on Die	Probability		
	Fraction		Decimal
1	1/6	=	.1667
2	1/6	=	.1667
3	1/6	=	.1667
4	1/6	=	.1667
5	1/6	=	.1667
6	1/6	=	.1667
Total	6/6	=	1.0000

There are several important features of the discrete probability distribution: (1) the listing is exhaustive; that is, all the possible outcomes are included. (2) The total (sum) of all possible outcomes is 1.0. (3) The probability of any particular outcome is between 0 and 1 inclusive. (See the table above.) (4) The outcomes are mutually exclusive meaning, for example, a 6 spot and a 2 spot cannot appear at the same time on the roll of one die.

This discrete probability distribution, presented above as a table, may also be portrayed in graphic form:

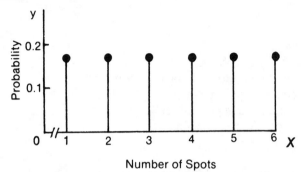

Number of Spots

By convention the probability is shown on the Y-axis (the vertical axis) and the outcomes on the X-axis (the horizontal axis). This probability distribution is often referred to as a uniform distribution.

A probability distribution can also be expressed in equation form. For example:

$P(X) = 1/6$, where X can assume the values 1, 2, 3, 4, 5, or 6.

What is the difference between a random variable and a probability distribution? A probability distribution lists all the possible outcomes as well as their corresponding probabilities. A random variable lists only the outcomes.

Mean and Variance of a Probability Distribution

In Chapters 3 and 4 we computed the mean and variance of a frequency distribution. The mean is a measure of central tendency and the variance is a measure of the spread of the data. In a similar fashion the mean (μ) and the variance (σ^2) summarize a probability distribution.

The mean, or expected value, of a probability distribution is its long-run average. It is computed by the following formula:

$$\mu = E(X) = \Sigma[XP(X)] \qquad 6-1$$

This formula directs you to multiply each outcome (X) by its probability $P(X)$; and then add the products.

While the mean describes the center of a probability distribution, it does not tell us anything about the spread in the distribution. The variance tells us about the spread or variation in the data. The variance is computed using the following formula:

$$\sigma^2 = \Sigma[(X - \mu)^2 P(X)] \qquad 6-2$$

The steps in computing the variance using formula 6–2 are:

1. Subtract the mean (μ) from each outcome (X) and square these differences.
2. Multiply each squared difference by its probability $P(X)$.
3. Sum these products to arrive at the variance.

The Binomial Probability Distribution

One of the most widely used discrete distributions is the **binomial probability distribution.** It has the following characteristics:

1. Each outcome is classified into one of two mutually exclusive categories. An outcome is classified as either a "success" or a "failure." For example, 40 percent of the students at a particular university are enrolled in the College of Business. For a selected student there are only two possible outcomes—the student is enrolled in the College of Business (designated a success) or he/she is not enrolled in the College of Business (designated a failure).
2. The binomial distribution is the result of counting the number of success in a fixed sample size. If we select 5 students 0, 1, 2, 3, 4, or 5 could be enrolled in the College of Business. This rules out the possibility of 3.45 of the students being enrolled in the College of Business. That is, there cannot be fractional counts.
3. Each sample item is independent. This means that if the first student selected is enrolled in the College of Business, it has no effect on whether the second or the fourth one selected will be in the College of Business.
4. The probability of a success remains the same from trial to trial. In the example regarding the College of Business, the probability of a success remains at 40 percent for all five students selected.

The number of trials, designated n, and the probability of success (p), must be known to construct a binomial distribution. The binomial probability distribution is constructed using the formula:

$$P(r) = \frac{n!}{r! \ (n - r)!} \ (p)^r \ (q)^{n-r} \qquad 6\text{--}3$$

where n is the number of trials, r the number of successes, p the probability of a success and q is equal to $1 - p$, the probability of a failure.

Hypergeometric Distribution

To qualify as a binomial distribution, the probability of a success must remain constant. What if this requirement is not met? This usually happens when the size of the population is small and samples are drawn from the population and not replaced. This causes the probability of a success to change from one trial (or sample) to the next. This means the trails are *not* independent. For example, if a class consisted of 20 students, 12 males and 8 females, what is the probability of selecting two females to serve on a committee? If Ms. Smith was selected on the first trial she cannot be selected again because she is already on the committee. Thus the outcome of the second trial depends on the outcome of the first trial. The probability of a female on the first selection is 8/20, and if a female is selected first there are 7 females out of the 19 remaining students. Hence the probability of selecting two females for the committee is .147 found by (8/20) (7/19).

This probability may also be calculated using the hypergeometric distribution, which is described by the formula:

$$P(r) = \frac{(_sC_r) \ (_{N-s}C_{n-r})}{_NC_n} \qquad 6\text{--}6$$

where N is the size of the population, S is the number of successes in the population, n is the number sampled, and r is the number of successes in the sample. In the example $N = 20$, $S = 8$, $n = 2$, and $r = 2$. Therefore,

$$P(2) = \frac{(_8C_2) \ (_{20-8}C_{2-2})}{_{20}C_2}$$

$$P(2) = \frac{\left(\dfrac{8!}{2! \ 6!}\right)\left(\dfrac{12!}{0! \ 12!}\right)}{\left(\dfrac{20!}{2! \ 18!}\right)} = .147$$

Hence, the probability of selecting two students to serve on a committee and having that committee consist of two females is .147. This is the same probability as computed above.

Poisson Probability

Another discrete probability distribution is the **Poisson probability distribution.** It has the same four characteristics as the binomial, but in addition the probability of success (p) is small, and n, the number of trials, is relatively large. The formula for computing the probability of a success is:

$$P(x) = \frac{\mu^x e^{-\mu}}{x!} \qquad 6\text{--}4$$

where X is the number of successes and μ is the mean number of occurrences (successes) found by $n \times p$, and e is 2.71828 which is the base of the Napierian logarithmic system.

As an example where the Poisson distribution is applicable, suppose electric utility bills are based on the actual reading of the electric meter. In 1 out of 100 cases the meter is incorrectly read ($p = .01$). Suppose the number of errors that appear in the processing of 500 customer bills approximates the Poisson distribution ($n = 500$). In this case the mean number of incorrect bills is 5, found by $\mu = np = 500 \ (.01)$.

Using formula 6–4 finding the probability of exactly two errors appearing in 500 customer bills is rather tedious. Instead we merely refer to the Poisson distribution in Appendix C. Locate μ (5.0) at the top of a set of columns. Then find the X of 2 in the left column and read across to the column headed by 5.0. The probability of exactly 2 billing errors is 0.0842.

GLOSSARY

Probability distribution—The listing of all possible outcomes of an experiment and the probability associated with each outcome. This listing is exhaustive and the outcomes are mutually exclusive.

Discrete probability distribution—A distribution that can assume only distinct values. It is the result of counting the number of favorable outcomes to an experiment.

Binomial probability distribution—A discrete probability distribution with the following characteristics: (1) The experiment consists of a sequence of *n* trials. (2) For each trial there are only two possible outcomes—one called a "success" and other a "failure." (3) The probability of a "success" remains the same from trial to trial. So does the probability of "failure." (4) The trials are independent.

Poisson probability distribution—A discrete probability distribution. It has the same characteristics as the binomial, but in addition, the probability of a success is usually small and the number of trials is large. The distribution is positively skewed.

Hypergeometric probability distribution—A discrete probability where the outcomes of consecutive observations are not independent.

Random variable—It is a numerical value determined by the outcome of an experiment.

CHAPTER PROBLEMS

Problem 1

Bill Russe, production manager at Ross Manufacturing, maintains detailed records on the number of times each machine breaks down and requires service during the week. Bill's records show that the Puret grinder has required repair service according to the following distribution. Compute the arithmetic mean and the variance of the number of breakdowns per week.

Number of breakdowns per week	Weeks	Probability
0	20	.333
1	20	.333
2	10	.167
3	10	.167
Total	60	1.000

Solution

The arithmetic mean, or expected number of breakdowns per week for the probability distribution is computed using formula 6–1.

Number of breakdowns per week X	Probability P(X)	XP(X)
0	.333	0
1	.333	.333
2	.167	.334
3	.167	.501
		E(X) = 1.168

The arithmetic mean number of times the Purett machine breaks down per week is 1.168. The variance of the number of breakdowns is computed using formula 6–2.

Number of breakdowns per week X	Probability P(X)	(X − μ)	(X − μ)² P(X)
0	.333	0 − 1.168	(1.364) (.333) = .454212
1	.333	1 − 1.168	(0.028) (.333) = .009324
2	.167	2 − 1.168	(0.692) (.167) = .115564
3	.167	3 − 1.168	(3.356) (.167) = .560452
		Total	1.139552

The variance of the number of breakdowns per week is about 1.140. The standard deviation of the number of breakdowns per week is 1.07, found by $\sqrt{1.140}$.

Exercise 1

Check your answers against those in the ANSWER section.

The safety engineer at Manellis Electronics reported the following probability distribution for the number of on-the-job accidents during a one-month period. Compute the mean and the variance.

Number of Accidents	Probability
0	.60
1	.30
2	.10

Problem 2

An insurance representative has appointments with four prospective clients tomorrow. From past experience she knows that the probability of making a sale on any appointment is 1 in 5 or .20. Use the rule of probability to determine the likelihood that she will sell a policy to 3 of the 4 prospective clients.

Solution

First note that the situation described meets the requirements of the binomial probability distribution. The conditions are:

1. There are a fixed number of trials—the representative visits four customers.
2. There are only two possible outcomes for each trial—she sells a policy or she does not sell a policy.
3. The probability of a success remains constant from trial to trial—for each appointment the probability of selling a policy (a success) is .20.
4. The trials are independent—if she sells a policy to the second appointment this does not alter the likelihood of selling to the third or the fourth appointment.

If S represents the outcome of a sale and NS the outcome of no sale, one possibility is that no sale is made on the first appointment but sales are made at the last 3.

$$(NS, S, S, S)$$

These events are independent, therefore the probability of their joint occurrence is the product of the individual probabilities. Therefore, the likelihood of no sale followed by three sales is (0.8) (0.2) (0.2) (0.2) = .0064. However, the requirements of the problem do not stipulate the location of NS. It could be the results of any one of the four appointments. The following summarizes the possible outcomes.

Location of NS	Order of Occurrence	Probability of Occurrence
1	NS, S, S, S	(0.8) (0.2) (0.2) (0.2) = .0064
2	S, NS, S, S	(0.2) (0.8) (0.2) (0.2) = .0064
3	S, S, NS, S	(0.2) (0.2) (0.8) (0.2) = .0064
4	S, S, S, NS	(0.2) (0.2) (0.2) (0.8) = .0064
		.0256

The probability of exactly three sales in the four appointments is the sum of the 4 possibilities. Hence, the probability of selling insurance to 3 out of 4 appointments is .0256.

Problem 3

Now lets use formula 6–3 for the binomial distribution to compute the probability that the sales representative in **Problem 2** will sell a policy to exactly 3 out of the 4 prospective clients.

Solution

To repeat, formula 6–3 for the binomial probability distribution is:

$$P(r) = \frac{n!}{r!\,(n-r)!}\,(p)^r\,(q)^{n-r}$$

where r is the number of successes, 3 in the example.
n is the number of trials, 4 in the example.
p is the probability of a success, .20
q is the where probability of a failure, $= .80$ found by $1 - .20$.

Applying the formula to find the probability of selling an insurance policy to exactly 3 out of 4 potential customers.

$$P(r) = \frac{n!}{r!\,(n-r)!}\,(p)^r\,(q)^{n-r}$$

$$= \frac{4!}{3!\,(4-3)!}\,(.20)^3\,(.80)^{4-3} = .0256$$

Thus the probability is .0256 that the representative will be able to sell policies to exactly 3 out of the 4 clients visited. This is the same probability as computed earlier. Clearly, formula 6–3 leads to a more direct solution, and better accommodates the situation where the number of trials is large.

Exercise 2

Check your answers against those in the ANSWER section.

It is known that 60 percent of all registered voters in the 42nd Congressional District are Republicans. Three registered voters are selected at random from the district. Compute the probability that exactly 2 of the 3 selected are Republicans, using both the rules of probability and the binomial formula.

Problem 4

In **Problems 2 and 3** the probability of 3 sales resulting from 4 appointments was computed using both the rules of addition and multiplication and the binomial formula. A more convenient way of arriving at the probabilities for 0, 1, 2, 3, or 4 sales out of 4 appointments is to refer to a binomial table. We will now use the binomial table to determine the probabilities for all possible outcomes.

Solution

Refer to Appendix A, the binomial table. Find the table where n, the number of trials, is 4. Within that table find the row where $r = 0$, and move horizontally to the column headed $p = .20$. The probability of 0 sales is .410. The list for all possible outcome number of successes is:

Binomial Probability Distribution

$$n = 4 \qquad p = .20$$

Number of Successes (r)	Probability
0	.410
1	.410
2	.154
3	.026
4	.002
	1.000*

*Slight discrepancy due to rounding.

Problem 5

Use the information regarding the insurance representative, where $n = 4$ and $p = .20$, to compute the probability that the representative sells more than two policies. Also determine the mean and variance.

Solution

The binomial table (Appendix A) can be used to compute the probability. First, note that the solution must include the probability that exactly 3 policies are sold and exactly 4 policies are sold, but not 2. From Appendix A, $P(3) = .026$ and $P(4) = .002$. The rule of addition is then used to combine these mutually exclusive events.

$$\begin{aligned} P(\text{more than } 2) &= P(3) + P(4) \\ &= .026 + .002 \\ &= .028 \end{aligned}$$

Thus the probability that a representative sells more than 2 policies is .028. Suppose the question asked is: "What is the probability of selling three or more policies in four trials?" Since there are no outcomes between greater than 2 and less than 3, the answer is exactly the same (.028).

To determine the mean and the variance of a binomial we use formulas 6–4 and 6–5. $\mu = np = 4(.20) = .80$. The variance of $\sigma^2 = np(1 - p) = 4(.20)(.80) = .64$. So the standard deviation is $\sqrt{.64} = .80$.

Exercise 3

Check your answers against those in the ANSWER section.

Labor negotiators estimate that 30 percent of all major contract negotiations result in a strike. During the next year, 12 major contracts must be negotiated. Determine the following probabilities using Appendix A: (a) no major strikes, (b) at least 5, and (c) between 2 and 4 (that is 2, 3, or 4).

Problem 6

Alden and Associates write weekend trip insurance at a very nominal charge. Records show that the probability a motorist will have an accident during the weekend and file a claim is quite small (.0005). Suppose Alden wrote 400 policies for the forthcoming weekend. Compute the probability that exactly two claims will be filed. Depict this distribution in a form of a chart.

Solution

The Poisson distribution is appropriate for this problem because the probability of filing a claim is small (p = .0005), and the number of trials n is large (400).
   The Poisson distribution is described by formula 6–7:

$$P(X) = \frac{\mu^x e^{-\mu}}{X!}$$

where X is the number of successes (claims filed). In this example $X = 2$
   μ is the expected or mean number of claims to be filed $\mu = np = (400)\,(.0005) = .2$
   e is a mathematical constant equal to 2.718.

The probability that exactly two claims are filed is 0.164, found by

$$P(2) = \frac{\mu^x e^{-\mu}}{X!} = \frac{(.2)^2(2.718)^{-0.2}}{2!} = .0164$$

This indicates that the probability is somewhat small (about .0164) that exactly 2 claims will be filed.

The calculations to determine the probability .0164 were not shown above. As noted previously, a more convenient way to determine Poisson probabilities is to refer to Appendix C. To use this table, first find the column where μ = 0.20, then go down that column to the row where $X = 2$ and read the value at the intersection. It is .0164.

The probabilities computed using formula 6–7 and those in Appendix C are the same. But those from the Appendix can be determined much more rapidly. The complete Poisson distribution and a graph for the case where μ = 0.20 are shown below.

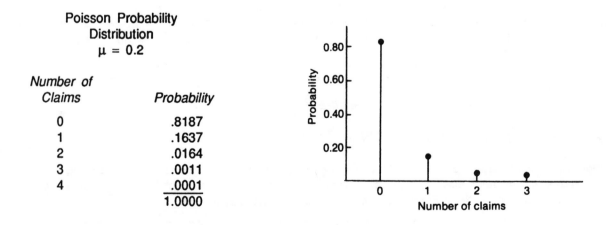

Poisson Probability
Distribution
μ = 0.2

Number of Claims	Probability
0	.8187
1	.1637
2	.0164
3	.0011
4	.0001
	1.0000

┌───┐

Exercise 4

Check your answers against those in the ANSWER section.

The probability of a typographical error on any page is .002. If a textbook contains 1,000 pages, compute the probability (a) that there are no typos on a page and (b) that there are at least 2.

Problem 7

The government of an underdeveloped country has 8 loans payable, 5 of which are overdue. If a representative of the International Monetary Fund randomly selects 3 loans, what is the probability that exactly 2 are overdue?

Solution

Note in this problem that successive observations are not independent. That is, the outcome of one sampled item influences the next sampled item. Because the observations are not independent, the binomial distribution is not appropriate and the hypergeometric distribution is used. To repeat formula 6–6 for the hypergeometric distribution:

$$P(r) = \frac{(_sC_r)\ (_{N-S}C_{n-r})}{_NC_n} \qquad\qquad 6\text{--}6$$

where N is the population size, S is the number of successes in the population, n is the number sampled, and r is the number of successes in the sample. The problem asks for the probability of exactly 2 loans overdue in a sample of 3, so $r = 2$ and $n = 3$. There are 8 loans in the population, 5 of which are overdue, so $N = 8$ and $S = 5$.

The probability is computed as follows:

$$P(2) = \frac{(_5C_2)\ (_3C_1)}{_8C_3} = \frac{\left(\dfrac{5!}{2!\ 3!}\right)\ \left(\dfrac{3!}{1!\ 2!}\right)}{\left(\dfrac{8}{3!\ 5!}\right)} = \frac{30}{56} = .536$$

Interpreting, the probability that exactly 2 of the 3 sampled loans are overdue is .536.

Exercise 5

Check your answers against those in the ANSWER section.

A retailer of personal computers just received a shipment of 30 units of a new model. The store has a quality agreement with the manufacturer which states that four of the machines are to be selected for a thorough performance check. If more than one fails a performance test the shipment is returned. Suppose the retailer did not know that 5 of the 30 incoming personal computers are defective. Compute the probability exactly two computers selected at random are defective.

CHAPTER ASSIGNMENT 6

Discrete Probability Distributions

Name _____ Section _____ Score _____

Part I Select the correct answer and write the appropriate letter in the space provided.

___ 1. A listing of all possible outcomes of an experiment and the corresponding probability is called
   a. a random variable.
   b. the complement rule.
   c. the normal rule.
   d. a probability distribution.

___ 2. A probability distribution that can assume only certain values within a range is called
   a. a discrete probability distribution.
   b. a continuous probability distribution.
   c. a random variable.
   d. none of the above.

___ 3. Which of the following is **not** a requirement of the binomial distribution?
   a. the trials must be independent
   b. the probability of a success changes from one trial to the next
   c. a fixed sample size
   d. only two possible outcomes

___ 4. The mean of a discrete probability distribution is also called the
   a. variance.
   b. standard deviation.
   c. expected value.
   d. median.

___ 5. The mean of a binomial distribution is found by
   a. *np.*
   b. *np* (1-*p*).
   c. 1/*p*
   d. none of the above

___ 6. Which of the following probability distributions is **not** always a discrete distribution?
   a. Poisson
   b. binomial
   c. hypergeometric
   d. normal

___ 7. A discrete distribution is usually the result of
   a. a measurement.
   b. a count.
   c. a small sample.
   d. a small probability.

___ 8. Which of the following is **not** a requirement for a discrete probability distribution?
   a. The sum of the probabilities is equal to 1.00.
   b. The probability of each outcome is between 0 and 1.00.

c. The outcomes are mutually exclusive.
d. The trials are independent.

___ 9. To construct a binomial probability distribution, we need to know
a. the mean and the standard deviation.
b. only the mean.
c. the size of the sample.
d. the values for n and p.

___ 10. The difference between the binomial distribution and the hypergeometric distribution is
a. the binomial requires a large sample.
b. the mean and the variance are equal for the binomial
c. the value of p is not the same for all trials in the hypergeometric.
d. the trials are not independent for the binomial.

Part III Fill in the blank with the correct answer.

11. What is the difference between a Poisson and a binomial probability distribution?_____
_____

12. What is the essential difference between a random variable and a probability distribution?_____
_____

13. List the four requirements of the binomial distribution.
a. _____
b. _____
c. _____
d. _____

14. What is the difference between a discrete and a continuous probability distribution?_____
_____

15. What is the difference between the hypergeometric probability distribution and the binomial probability
distribution?_____
_____

Part III Record your answer in the space provided. Show all your work.

16. Tom Schmidt, the service manager at Schmidt Jeep/Eagle, estimated the number of times new cars sold
at the dealership are brought in during the warranty period for adjustments. The estimates are:

Number of times	Proportion
0	.30
1	.40
2	.20
3	.10

a. Determine the mean number of times a car is returned for warranty work.

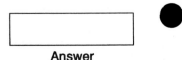

Answer

82

b. Determine the standard deviation of the number of times the car is returned.

Answer

17. According to a recent survey 80 percent of customers pay by cash at retail stores. Suppose eight customers are selected at random.
a. How many of the eight customers would you expect to purchase with cash?

Answer

b. What is the probability that exactly 6 purchase with cash?

Answer

c. What is the probability that at least 6 purchase with cash?

Answer

18. The Foreign Relations Committee is comprised of seven Republicans and five Democrats. Four members of the committee are selected at random to participate in foreign policy talks. What is the probability that two Republicans and two Democrats are selected?

Answer

19. On the average two new checking accounts are opened per day at the Marine National Bank. What is the likelihood that for a particular day:

a. no new accounts are opened?

Answer

b. at least one new account is opened?

Answer

7

THE NORMAL PROBABILITY DISTRIBUTION

CHAPTER GOALS

After completing this chapter, you will be able to:

1. List the characteristics of the normal distribution.
2. Calculate probabilities using the standard normal distribution.
3. Use the normal distribution to approximate binomial probabilities.

Introduction

The previous chapter dealt with discrete probability distributions. Recall that for a discrete distribution, the outcome can assume only a specific set of values. For example, the number of correct responses to ten true-false questions can only be the numbers 0, 1, 2, ..., 10.

This chapter examines an important *continuous probability distribution*—the normal distribution. Recall that a continuous probability distribution can assume an infinite number of values within a given range. As an example, the weight of an engine block could be 54, 54.1, or 54.1437 pounds depending on the accuracy of the measuring device.

Characteristics of the Normal Distribution

The mean of a normal distribution is represented by the Greek letter μ (lower case mu), and standard deviation by the Greek letter σ (lower case sigma). The major characteristics of the normal distribution are:

1. *The normal distribution is "bell-shaped" and the mean, median, and mode are all equal.* Exactly one-half of the observations are larger than this center value, and one-half are smaller.
2. *The distribution is symmetrical.* A vertical line drawn at the mean divides the distribution into two equal halves and these halves have exactly the same shape.
3. *It is asymptotic.* That is, the curve approaches the X-axis but never actually touches it.
4. *A normal distribution is completely described by its mean and standard deviation.* This indicates that if the mean and standard deviation are known, a normal distribution can be constructed and its curve drawn.
5. *There is a "family" of normal distributions.* This means that there is a different normal distribution for each combination of μ and σ.

These characteristics are summarized in the following graph.

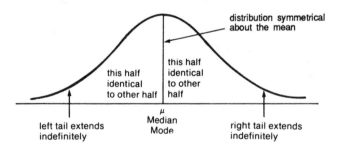

The Standard Normal Distribution

As noted in the previous discussion, there are many normal probability distributions, a different one for each pair of values for a mean and standard deviation. This principle makes the normal probability distribution applicable to a wide range of real-world situations. However, since there is an infinite number of probability distributions, it would be awkward to construct tables of probabilities for so many different normal distributions. An efficient method for overcoming this difficulty is to *standardize* each normal distribution. To obtain the probability of a value falling in the interval between the variable of interest (X) and the mean (μ), we first compute the distance between the value (X) and the mean (μ). Then we express that difference in units of the standard deviation by dividing ($X - \mu$) by the standard deviation. This process is called **standardizing**.

The formula for a specific standardized value, called a z value, is:

$$z = \frac{X - \mu}{\sigma} \qquad 7\text{--}1$$

where X is any observation of interest, μ is the mean of the normal distribution, σ is the standard deviation of the normal distribution, and z is the **standardized normal value**, usually called the **z value**.

To illustrate the probability of a value being between a selected X value and the mean μ, suppose the mean useful life of a car battery is 36 months, with a standardized deviation of 3 months. What is the probability that such a battery will last between 36 and 40 months?

The first step is to convert the 40 months to an equivalent standard normal value, using formula 7–1. The computation is:

$$z = \frac{X - \mu}{\sigma} = \frac{40 - 36}{3} = 1.33$$

Next refer to Appendix D, a table for the areas under the normal curve. A partial table is shown below. To obtain the probability go down the left-hand column to 1.3, then move over to the column headed 0.03 and read the probability. It is .4082.

z	0.00	0.01	0.02	0.03	0.04	0.05
		•	•	•	•	
		•	•	•	•	
		•	•	•	•	
1.0						
1.1		.3665	.3686	.3708	.3729	
1.2		.3869	.3888	.3907	.3925	
1.3		.4049	.4066	.4082	.4099	
1.4		.4207	.4222	.4236	.4251	

The probability that a battery will last between 36 and 40 months is .4082. Other probabilities may be calculated, such as more than 46 months, and less than 33 months. Further details are given in Problems 1 through 5.

The Normal Approximation to the Binomial

The binomial table (Appendix A) goes from a sample size of 1 to 25. What do we do when the sample size is greater than 25? A binomial probability can be estimated using the normal distribution. To apply it both np and $n(1 - p)$ must be greater than 5. The sample size, or the number of trials, is designated by n, and p is the probability of a success. The mean and the standard deviation of the binomial are computed by:

$$\mu = np$$

$$\sigma = \sqrt{np(1 - p)}$$

To illustrate, suppose 60 percent of the applications for an exclusive credit card are approved. In a sample of 200 applications, what is the probability that 130 or more applications are approved? Since both np and $n(1 - p)$ exceed 5 (that is, $np = 200(0.6) = 120$ and $n(1 - p) = 200(1 - 0.60) = 80$), the normal approximation to the binomial may be used.

The mean and standard deviation are computed as follows:

$$\mu = np = 200(0.60) = 120$$

$$\sigma = \sqrt{np(1 - p)} = \sqrt{200(0.6)(0.4)} = 6.93$$

This distribution is standardized by:

$$z = \frac{X - \mu}{\sigma} = \frac{129.5 - 120}{6.93} = 1.37$$

Note in the solution that 129.5 is used instead of 130.0.

The probability of a z value between 0 and 1.37 is .4147 (See Appendix D). Therefore the probability of a z value greater than .4147 is .0853, found by .5000 − .4147. So, the probability that more than 130 applications will be approved is .0853. Why is 129.5 used instead of 130? Namely to "correct" for the fact that a continuous distribution (the normal) is used to approximate a discrete distribution (the binomial). On a continuous scale the value 130 would range from 129.5 to 130.5. On a discrete scale there would be a "gap" between 129 and 130 where there would not be any probability. The .50 is called the **correction for continuity**.

GLOSSARY

Normal distribution—A continuous probability distribution that is uniquely determined by μ and σ. Portrayed graphically, it is symmetrical and bell–shaped. The curve approaches the **X**–axis asymptotically as **X** approaches $-\infty$ or $+\infty$. For a normal distribution, the mean, median, and mode are equal. Half the observations are above the mean and half below it.

Standard normal distribution—A special normal distribution where the mean is 0 and the standard deviation 1.0. A table of areas is available for computing probabilities using the standard normal distribution. The total area under the normal curve is 1.0. Thus, the area to the right of the mean μ is .5000. The area to the left of the mean is also .5000.

Normal approximation to the binomial—A binomial probability may be approximated by the normal distribution when both np and $n(1 - p)$ are greater than 5.0.

z values—It is a unit of measure with respect to the standard normal distribution. A z value is the number of standard deviations from the mean. z may be positive or negative. A z value to the right of the mean is positive, to the left negative.

Correction for continuity—A correction factor of .5 used to improve the accuracy of the approximation of a binomial probability distribution by the normal distribution.

CHAPTER PROBLEMS

Problem 1

The mean amount of gasoline and services charged by Key Refining Company credit customers is $70 per month. The distribution of amounts spent is approximately normal with a standard deviation of $10. Compute the probability of selecting a credit card customer at random and finding the customer charged between $70 and $83 last month.

Solution

The first step is to convert the area between $70 and $83 to a z value using formula 7–1.

$$z = \frac{X - \mu}{\sigma}$$

where X is any value of the random variable ($83 in this problem), μ is the arithmetic mean of the normal distribution ($70), σ is its standard deviation ($10). Solving for z:

$$z = \frac{X - \mu}{\sigma} = \frac{\$83 - \$70}{\$10} = 1.30$$

This indicates that $83 is 1.30 standard deviations to the right of the mean of $70. Showing the problem graphically:

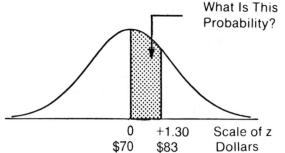

0   +1.30   Scale of z
$70 $83   Dollars

The probability of a z value from 0 to 1.30 is given in a table of areas of the normal curve, Appendix D. To obtain the probability, go down the left-hand column to 1.3, then move over to the column headed 0.00, and read the probability. It is .4032. To put it another way, 40.32 percent of the credit card customers charge between $70 and $83 per month.

Problem 2

Again using the Key Refinery data from **Problem 1**, compute the probability of customers charging between $57 and $83 per month.

Solution

As shown in the following graph, the probability of a customer charging between $57 and $70 per month must be combined with the probability of charging between $70 and $83 in a month to obtain the combined probability.

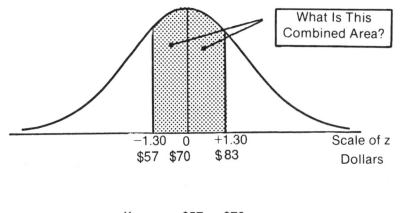

−1.30   0   +1.30   Scale of z
$57 $70 $83   Dollars

$$z = \frac{X - \mu}{\sigma} = \frac{\$57 - \$70}{\$10} = 1.30$$

The probability of between $70 and $83 was computed in Problem 1. Due to the symmetry of the normal distribution, the probability between 0 and 1.30 is the same as the probability between −1.30 and 0. It is .4032. The probability that customers will charge between $57 and $83 is .8064, found by adding .4032 and .4032.

Problem 3

Using the Key Refining data from **Problem 1**, what is the probability that a particular customer charges less than $54?

Solution

The area to be determined is shown below.

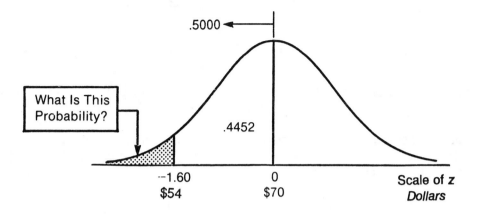

The z value for the area of the normal curve between $70 and $54 is −1.60, found by:

$$z = \frac{X - \mu}{\sigma} = \frac{\$54 - \$70}{\$10} = \frac{-\$16}{\$10} = -1.60$$

Referring to Appendix D, and a z of 1.60, the area of the normal curve between μ ($70) and X ($54) is .4452. Recall that for a symmetrical distribution half of the observations are above the mean, and half below it. In this problem, the probability of an observation being below $70 is, therefore, .5000. Since the probability of an observation being between $54 and $70 is .4452, it follows that .5000 - .4452 = .0548, is the probability that an observation is below $54. To put it another way, 5.48 percent of the customers charge less than $54 per month.

Problem 4

Again using the Key Refining data from Problem 1 compute the probability of a customer charging between $82 and $92.

Solution

The area to be determined is depicted in the following diagram.

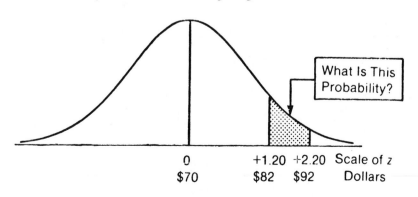

The areas of the normal curve between $70 and $82, and $70 and $92 are determined using formula 7-1.

$$z = \frac{X - \mu}{\sigma}$$

$$= \frac{\$82 - \$70}{\$10}$$

$$= 1.20$$

$$z = \frac{X - \mu}{\sigma}$$

$$= \frac{\$92 - \$70}{\$10}$$

$$= 2.20$$

The probability corresponding to a z of 1.20 is .3849 (from Appendix D).

The probability corresponding to a z of 2.20 is .4861 (from Appendix D).

The probability of a credit card customer charging between $82 and $92 a month, therefore, is the difference between these two probabilities. Thus, .4861 − .3849 = .1012. That is, 10.12 percent of the charge account customers charge between $82 and $92 monthly.

Problem 5

Key Refining (*Problem 1*) decided to send a special financing plan to charge account customers having the highest 10 percent of the money charges. What is the dividing point between the customers who receive the special plan and those who do not?

Solution

The shaded area in the following diagram represents the upper 10 percent who receive the special plan. X represents the unknown value that divides the customers into two groups—those who receive the special financing plan (the shaded area), and those who do not receive it. The area from the mean of $70 to this unknown X value is .4000, found by .5000 − .1000. From the table of areas of the normal curve (Appendix D) the closest z value corresponding to the area .4000 is 1.28. This indicates that the unknown X value is 1.28 standard deviations above the mean. Substituting 1.28 in the equation 7–1 for z:

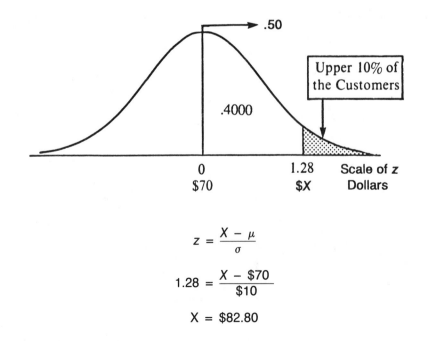

$$z = \frac{X - \mu}{\sigma}$$

$$1.28 = \frac{X - \$70}{\$10}$$

$$X = \$82.80$$

Key Refining should send the special financing plan to those charge account customers having a monthly charge of $82.80 and above.

Exercise 1

Check your answers against those in the ANSWER section.

A cola dispensing machine is set to dispense a mean of 2.02 liters into a container labeled 2 liters. Actual quantities dispensed vary and the amounts are normally distributed with a standard deviation of .015 liters.

a. What is the probability a container will contain less than 2 liters?
b. What is the probability a container will contain between 2.00 and 2.03 liters?
c. Two percent of the containers will contain how much cola or more?

Problem 6

The Key Refining Company, referred to in the earlier problems, determined that 15 percent of its customers will not pay their bill by the due date. What is the probability that for a sample of 80 customers, less than 10 will not pay their bill by the due date?

Solution

The answer could be determined by using the binomial distribution where p, the probability of a success, is 0.15, and where n, the number of trials, is 80. However, most binomial tables do not go beyond an n of 25 and the calculations by hand would be very tedious.

As noted previously, the probability can be accurately estimated by using the normal approximation to the binomial. The approximations are quite good when both np and $n(1 - p)$ are greater than 5. In this case, np = (80)(0.15) = 12, and $n(1 - p)$ = (80)(0.85) = 68. Both are greater than 5.

Recall the mean and variance of a binomial distribution are computed as follows:

$$\mu = np = (80)(0.15) = 12$$
$$\sigma^2 = np(1 - p) = (80)(0.15)(0.85) = 10.2$$

The standard deviation is 3.19, found by $\sqrt{10.2}$. The area less than 9.5 is shown on the following diagram. Because we are estimating a discrete distribution using a continuous distribution, the continuity correction factor is needed. In this instance if we were actually using the binomial distribution we would add the probabilities of 0 customers not paying, one customer not paying and so on up to nine customers not paying the bill. With the discrete distribution there would be no probability of 8.6 customers not paying their bill. When we estimate binomial probabilities using the normal distribution, the area for nine corresponds to the area from 8.5 up to 9.5. In this case, we want all the area below (to the left of) 9.5. This area is depicted schematically as:

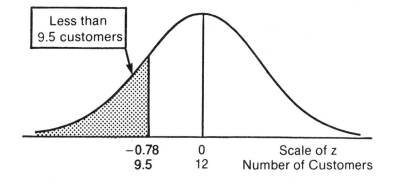

91

The *z* value associated with less than 9.5 customers is -0.78, found by

$$z = \frac{9.5 - 12.0}{3.19} = -0.78$$

The area to the left of -0.78 is .2177 found by .5000 $-$ .2823. The probability that less than ten customers will not pay their bill is .2177. The following output from MINITAB shows the cumulative distribution for the case where n = 80 and p = .15. Look down the column labeled *X* to the row for 9 and read the probability. It is .2211. Very close to our estimate of .2177.

```
MTB > cdf;
SUBC> binomial 80 .15.

Cumulative Distribution Function

Binomial with n = 80 and p = 0.150000

        x       P( X <= x)
        1         0.0000
        2         0.0003
        3         0.0013
        4         0.0047
        5         0.0140
        6         0.0345
        7         0.0727
        8         0.1342
        9         0.2211
       10         0.3300
       11         0.4522
       12         0.5762
       13         0.6907
       14         0.7874
       15         0.8625
       16         0.9163
       17         0.9520
       18         0.9741
       19         0.9868
       20         0.9937
       21         0.9971
       22         0.9988
       23         0.9995
       24         0.9998
       25         0.9999
       26         1.0000
```

Exercise 2

Check your answers against those in the ANSWER section.

A new drug has been developed that is found to relieve nasal congestion in 90 percent of those with the condition. The new drug is administered to 300 patients with this condition. What is the probability that more than 265 will be relieved of the nasal congestion?

CHAPTER ASSIGNMENT 7

The Normal Probability Distribution

Name _____ Section _____ Score _____

Part I Select the correct answer and write the appropriate letter in the space provided.

___ 1. In a normal distribution the mean
    a. and the median are always equal.
    b. and the standard deviation are always equal.
    c. is always larger than the mode.
    d. is always smaller than the median.

___ 2. The normal distribution is
    a. bell-shaped distribution.
    b. a continuous distribution.
    c. symmetric.
    d. all of the above

___ 3. The standard normal distribution
    a. is a special case of the normal distribution.
    b. has a mean equal to 0 and a standard deviation equal to 1.
    c. measures the distance from the mean in units of the standard deviation.
    d. all of the above

___ 4. A normal distribution is completely described by
    a. its mean.
    b. its standard deviation.
    c. its mean and standard deviation.
    d. none of the above

___ 5. Any normal distribution can be converted to a standard normal distribution
    a. by squaring the mean.
    b. if np is greater than 5.
    c. by the formula $(X - \mu) / \sigma$
    d. by the formula $np(1 - p)$.

___ 6. A normal distribution
    a. has at least two peaks.
    b. is asymptotic.
    c. increases as X increases.
    d. is discrete.

___ 7. The normal distribution can be used to approximate the binomial when
    a. np is at least 30.
    b. np and $n(1 - p)$ are both greater than 5.
    c. $np(1 - p)$ is larger than 5.
    d. None of the above. We approximate the normal with the binomial.

___ 8. The area under the normal curve between 0 and 1.00 and 0 and -1.00
    a. is the same.
    b. is negative.

        c. equal to 0.
        d. none of the above.

___ 9. A z value
        a. can not be negative.
        b. is always 0.
        c. is found by *np*.
        d. can assume both positive and negative values.

___ 10. To construct a normal approximation to the binomial
        a. the binomial conditions must be met.
        b. both *n* and *p* must be known.
        c. *np* and $n(1 - p)$ must be greater than 5.
        d. all of the above

Part II Fill in the blanks with the correct answer.

11. When is the correction for continuity used?_____
_____

12. Explain the difference between a normal distribution and the standard normal distribution._____
_____

13. Under what conditions can the normal distribution be used to approximate the binomial distribution?_____
_____

14. In a binomial distribution $n = 30$ and $p = .6$. The mean and the variance of the binomial distribution are:
        a. $\mu =$_____
        b. $\sigma^2 =$_____

15. List the characteristics of the normal distribution.
        a. _____
        b. _____
        c. _____
        d. _____

Part III Record your answer in the space provided. Show essential work.

16. Dan, owner of Dan's TV Repair Service, reports that the mean time for an in home service call is 75 minutes, with a standard deviation of 20 minutes. This includes the transportation time.

a. What proportion of the calls take less than 100 minutes?

Answer

b. What proportion of the calls take less than 70 minutes?

Answer

c. What proportion of the calls take between 70 and 100 minutes?

[ ]
Answer

d. What proportion of the calls take between 90 and 100 minutes?

[ ]
Answer

e. Some of the calls can be handled quickly. Ten percent of the calls take less than home much time?

[ ]
Answer

17. It is very difficult for small businesses to be successful. The Small Business Administration estimates that 20 percent will dissolve or go bankrupt within two years. A sample of 50 new business is selected.

a. What is the mean and the standard deviation of this distribution?

[ ]
Answer

b. What is the probability that more than 15 in the sample will go bankrupt?

[ ]
Answer

c. What is the probability that exactly 15 will go bankrupt?

[ ]
Answer

d. What is the probability that between 7 and 9 will go bankrupt? (This means that 7, 8, or 9 of the sample will go bankrupt.)

[ ]
Answer

e. What is the probability that between 7 and 15 will go bankrupt?

[ ]
Answer

8

SAMPLING METHODS AND SAMPLING DISTRIBUTIONS

CHAPTER GOALS

After completing this chapter, you will be able to:

1. List the reasons for sampling.
2. Explain the various methods of sampling.
3. Distinguish between probability and nonprobability sampling.
4. Define and construct a sampling distribution of means.
5. Explain the central limit theorem and its importance to statistical inference.
6. Calculate and interpret confidence interval for means and proportions.
7. Understand and apply the finite population correction factor.
8. Determine the size of a sample.

Introduction

With this chapter we begin our study of sampling. Sampling is necessary because we want to make statements about a population but we do not want to (or cannot) examine all the items in that population. Recall from Chapter 1 that a **population** refers to the entire group of objects or persons of interest. The population of interest might be all the persons in the city receiving welfare payments or all the computer chips produced during the last hour. A **sample** is a portion, a part, or a subset of the population. Fifty welfare recipients out of 4,000 receiving payments might constitute the sample, or 20 computer chips might be sampled out of 1,500 produced last hour.

Reasons for Sampling

Why is it necessary to sample? Why can't we just inspect all the items? There are several reasons.

1. *The destructive nature of certain tests.* The manufacturer of fuses cannot test all of them because in the testing the fuse is destroyed and none would be available for sale!
2. *The physical impossibility of checking all the items in the population.* The South Dakota Game Commission, for example, cannot check all the deer, grouse, and other wild game because they are always moving.

3. *The cost of studying all the items in the population is prohibitive.* Some televisions ratings are established by analyzing the viewing habits of about 1,200 viewers. The cost of studying all the homes having television would be exorbitant.
4. *The adequacy of sample results.* If the sample results of the viewing habits of 1,200 homes revealed that only 1.1 percent of the homes watched "Mama Knows Best," no doubt the program would be replaced by another series. Checking the viewing habits of all the homes regarding "Mama Knows Best" probably would not change the percent significantly.
5. *To contact the entire population in most cases would be very time consuming.* To ask every eligible voter regarding the chances of Senator Tolson in the forthcoming election would take months. The election would probably be over before the survey was completed.

Types of Sampling

There are two basic types of sampling, probability sampling and nonprobability sampling. If all the items in the population have a chance to be included in the sample, the method is referred to as **probability sampling.** If the items included in the sample are based on the judgment of the person selecting the sample, the method is called **nonprobability sampling.**

Types of Probability Sampling

Four types of probability sampling are commonly used: simple random sampling, systematic sampling, stratified sampling, and cluster sampling.

In a simple random sample each item in the population has the *same* chance of being selected for inclusion in the sample.

Several ways of selecting a simple random sample are:

1. The name or identifying number of each item in the population is recorded on a slip of paper and placed in a box. The slips of paper are shuffled and the required sample size is chosen from the box.
2. Each item is numbered and a table of random numbers, such as the one in Appendix E, is used to select the members of the sample.
3. Many computers have routines that randomly select a given number of items from the population.

In a **systematic sample** the items in the population are numbered 1, 2, 3, ... Next, a random starting point is selected—let's say 39. Every *n*th item thereafter, such as every 100th, is selected for the sample. This means that 39, 139, 239, 339, and so on would be a part of the sample.

In a **stratified sample** the population is divided into subgroups, or strata, and a sample is drawn from each stratum. For example, if our study involved Army personnel, we might decide to stratify the population (all Army personnel) into generals, other officers, and enlisted personnel. The number selected from each of the three strata could be proportional to the total number in the population for the corresponding strata. Each member of the population can belong to only one of the strata. That is, a military person cannot be a general and a private at the same time.

Cluster sampling is often used to reduce the cost of sampling when the population is scattered over a large geographic area. Suppose the objective is to study household waste collection in a large city. As a first step you divide the city into smaller units (perhaps precincts). Next, the precincts are numbered and several selected randomly. Finally, households within each of these precincts are randomly selected and interviewed.

Sampling Error

It is not logical to expect that the results obtained from a sample will coincide *exactly* with those from a population. For example, it is unlikely that the mean welfare payment for a sample of 50 recipients is exactly the same as the mean for all 4,000 welfare recipients. The difference between the actual population value (a **parameter**) and the sample value (the **statistic**) is called **sample error**. Because these errors happen by chance, they are referred to as **chance variations.**

The Sampling Distribution of the Mean

Suppose all possible samples of size *n* are selected from a specified population, and the mean of each of these samples is computed. The distribution of these sample means is called the **sampling distribution of the sample means**. The sampling distribution of the mean is a probability distribution and has the following major characteristics.

1. The mean of all the sample means will be exactly equal to the population mean.
2. If the population from which the samples are drawn is normal, the distribution of sample means is also normally distributed.
3. If the population from which the samples are drawn is not normal, the sampling distribution is approximately normal, provided the samples are "sufficiently" large (usually accepted to include at least 30 observations). This phenomenon is called the **Central Limit Theorem.**

Point Estimates

A point estimate is based on the sample information. It is one value used to estimate an unknown population parameter. For example, a sample of 100 recent accounting graduates revealed a mean starting salary of $30,000. The $30,000 is a point estimate. The sample mean is our best estimate of the mean starting salary of all (population) accounting graduates.

Confidence Interval Estimates

Why is the above mentioned central limit theorem so important? It can be used to specify a range of values within which a population parameter, such as the population mean, can be expected to occur. The range of values, within which a population parameter is expected to lie, is called the **confidence interval.** The end points of the confidence interval are called the **confidence limits.** The measure of the confidence we have that an interval estimate will include the population parameter is called the **level of confidence.** A confidence interval for the population mean is determined by:

$$\bar{X} \pm z \frac{\sigma}{\sqrt{n}}$$

where $\bar{X}$ is the sample mean, z is the value associated with the given level of confidence, σ the population standard deviation, and n the size of the sample. How this z value is determined will be explained in Problem 3. If σ is not known, but the sample size is 30 or more, then s, the sample standard deviation, is used in place of σ.

The confidence interval for a **population proportion** is found by:

$$\bar{p} \pm z \sqrt{\frac{\bar{p}(1-\bar{p})}{n}} \qquad 8-8$$

where $\bar{p}$ is the sample proportion, found by X/n. X is the number of "successes" in a sample of size n. If 451 out of 2,000 voters surveyed plan to vote for the incumbent governor, $X = 451$ and $n = 2,000$. So, $p = 451/2,000 = .2255$. z is the z value, corresponding to the selected level of confidence.

Finite-Correction Factor

If the sampling is done without replacement from a small population, the **finite-population correction factor** is used. If the sample constitutes more than 5 percent of the population, the finite correction factor is applied. Its purpose is to account for the fact that a parameter can be more accurately estimated from a small population when a large portion of that population's units are sampled. The correction factor is:

$$\sqrt{\frac{N-n}{N-1}}$$

What is the effect of this term? If N, the number of units in the population is large relative to n, the sample size, the value of this correction factor is near 1.00. For example, if $N = 10,000$ and a sample of 40 is selected the value of the correction factor is .9980, found by $\sqrt{(10,000 - 40)/(10,000 - 1)}$. However, if N is only 500 the correction factor is .9601, found by $\sqrt{(500 - 40)/(500 - 1)}$. Logically, we can estimate a population parameter with a sample of 40 from a population of 500 more accurately than with a sample of 40 from a population of 10,000.

The standard error of the mean or the standard error of the proportion is multiplied by the correction factor. Because the correction factor will always be less than 1.00, the effect is to reduce the standard error. Stated differently, because the sample consti-

tuted a substantial proportion of the population, the standard error is reduced. The confidence interval for the population mean, therefore, is computed as follows:

$$\bar{X} \pm z \frac{s}{\sqrt{n}} \left(\sqrt{\frac{N-n}{N-1}} \right)$$

The confidence interval for a population proportion is:

$$\bar{p} \pm z \sqrt{\frac{\bar{p}(1-\bar{p})}{n}} \left(\sqrt{\frac{N-n}{N-1}} \right)$$

Required Sample Size

The size of a sample required for a particular study is based on three factors.

1. The desired level of confidence. This is expressed in terms of z.
2. The variability in the population under study (as measured by s).
3. The maximum allowable error (E).

The sample size is computed using the formula:

$$n = \left(\frac{z \cdot s}{E} \right)^2 \qquad 8-12$$

A population with considerable variability (reflected by a large s) will require a larger sample than a population with a smaller standard deviation. E is the maximum allowable error that you, the researcher, are willing to accept. It is the amount that is added and subtracted from the mean to obtain the end points of the confidence limits.

To determine the required sample size for a proportion p, the following formula is used.

$$n = \bar{p}(1 - \bar{p}) \left(\frac{z}{E} \right)^2 \qquad 8-13$$

where $\bar{p}$ is based on a pilot study. If no estimate of $\bar{p}$ is available then let $\bar{p} = .50$. The sample size will never be larger than that obtained when $\bar{p} = .50$.

GLOSSARY

Population—The total group of persons, or objects, of interest.

Sample—A portion, or part, of the population.

Statistical inference—Reasoning from a small group (a sample) to the large entire group (the population).

Probability sample—All the items in the population of interest have a chance to be included in the sample.

Nonprobability sample—The items included in the sample are based on the judgment of the person selecting the sample.

Simple random sample—Each item in the population has the same likelihood of being selected for the sample.

Systematic sample—The elements of the population are numbers, 1, 2, 3, 4, . . . etc. A random starting point is elected. Then every nth element thereafter is chosen for the sample.

Stratified random sample—The population is divided into some logical strata. Samples are drawn from each stratum, either proportional to the number in each stratum, or in a nonproportional manner depending on a specified criterion.

Sampling error—The difference between the sample statistic and the population parameter.

Chance variation—Variation that is not attributable to any specific cause. It is random in nature.

Finite-population correction factor—A factor used to correct the standard error of the mean, or the standard error of the proportion. It is usually applied when $n/N > .05$

Statistic—Refers to any sample value (such as the sample mean).

Parameter—Refers to any population value (such as the population mean).

Point estimate—A single value resulting from a sample used as an estimate of a corresponding population value.

Interval estimate—The interval within which a population value, such as the population mean, is likely to occur.

Sampling distribution of the mean—A probability distribution of all possible sample means of a given size selected from a population.

Central Limit Theorem—The distribution of the sample means approaches the normal distribution as the sample size increases, regardless of the shape of the population.

Level of confidence—The degree of confidence the researcher has that the population value (such as the mean) will lie in a specified interval.

Cluster sample—A form of stratified sampling. The population is divided into homogeneous groups called clusters. Samples are then randomly obtained from these clusters.

CHAPTER PROBLEMS

Problem 1

Suppose that a population consists of the six families living in Brentwood Circle. You are studying the number of children in the six families. The population information is:

Family	Number of Children
Clark	1
Walston	2
Dodd	3
Marshall	5
Saner	3
White	4

List the possible samples of size 2 that could be selected from this population and compute the arithmetic mean of each sample. Organize these sample means into a probability distribution.

Solution

There are 15 different samples. The formula for the number of combinations from Chapter 5 is used to determine the total number of samples. There are six members of the population and the sample size is two.

$$_6C_2 = \frac{6!}{2! \; 4!} = 15$$

The 15 possible samples and the sample means are:

Sample Number	Families in the Sample	Total Number of Children in Sample	Mean Number of Children Per Family in Sample
1	Clark, Walston	3	1.5 ← 3/2
2	Clark, Dodd	4	2.0
3	Clark, Marshall	6	3.0
4	Clark, Saner	4	2.0
5	Clark, White	5	2.5
6	Walston, Dodd	5	2.5
7	Walston, Marshall	7	3.5
8	Walston, Saner	5	2.5
9	Walston, White	6	3.0
10	Dodd, Marshall	8	4.0
11	Dodd, Saner	6	3.0
12	Dood, White	7	3.5
13	Marshall, Saner	8	4.0
14	Marshall, White	9	4.5
15	Saner, White	7	3.5
		Total	45.0

This information is organized into the following probability distribution called the sampling distribution of the means.

Mean Number of Children	Frequency	Probability
1.5	1	.067 ← 1/15
2.0	2	.133
2.5	3	.200
3.0	3	.200 ← 3/15
3.5	3	.200
4.0	2	.133
4.5	1	.067
	15	1.000

Problem 2

Using the Brentwood Circle data in **Problem 1,** compare the mean of the sampling distribution with the mean of the population. Compare the spread of the sample means with that of the population.

Solution

The mean of the sampling distribution and the mean of the population are the same. The population mean, written μ, is found by $\mu = (1 + 2 + 3 + 5 + 3 + 4)/6 = 3.0$. The mean of the sampling distribution (written $\mu_{\bar{x}}$ because it is the mean of a group of sample means) is also 3.0, found by 45.0/15.
The calculations for the mean of the sample means are:

$\bar{X}$ Sample Means	f Frequency	$f\bar{X}$
1.5	1	1.5
2.0	2	4.0
2.5	3	7.5
3.0	3	9.0
3.5	3	10.5
4.0	2	8.0
4.5	1	4.5
	15	45.0

$$\mu_{\bar{x}} = \frac{f\bar{X}}{-f} = \frac{45.0}{15} = 3.0$$

The population mean μ is exactly equal to the mean of the sampling distribution $\mu_{\bar{x}}$ (3.0). This is always true. Note in the following graphs that there is less spread in the sampling distribution of the means (bottom chart) than in the population distribution (top chart). The sample means range from 1.5 to 4.5, whereas the population values ranged from 1 to 5.

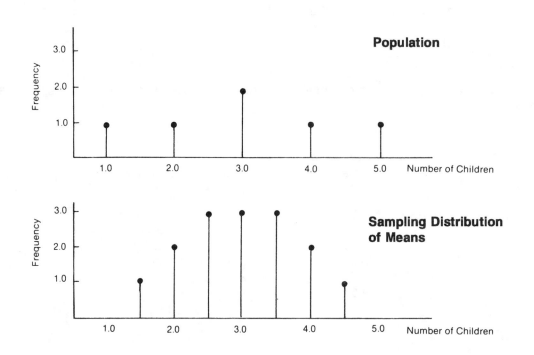

Also note that the shape of the population is different than that of the sampling distribution. This phenomenon is described by the central limit theorem. Recall the central limit theorem states that regardless of the shape of the population the sampling distribution will tend toward normal as n increases.

Exercise 1

Check your answers against those in the ANSWER section.

The real estate company of Kuhlman and Associates has five sales people. Listed below is the number of homes sold last month by each of the five associates. Bruce Kuhlman, the owner, wants to estimate the population mean number of homes sold based on samples of three.

	Associate	Number of Homes Sold
A.	Sue Klaus	6
B.	John Bardo	2
C.	Jean Cannon	5
D.	A. J. Kemper	9
E.	Carol Ford	3

a. If samples of size 3 are selected, how many different samples are possible?
b. List the various samples and compute the mean of each.
c. Develop a sampling distribution of the means.
d. Draw graphs to compare the variability of the sampling distribution of the mean with that of the population.

Problem 3

Crossett Truck Rental has a large fleet of rental trucks. Many of the trucks need substantial repairs from time to time. Mr. Crossett, the owner, has requested a study of the repair costs. A random sample of 64 trucks is selected. The mean annual repair cost is $1,200, with a standard deviation of $280. Estimate the mean annual repair cost for all rental trucks. Develop the 95 percent confidence interval for the population mean.

Solution

The population parameter being estimated is the population mean—the mean annual repair cost of all Crossett rental trucks. This value is not known, but the best estimate we have of that value is the sample mean of $1,200. Hence, $1,200 is a *point estimate* of the unknown population parameter. A *confidence interval* is a range of values within which the population parameter is expected to occur. The 95 percent refers to the approximate percent of time that similarly constructed intervals would include the parameter being estimated.

The confidence interval for a mean is obtained by applying formula 8–3.

$$\bar{X} \pm z\,\frac{s}{\sqrt{n}}$$

How is the z value determined? In this problem the 95 percent level of confidence is used. This refers to the middle 95 percent of the values. The remaining 5 percent is divided equally between the two tails of curve. (See the following diagram.)

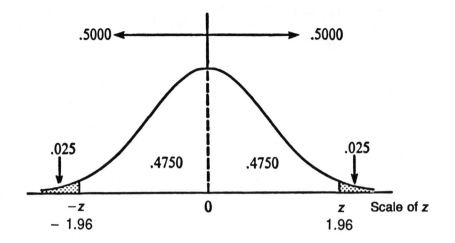

To find z, the standard normal distribution is used. Referring to Appendix D, the first step is to locate the value of .4750 in the body of the table, and then read the corresponding row and column values. The z value is 1.96.

Substitute the z value into the equation. Solving, the confidence interval is \$1,131.40 to \$1,268.60

$$\bar{X} \pm z \frac{s}{\sqrt{n}} = \$1,200 \pm 1.96 \frac{\$280}{\sqrt{64}}$$

$$= \$1,200 \pm \$68.6$$

$$= \$1,131.40 \text{ to } \$1,268.60$$

This indicates that if 100 similar intervals were constructed about 95 would be expected to include the population mean.

Exercise 2

Check your answers against those in the ANSWER section.

The Internal Revenue Service is studying contributions to charity. A random sample of 36 returns is selected. The mean contribution is \$150 and the standard deviation of the sample is \$20. Construct a 98 percent confidence interval for the population mean.

Problem 4

Refer to the information on Crossett Truck Rental in Problem 3. Suppose Crossett's fleet consists of 500 trucks. Develop a 95 percent confidence interval for the population mean.

Solution

When the sample is more than 5 percent of the population, the finite population correction factor is used. In this case the sample size is 64 and the population size is 500. Thus, $n/N = 64/500 = .128$ or 12.8 percent. The confidence interval is adjusted as follows.

$$\bar{X} \pm z \frac{s}{\sqrt{n}} \left(\sqrt{\frac{N-n}{N-1}} \right) = \$1{,}200 \pm 1.96 \frac{\$280}{\sqrt{64}} \left(\sqrt{\frac{500-64}{500-1}} \right)$$

$$= \$1{,}200 \pm \$68.6(.9347)$$

$$= \$1{,}200 \pm \$64.12$$

$$= \$1{,}135.88 \text{ to } \$1{,}264.12$$

Notice that when the correction factor is included the confidence interval becomes smaller. This is logical because the number of items sampled is large relative to the population.

Exercise 3

Check your answers against those in the ANSWER section.

Refer to Exercise 2. Compute the 98 percent confidence interval, if the population consists of 200 tax returns.

Problem 5

The Independent Department Store wants to determine the proportion of their charge accounts having an unpaid balance of $500 or more. A sample of 250 accounts revealed that 100 of them had an unpaid balance of $500 or over. What is the 99 percent confidence interval for the population proportion?

Solution

In the sample of 250 charge accounts, there were 100 with unpaid balances of over $500. The point estimate of the proportion of charge customers with balances of more than $500 is .40, found by 100/250. The z value corresponding to a 99 percent level of confidence is 2.58 (from Appendix D). The formula for the confidence interval for the population proportion is: (See formula 8–5.)

$$\bar{p} \pm z \sqrt{\frac{\bar{p}(1-\bar{p})}{n}} = .40 \pm 2.58 \sqrt{\frac{(.40)(1-.40)}{250}}$$

$$= .40 \pm (2.58) \sqrt{.00096}$$

$$= .40 \pm .08$$

The confidence interval is .32 to .48. This means that about 99 percent of the similarly constructed intervals would include the population proportion.

Exercise 4

Check your answers against those in the ANSWER section.

A random sample of 100 light bulbs was selected. Sixty were found to burn for more than 1,000 hours. Develop a 90 percent confidence interval for the proportion of bulbs that will burn more than 1,000 hours.

Problem 6

Refer to the charge account data of Independent Department Stores in **Problem 5.** Recall that 250 accounts were sampled. Suppose there is a total of 900 charge customers. Develop the 99 percent confidence interval for the proportion of charge customers with an unpaid account balance of over $500.

Solution

The finite population correction factor should be used because the sample is 28 percent of the population, found by 250/900. (Note that 28 percent is more than 5% of the population.)

$$\bar{p} \pm z \sqrt{\frac{\bar{p}(1-\bar{p})}{n}} \sqrt{\frac{N-n}{N-1}} = .40 \pm 2.58 \sqrt{\frac{.40(1-.40)}{250}} \left(\sqrt{\frac{900-250}{900-1}} \right)$$

$$.40 \pm .08(.8503)$$

$$.40 \pm .068$$

Using the correction factor the interval is reduced from .40 ± .08 to .40 ± .068. Again, this is because Independent Stores has sampled a large proportion (28 percent) of its customers.

Problem 7

The manager of the Jiffy Supermarket wants to estimate the mean time a customer spends in the store. A 95 percent level of confidence is to be used. The standard deviation of the population based on a pilot survey is estimated to be 3.0 minutes. The manager requires the estimate to be within plus or minus 1.00 minute of the population value. What sample size is needed?

Solution

The size of the sample is dependent on three factors.

1. The allowable error (E).
2. The level of confidence. (z).
3. The estimated variation in the population, usually measured by s, the sample standard deviation.

In this problem, the store manager has indicated that the estimate must be within 1.0 minute of the population parameter. The level of confidence is .95 and the population standard deviation is estimated to be 3.0 minutes. The formula (8–12) for determining the size of the sample is:

$$n = \left(\frac{z \cdot s}{E} \right)^2$$

where z refers to the level of confidence, s is the estimated population standard deviation, and E the allowable error.

$$z = \left(\frac{(1.96)(3.0)}{1.0}\right)^2 = (5.88)^2 = 34.57 = 35$$

Hence, the manager should randomly select 35 customers and determine the amount of time they spend in the store.

Exercise 5

Check your answers against those in the ANSWER section.

A health maintenance organization (HMO) wants to estimate the mean length of a hospital stay. How large a sample of patient records is necessary if the HMO wants to be 99 percent confident of the estimate, and wants the estimate to be within plus or minus .2 days? An earlier study showed the standard deviation of the length of stay to be .25 days.

Problem 8

The Ohio Unemployment Commission wants to estimate the proportion of the labor force that was unemployed during last year in a certain depressed region. The Commission wants to be 95 percent confident that their estimate is within 5 percentage points (written .05) of the population proportion. If the population proportion has been estimated to be .15, how large a sample is required? If no estimate of p was available, how large a sample would be required?

Solution

Note that the estimate of the population proportion $(\bar{p})$ is .15. The allowable error (E) is .05. Using the 95 percent level of confidence the z value is 1.96. Applying formula 8–13 to determine the sample size:

$$n = \bar{p}(1-\bar{p})\left(\frac{z}{E}\right)^2 = .15(1-.15)\left(\frac{1.96}{.05}\right)^2 = 196$$

The required sample size is 196.

When no estimate of $\bar{p}$ is available, .50 is used. The size of the sample will never be larger than that obtained when $\bar{p} = .50$. The calculations for the sample size when $\bar{p} = .50$ are:

$$n = \bar{p}(1-\bar{p})\left(\frac{z}{E}\right)^2 = .5(1-.5)\left(\frac{1.96}{.05}\right)^2 = 385$$

Note that the required sample size is considerably larger (385 versus 196) when $\bar{p}$ is set at .50.

Exercise 6

Check your answers against those in the ANSWER section.

A large bank believes that one-third of its checking customers have used at least one of the bank's other services during the past year. How large a sample is required to estimate the actual proportion within a range of plus and minus .04? Use the 98 percent level of confidence.

CHAPTER ASSIGNMENT 8

Sampling Methods and Sampling Distributions

Name _____ Section _____ Score _____

Part I Select the correct answer and write the appropriate letter in the space provided.

___ 1. The population proportion is an example of a
   a. sample statistic
   b. normal population.
   c. *z* value.
   d. population parameter.

___ 2. In a probability sample each item in the population has
   a. a chance of being selected.
   b. the same chance of being selected.
   c. a 50 percent chance of being selected.
   d. no chance of being selected.

___ 3. In a simple random sample each item in the population has
   a. a chance of being selected.
   b. the same chance of being selected.
   c. a 50 percent chance of being selected.
   d. no chance of being selected.

___ 4. The sampling error is
   a. the difference between a sample statistic and a population parameter.
   b. always positive.
   c. also called the Central Limit Theorem.
   d. equal to the population value.

___ 5. The sample mean is an example of a
   a. sample statistic.
   b. normal population.
   c. *z* value.
   d. population parameter.

___ 6. Suppose we have a negatively skewed population. According to the Central Limit Theorem, the distribution of the sample means of a particular size will
   a. also be negatively skewed.
   b. form a binomial distribution.
   c. approach a normal distribution.
   d. become positively skewed.

___ 7. If the level of confidence is decreased from 95 percent to 90 percent, the width of the corresponding interval will
   a. be increased.
   b. be decreased.
   c. stay the same.
   d. the level of confidence doesn't have an effect on the width of the interval

___ 8. The population is the five employees in a physician's office. The number of possible samples of 2 that could be selected from this population is
   a. 15
   b. 60
   c. 5
   d. 10

___ 9. The finite population correction factor is used when
   a. the sample is more than 5 percent of the population.
   b. the sample is less than 5 percent of the population.
   c. the sample is larger than the population.
   d. the population cannot be estimated.

___ 10. A 90 percent confidence interval for means indicates that 90 out of 100 similarly constructed intervals will include the
   a. sample mean.
   b. sampling error
   c. z value.
   d. population mean.

Part II Fill in the blank with the correct answer.

11. List the three factors that determine the size of the sample.
   a. _____
   b. _____
   c. _____

12. Describe the conditions when the finite population correction factor is used._____
_____

13. Define the term sample statistic._____
_____

14. The difference between a population parameter and a sample statistic is called the_____

15. Variation not associate with any particular cause is called_____variation.

Part III Record your answer in the space provided. Show essential work.

16. Ralph's Supermarket has five 5-pound bags of apples. Ralph counted the number of apples in each bag.

Bag number	Number of apples in the bag
1	8
2	10
3	10
4	12
5	12

   a. If all possible samples of size 2 are selected, how many different samples are possible?

b. List all possible samples of size 2 and compute the mean of each sample,

c. Compute the population mean and compare it to the mean of the sampling distribution.

17. As part of a safety check, the Pennsylvania Highway Patrol randomly stopped 35 cars and checked their tire pressure. The sample mean was 32 pounds per square inch with a sample standard deviation of 2 pounds per square inch. Develop a 95 percent confidence interval for the population mean.

18. Of a random sample of 90 firms with employee stock ownership plans, 50 indicated that the primary reason for setting up the plan was tax related. Develop a 90 percent confidence interval for the population proportion of all such firms with this as the primary motivation.

19. The Customer Relations Department at Commuter Airlines, Inc. wants to estimated the proportion of customers that carry only hand luggage. The estimate is to be within .03 of the true proportion with a 95 percent level of confidence. No estimate of the population proportion is available. How large a sample is required?

20. The *Corporate Lawyer,* a magazine for corporate lawyers, would like to report the mean amount earned by lawyers in their area of specialization. How large a sample is required if the 97 percent level of confidence is used and the estimate is to be within $2500? The standard deviation is $16,000.

9

TESTS OF HYPOTHESES: LARGE SAMPLES

CHAPTER GOALS

After completing this chapter, you will be able to:

1. Define what is meant by a hypothesis and hypothesis testing.
2. Describe and employ the five step hypothesis testing procedure.
3. Distinguish between one and two-tailed statistical tests.
4. Determine *p*-values.
5. Identify and describe possible statistical errors in hypothesis testing.
6. Conduct a test of hypothesis about a population mean.
7. Conduct a hypothesis test about two population means.
8. Conduct a test of hypothesis about one and two proportions.

Introduction

In the previous chapter we used the normal probability distribution to describe a sampling distribution of means. In this chapter we will extend this knowledge to use *sample* information to draw conclusions regarding the value of the *population parameter.* Recall that a sample is a part or subset of the population, while a parameter is a value calculated from the entire population. Two statements called **hypotheses** are made regarding the possible values of population parameters. What is **statistical hypothesis testing**? It is a method for choosing between statements or courses of action.

For example, one statement about the performance of a new model car is that the mean miles per gallon is 30. The other statement is that the mean miles per gallon is not 30. Only one of these statements is correct.

Steps in Hypothesis Testing

Statistical hypothesis testing is a five-step procedure. These steps are:

1. State the null hypothesis and the alternate hypothesis.
2. Select a level of significance.
3. Select an appropriate test statistic.
4. Formulate a decision rule based on the selected test statistic and level of significance.

5. Take a sample and make a decision whether or not to reject the null hypothesis.

(Each step will be discussed in detail shortly.)

When conducting hypothesis tests we actually employ a strategy of "proof by contradiction." That is, we hope to accept a statement to be true by rejecting or ruling out another statement. The steps involved in hypothesis testing will now be described in more detail. First we will concentrate on testing a hypothesis about a population mean, or means. Then we will consider one or two population proportions. For a mean or means:

Step 1. State the null hypothesis and the alternate hypothesis.

The **null hypothesis** is a claim about the value of a population parameter. For example, a recent newspaper report made the claim that the mean length of a hospital stay was 3.3 days. You think that the true length of stay is some other length than 3.3 days. The null hypothesis is written H_0: $\mu = 3.3$, where H_0 is an abbreviation of the null hypothesis. It is the statement about the value of the population parameter—in this case the population mean. The null hypothesis is established for the purpose of testing. On the basis of the sample evidence, it is either rejected or not rejected.

The **alternate hypothesis**, written H_1, is the claim that is accepted if the null hypothesis is rejected. The alternate hypothesis is that the mean length of stay is not 3.3 days. It is written H_1: $\mu \neq 3.3$ ($\neq$ is read "not equal to"). H_1 is accepted only if H_0 is rejected. When the "$\neq$" sign appears in the alternate hypothesis, the test is called a **two-tailed test.**

There are two other formats for writing the null and alternate hypotheses. Suppose you think that the mean length of stay is greater than 3.3 days. The null and alternate hypotheses would be written as follows: ($\leqslant$ is read "equal to or less than")

$$H_0: \mu \leqslant 3.3$$
$$H_1: \mu > 3.3$$

Notice that in this case the null hypothesis indicates "no change or that μ is less than 3.3." The alternate hypothesis states that the mean length of stay is greater than 3.3 days. Acceptance of the alternate hypothesis would allow us to conclude that the mean length of stay is greater than 3.3 days.

What if you think that the mean length of stay is *less than* 3.3 days? The null and alternate hypotheses would be written as:

$$H_0: \mu \geqslant 3.3$$
$$H_1: \mu < 3.3$$

Acceptance of the alternate hypothesis in this instance would allow you to conclude the mean length of stay is less than 3.3 days. When a direction is expressed in the alternate hypothesis, such as $>$ or $<$, the test is referred to as being **one-tailed.**

Step 2. Select the level of significance.

The **level of significance** is the probability that the null hypothesis is rejected when, in fact, it is true. It will indicate when the sample mean is too far away from the hypothesized mean for the null hypothesis to be true. Usually the significance level is set at either .01 or .05, although other values may be chosen. Testing a null hypothesis at the .05 significance level, for example, indicates that the probability of rejecting the null hypothesis, even though it is true, is .05. When a true hypothesis is rejected it is referred to as a **Type I error.** The decision whether to use the .01 or the .05 significance level, or some other value, depends on the consequences of making a Type I error. The significance level is chosen *before* the sample is selected.

A **Type II error** is accepting a false null hypothesis. That is, the null hypothesis is not true, but our sample results indicate that it is. For example, if H_0 asserts that the mean length of a hospital stay is 3.3 days and we accept this hypothesis when, in fact, the mean length of stay is 4.0 days, then a Type II error is committed.

Step 3. Identify the test statistic.

A **test statistic** is a quantity calculated from the sample information and is used as the basis for deciding whether or not to reject the null hypothesis. Ex-

actly which test statistic to employ is determined by factors such as whether the population standard deviation is known, and the size of the sample. The standard normal distribution, the z statistic, is the test statistic used in this chapter.

Step 4. Formulate a decision rule.

A decision rule is based on H_0 and H_1, the level of significance, and the test statistic. The **decision rule** is a statement of the conditions under which the null hypothesis is rejected. If we are applying a one-tailed test, the dividing point between the condition under which the null hypothesis is rejected and under which it is not rejected is called the **critical value.** If we are applying a two-tailed test, there are two critical values. The following diagram shows the conditions under which the null hypothesis is rejected, using the .05 significance level, a one-tailed test, and the standard normal distribution—the test statistic used in this chapter.

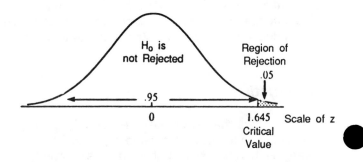

When is the standard normal distribution used? It is appropriate when the population is normal and the population standard deviation is known. When the population standard deviation is not known, the sample standard deviation is used instead. If the sample is at least 30, then the standard normal distribution is appropriate. If the computed value of z is greater than 1.645, the null hypothesis is rejected. If the computed value of z is smaller than 1.645, the null hypothesis is not rejected.

Step 5. Select the sample and make a decision.

The final step is to select the sample and compute the value of the test statistic. This value is compared to the critical value, or values, and a decision is made whether to accept or reject the null hypothesis.

A p-value is the probability that the test statistic is as extreme or more extreme than that actually observed, when the null hypothesis is true. The p-value for a given test depends on three factors: (1) whether the alternate hypothesis is one-tailed or two-tailed, (2) the particular test statistic that is used, and (3) the computed value of the test statistic.

A p-value is frequently compared to the significance level to evaluate the decision regarding the null hypothesis. If the p-value is greater than the signifi-

level, then H_0 is not rejected. If it is less than the significance level, then H_0 is rejected. For example, if $\alpha = .05$ and the p-value is .0025, H_0 is rejected and there is only a .0025 likelihood that H_0 is true.

Types of Tests for Means

Hypothesis tests for two situations will now be considered. One involves a single population; the other, two populations.

Suppose we are concerned with a single population mean. We want to test if our sample mean could have been obtained from a population with a hypothesized mean. For example, we may be interested in testing whether the mean starting salary of recent marketing graduates is equal to $32,000 per year. It is assumed that (1) the population is normally distributed and (2) the population standard deviation is known. If σ is not known, the sample standard deviation is substituted for the population standard deviation provided the sample size is 30 or more.

Under these conditions the test statistic is the standard normal distribution and is given by formula 9–1:

$$z = \frac{\bar{X} - \mu}{\sigma / \sqrt{n}} \qquad 9\text{–}1$$

where X is the sample mean, μ is the population mean, σ is the population standard deviation. The sample standard deviation s could be substituted for σ providing that the sample size is 30 or more. n is the sample size, and z the value of the test statistic.

If there are two populations, we can compare two sample means to determine if they came from populations with the same or equal means. For example, a purchasing agent is considering two brands of tires for use on the company's fleet of cars. A sample of 60 Rossford tires indicates the mean useful life to be 45,000 miles. A sample of 50 Maumee tires revealed the useful life to be 48,000 miles. Could the difference between the two sample means be due to chance? The assumption is that for both populations (Rossford and Maumee) the standard deviations are either known or have been computed from samples greater than 30. The test statistic used is the standard normal distribution and its value is computed from the following formula:

$$z = \frac{\bar{X}_1 - \bar{X}_2}{\sqrt{\dfrac{s_1^2}{n_1} + \dfrac{s_2^2}{n_2}}} \qquad 9\text{–}3$$

where $\bar{X}_1$ and $\bar{X}_2$ refer to the two sample means, s_1^2

and s_2^2 to the two sample variances, and n_1 and n_2 to the two sample sizes.

Test Requirements for Proportions

We continue our study of hypothesis testing but expand the idea to a proportion. What is a proportion? A **proportion** is a fraction, or a percent, that indicates what part of the sample or population has a particular trait. For example, we want to estimate the proportion of all home sales made to first time buyers. A random sample of 200 recent transactions showed that 40 were first time buyers. Therefore, we estimate that .20, or 20 percent, of all sales are made to first time buyers, found by 40/200.

To conduct a test of hypothesis for proportions, the same assumptions required for the binomial distribution must be met. Recall from Chapter 6 that those assumptions are:

1. Each outcome is classified into one of two categories such as, buyers were either first time home buyers or they were not.
2. The number of trials is fixed. In this case it is 200.
3. Each trial is independent, meaning that the outcome of one trial has no bearing on the outcome of any other. Whether the 20th sampled person was a first time buyer does not affect the outcome of any other trial.
4. The probability of a success is fixed—the probability is .20 for all 200 buyers in the sample.

Recall from Chapter 7 that the normal distribution is a good approximation of the binomial distribution when np and $n(1 - p)$ are both greater than 5. In this instance n refers to the sample size and p to the probability of a success. The test statistic that is employed for testing hypotheses about proportions is the standard normal distribution.

Types of Tests of Hypothesis

There are three formats for testing a hypothesis about a proportion. For a one-tailed test there are two possibilities, depending on the intent of the researcher. For example, if we wanted to determine whether more than 25 percent of the sales of homes were sold to first time buyers, the hypotheses would be given as follows:

$$H_0: p \leqslant .25$$
$$H_1: p > .25$$

If we wanted to find out whether fewer than 25 percent of the homes were sold to first time buyers, the hypotheses would be given as:

117

$$H_0: p \geq .25$$
$$H_1: p < .25$$

For a two-tailed test the null and alternate hypotheses are:

$$H_0: p = .25$$
$$H_1: p \neq .25$$

where $\neq$ means "not equal to." Rejection of H_0 and acceptance of H_1 allows us to conclude only that the population proportion is "different from" or "not equal to" the population value. It does not allow us to make any statement about the direction of the difference.

Test Statistic

Two tests are considered about proportions. The first is for a *single population*. In the illustration a sample was drawn and the results tested against a hypothesized population proportion. The test statistic is z and it is found by the formula:

$$z = \frac{\bar{p} - p}{\sqrt{\dfrac{p(1 - p)}{n}}} \qquad 9\text{–}6$$

where $\bar{p}$ is the proportion of "successes" in the sample of size n and p is the hypothesized population proportion.

The second test of population compares the proportions of *two populations*. For example, we want to compare the proportion of rural voters planning to vote for the incumbent governor, with the proportion of urban voters. The test statistic is:

$$z = \frac{\bar{p}_1 - \bar{p}_2}{\sqrt{\dfrac{\bar{p}_c(1 - \bar{p}_c)}{n_1} + \dfrac{\bar{p}_c(1 - \bar{p}_c)}{n_2}}} \qquad 9\text{–}7$$

If we let X_1 be the number in the first sample possessing the trait of interest, X_2 the number in the second sample possessing the trait, and n_1 and n_2 the respective sample sizes, then $\bar{p}_1 = Z/n_1$ and $\bar{p}_2 = Z_2/n_2$. The value $\bar{p}_c$ refers to a combined or **pooled estimate** of the population proportion and is found by applying formula 9–8.

$$\bar{p}_c = \frac{\text{total number of successes}}{\text{total number of items}} = \frac{X_1 + X_2}{n_1 + n_2} \qquad 9\text{–}8$$

Use of these formulas will be examined in the Problem/Solution section.

GLOSSARY

Statistical inference—it involves drawing a conclusion about a population parameter based on sample information.

Hypothesis testing—A procedure for choosing between alternative statements or courses of action.

Null hypothesis—A claim about the value of a population parameter. It is designated H_0. Based on sample information, a decision is made to reject or not to reject the null hypothesis.

Alternate hypothesis—The claim that is accepted if the null hypothesis is rejected. It is denoted H_1. If the null hypothesis is rejected, the alternate hypothesis is accepted.

Level of significance—It is selected by the researcher, and defined as the probability that the null hypothesis will be rejected when it is actually true. It is referred to as the Type I error.

Type II error—Accepting a false null hypothesis.

Test statistic—A random variable used as a basis for making a decision to reject or not to reject the hypothesis.

Decision rule—A statement of the condition or conditions under which the null hypothesis is rejected and conditions under which it is not rejected.

Rejection region—A region of values for a particular test statistic. When the computed value of z (or any other value computed in the forthcoming chapters) falls in this region, the null hypothesis is rejected.

Critical value—A value, or values, that separates the rejection region from the region where the null hypothesis is not rejected.

p-value—The probability that the test statistic is as extreme or more extreme than that actually observed, when the null hypothesis is actually true.

Proportion—A fraction or a percent indicating what part of the sample or population has a particular trait of interest.

CHAPTER PROBLEMS

Problem 1

The manufacturer of the new subcompact Clipper claims in their TV advertisements that it will average "40 or more miles per gallon on the open road." Some of the competitors believe this claim is too high. To investigate, an independent testing agency is hired to conduct highway mileage tests. A random sample of 64 Clippers showed their mean miles per gallon to be 38.9, with a sample standard deviation of 4.00 miles per gallon. At the .01 significance level can the manufacturer's claim be refuted? Determine the p-value. Interpret the result.

Solution

The first step is to state the null and alternate hypotheses. The null hypothesis refers to the "no change" situation. That is, there has been no change in the Clipper's mileage, it is 40 mpg. It is written $H_0: \mu \geq 40$ and is read that the population mean is greater than or equal to 40. The alternate hypothesis is that the population mean is less than 40. It is written $H_1: \mu < 40$. If the null hypothesis is rejected, then the alternate is accepted. It would be concluded that the Clipper's mileage is less than 40 mpg.

The second step is to select the level of significance. The testing agency decided on the .01 significance level. This is the probability that the null hypothesis will be rejected, when in fact it is true.

The third step is to decide on a test statistic. The use of the standard normal distribution requires that the population standard deviation σ be known. When it is not known, as in this problem, the sample standard deviation, designated by s, is used as an estimate of σ. When this sample standard deviation is based on a large sample, the standard normal distribution is still an appropriate test statistic. "Large" is usually defined as being more than 30. To determine z we use formula 9–2.

$$z = \frac{\bar{X} - \mu}{s / \sqrt{n}}$$

where $\bar{X}$ is the sample mean, μ is the population mean, s is the standard deviation computed from the sample, and n is the sample size.

The fourth step is to develop the decision rule. The decision rule is a statement of the conditions under which the null hypothesis is rejected. The decision rule is shown in the following diagram. If the computed value of z is to the left of -2.33, the null hypothesis is rejected. The -2.33 is the critical value. How is it determined? Remember that the significance level stated in the problem is .01. This indicates that the area to the left of the critical value under the normal curve is .01. For the standard normal distribution the total area to the left of 0 is .5000. Therefore, the area between the critical value and 0 is .4900, found by .5000 − .0100. Now refer to Appendix D, and search the body of the table for a value close to .4900. The closest value is .4901. Read 2.3 in the left margin and .03 in the column containing .4901. Thus the z value corresponding to .4901 is 2.33.

Recall from Step 1 that the alternate hypothesis is $H_1: \mu < 40$. The inequality sign points in the negative direction. Thus the critical value is −2.33 and the rejection region is all in the lower left tail.

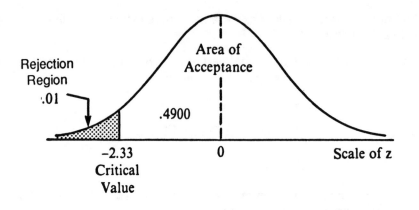

The fifth step is to compute the value of the test statistic, make a decision regarding the null hypothesis, and interpret the results. Since the standard deviation of the population is not known, the sample standard deviation is used as its estimate. Repeating the formula for z:

$$z = \frac{\bar{X} - \mu}{s / \sqrt{n}}$$

Recall that the manufacturer claims 40 mpg and the mean of the sample is 38.9 mpg.

Solving for z: $z = \frac{38.9 - 40.0}{4.0 / \sqrt{64}} = \frac{-1.1}{0.5} = -2.20$

The computed value of -2.20 is to the right of -2.33, so the null hypothesis is not rejected. We do not reject claim of the manufacturer that the Clipper gets at least 40.0 miles per gallon. It is reasonable that the 1.1 miles per gallon between (40.0 and 38.9) could be due to chance.

We do observe, however, that -2.20 is fairly close to the critical value of -2.33. What is the likelihood of a z value to the left of -2.20? It is .0139, found by .5000–.4861 where .4861 is the likelihood of a z value between 0 and 2.20.

The .0139 is referred to as the p-value. It is the probability of getting a value of the test statistic (z in this case) more extreme than that actually observed, if the null hypothesis is true. Had the significance level been set at .02 instead of .01, the null hypothesis would have been rejected. By reporting the p-value we give information on the strength of the decision regarding the null hypothesis.

Exercise 1

Check your answers against those in the ANSWER section.

Last year the records of Ski and Golf, Inc., a sporting goods chain, showed the mean amount spent by a customer was $30. A sample of 40 transactions this month revealed the mean amount spent was $33 with a standard deviation of $12. At the .05 significance level can we conclude that the mean amount spent has increased? What is the p-value?

Problem 2

Two manufacturers of sinus relief tablets, SINUS and ANTIDRIP, have made conflicting claims regarding the effectiveness of their tablets. A private testing organization was hired to evaluate the two tablets. The test company tried SINUS on 100 sinus congestion sufferers and found the mean time to relief was 85.0 minutes with a sample standard deviation of 6.0 minutes. A sample of 81 sinus congestion sufferers used ANTIDRIP. The mean time relief was 86.2 minutes, the sample standard deviation 6.8 minutes. Does the evidence suggest a difference in amount of time required to obtain relief? Use the .05 significance level and the five-step procedure. What is the *p*-value? Interpret it.

Solution

Note that the testing company is attempting to show only that there is a difference in the time required to affect relief. There is no attempt to show one tablet is "better than" or "worse than" the other. Thus, a two-tailed test is applied.

$$H_0: \mu_1 = \mu_2$$
$$H_1: \mu_1 \neq \mu_2$$

Let μ_1 refer to the mean time to obtain relief using SINUS and μ_2 to the mean time to obtain relief using ANTIDRIP.

The .05 significance level is to be used. Because both samples are large (greater than 30) the standard normal distribution is used as the test statistic. The alternate hypothesis does not state a direction, so this is a two-tailed test. The .05 significance level is divided equally into two tails of the standard normal distribution. Hence the area in the left tail is .0250 and .0250 in the right tail.

The critical values which separate the two rejection regions from the region of acceptance are −1.96 and +1.96. To explain: if the area in a rejection region is .0250, the acceptance area is .4750, found by .5000 − .0250. The z value corresponding to an area of .4750 is obtained by referring to the table of areas of the normal curve (Appendix D). Search the body of the table for a value as close to .4750 as possible and read the corresponding row and column values. The area of .4750 is found in the row 1.9 and the column .06. Hence, the critical values are ± 1.96. This is shown on the following diagram.

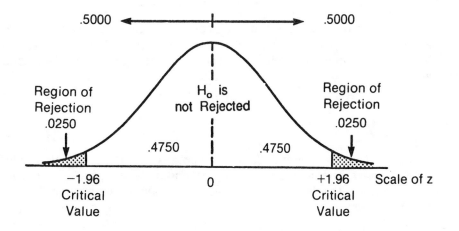

The computed value of z is − 1.24, found by using formula 9–3. Because the population standard deviations are not known, the sample standard deviations are substituted.

$$z = \frac{\bar{X}_1 - \bar{X}_2}{\sqrt{\dfrac{s_1^2}{n_1} + \dfrac{s_2^2}{n_2}}} = \frac{85.0 - 86.2}{\sqrt{\dfrac{(6.0)^2}{100} + \dfrac{(6.8)^2}{81}}} = -1.24$$

The computed value of z falls in the acceptance region between -1.96 and $+1.96$. The null hypothesis is, therefore, not rejected. There is no difference in the mean time it takes SINUS and ANTIDRIP to bring relief. The difference of 1.2 minutes ($85.0 - 86.2$) can be attributed to sampling error (chance).

To determine the p-value we need to find the area to the left of -1.24 and add to it the area to the right of 1.24. Why are we concerned with both tails? Because H_1 is two-tailed. The p-value is .2150, found by 2(.5000 − .3925).

Exercise 2

Check your answers against those in the ANSWER section.

The county commissioners received a number of complaints from county residents that the Youngsville Fire Department takes longer to respond to fires than the Claredon Fire Department. To check the validity of these complaints, a random sample of 60 fires handled by the Youngsville Fire Department was selected. It was found that the mean response time was 6.9 minutes and the standard deviation of the sample 3.8 minutes. A sample of 70 fires handled by the Claredon Fire Department found the mean response time was 4.9 minutes with a sample standard deviation of 3.0 minutes. Does the data suggest that it takes longer for the Youngsville Department to respond? Use the .05 significance level.

Problem 3

The Dean of Students at Scandia Tech believes that 30 percent of the students are employed. You, as President of the Student Government, believe the proportion employed is less than 30 percent and decide to conduct a study. A random sample of 100 students revealed 25 were employed. At the .01 significance level, can the Dean's claim be refuted?

Solution

As usual, the first step is to state the null and alternate hypotheses. The null hypothesis is that there is no change in the percent employed. That is, the population proportion is at least .30. The alternate hypothesis is the proportion is less than .30. This is the statement we are trying to test empirically. Symbolically, these statements are written as follows:

$$H_0\colon p \geqslant .30$$
$$H_1\colon p < .30$$

The .01 significance level is to be used. The assumptions of the binomial distribution are met in the problem. That is (1) there are only two outcomes for each trial—the student is either employed or isn't employed; (2) the number of trials is fixed—100 students; (3) each trial is independent, meaning that the employment of one student selected does not affect another; (4) the probability that any randomly selected student is employed is .30.

The normal approximation to the binomial is used because both np and $n(1 - p)$ exceed 5. ($np = 100(.30)$ = 30 and $n(1 - p) = 100(.70) = 70$). The standard normal distribution, z, is the test statistic. To formulate the decision rule, we need the critical value of z. Using the .01 significance level, the area is .4900 (.500 − .0100).

Search the body of Appendix D for a value as close to .4900 as possible. It is .4901. The value associated with .4901 is 2.33. The alternate hypothesis points in the negative direction, hence the rejection region is in the left tail and the critical value of z is −2.33.

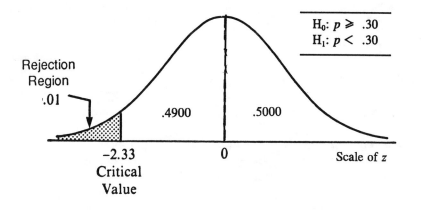

The decision rule is to reject the null hypothesis if the computed value of the test statistic lies in the rejection region to the left of −2.33.

Recall that the sample of 100 Scandia Tech students revealed that 25 were employed. The question is whether the sample proportion of .25, found by 25/100, is significantly less than .30.

$$z = \frac{\bar{p} - p}{\sqrt{\dfrac{p(1 - p)}{n}}} = \frac{.25 - .30}{\sqrt{\dfrac{(.30)(1 - .30)}{100}}} = -1.09$$

The computed value of z falls in the region between 0 and −2.33. H_0 is not rejected. There is a difference between the Dean's hypothesized proportion (.30) and the sample proportion (.25), but this difference of .05 is not sufficient to reject the null hypothesis. The .05 can be attributed to sampling (chance). The Dean's claim cannot be refuted.

The p-value is the probability of a z value to the left of −1.09. It is .1379, found by .5000 − .3621. The p-value is larger than the significance level of .01, which is consistent with our decision not to reject the null hypothesis.

Exercise 3

Check your answers against those in the ANSWER section.

The producer of a TV special expected about 40 percent of the viewing audience to watch a rerun of a 1965 Beatles Concert. A sample of 200 homes revealed 60 to be watching the concert. At the .10 significance level, does the evidence suggest that less than 40 percent were watching? Use the usual hypothesis testing format. What is the p-value?

Problem 4

Two different sites are being considered for a day-care center. One is on the south side of the city and the other is on the east side. The decision where to locate the day-care center depends in part on how many mothers work and have children under 5 years old.

A sample of 200 family units on the south side revealed that 88 working mothers have children under 5 years.

A sample of 150 family units on the east side revealed that 57 have children under 5 years and the mother worked. Summarizing the data:

	South Side	East Side
Number of working mothers with children under 5	$X_1 = 88$	$X_2 = 57$
Number in sample	$n_1 = 200$	$n_2 = 150$
Proportion with children under 5 and mothers work	$p_1 = .44$	$p_2 = .38$

The question to be explored is: Is there a significantly higher proportion of mothers on the south side (.44) who work and have children under 5 years compared with those on the east side (.38)? Or, can the difference be attributed to sampling variation (chance)? Use the .05 level of significance.

Solution

The problem is to examine whether a higher proportion of working mothers of young children live on the south side. The hypotheses will therefore be:

$$H_0: p_1 \leqslant p_2$$
$$H_1: p_1 > p_2$$

The standard normal distribution is the test statistic to be used. The significance level is .05. The critical value is 1.645 obtained from Appendix D. The area in the upper tail of the curve is .05, therefore the area between $z = 0$ and the critical value is .4500, found by .5000 − .0500. Search the body of the table for a value close to .4500. Since 1.64 is equal to .4495 and 1.65 is equal to .4505, a value between 1.64 and 1.65 or (1.645) is used as the critical value. The null hypothesis is rejected if the calculated value is greater than 1.645. This information is shown in the following diagram.

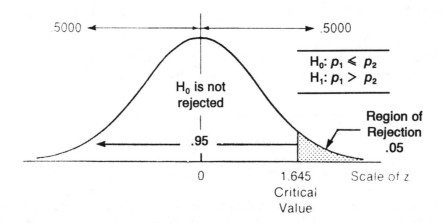

Formula 9–7 for z is repeated below.

$$z = \frac{\bar{p}_1 - \bar{p}_2}{\sqrt{\dfrac{\bar{p}_c(1 - \bar{p}_c)}{n_1} + \dfrac{\bar{p}_c(1 - \bar{p}_c)}{n_2}}}$$

where $\bar{p}_c$ is a pooled estimate of the population proportion and is computed using formula 9–8.

$$\bar{p}_c = \frac{X_1 + X_2}{n_1 + n_2}$$

In this problem X_1 and X_2 refer to the number of "successes" in each sample (number of working mothers with children under 5 years). n_1 and n_2 refer to the number of housing units sampled in the south side and east side, respectively.

The pooled estimate of the population proportion is .4143, found as follows:

$$\bar{p}_c = \frac{X_1 + X_2}{n_1 + n_2} = \frac{88 + 57}{200 + 150} = .4143$$

Inserting the pooled estimate of .4143 in the formula and solving for z in formula 9–8 gives 1.13.

$$z = \frac{\bar{p}_1 - \bar{p}_2}{\sqrt{\dfrac{\bar{p}_c(1 - \bar{p}_c)}{n_1} + \dfrac{\bar{p}_c(1 - \bar{p}_c)}{n_2}}}$$

$$= \frac{.44 - .38}{\sqrt{\dfrac{(.4143)(1 - .4143)}{200} + \dfrac{(.4143)(1 - .4143)}{150}}} = 1.13$$

The computed value of z (1.13) is less than the critical value of 1.645 so the null hypothesis is not rejected. The difference of .06 can be attributed to sampling error (chance). To put it another way, the proportion of mothers who work and have children under 5 on the south side and east side is not significantly different. The p-value is .1292, found by .5000 − .3708. So, the probability of finding a value of the test statistic this large or larger is .1292.

Exercise 4

Check your answers against those in the ANSWER section.

A recent study was designed to compare smoking habits of young women with those of young men. A random sample of 150 women revealed that 45 smoked. A random sample of 100 men indicated that 25 smoked. At the .05 significance level does the evidence show that a higher proportion of women smoke? Compute the p-value.

CHAPTER ASSIGNMENT 9

Tests of Hypotheses: Large Samples

Name _____ Section _____ Score _____

Part I Select the correct answer and write the appropriate letter in the space provided.

___ 1. The null hypothesis is a claim about
    a. the size of the sample.
    b. the size of the population.
    c. the value of a sample statistic.
    d. the value of a population parameter.

___ 2. When the null hypothesis is rejected, we conclude that
    a. the alternate hypothesis is false also.
    b. the alternate hypothesis is true.
    c. the sample size is too large.
    d. we used the wrong test statistic.

___ 3. The probability of committing a Type I error is
    a. always greater than the p-value.
    b. equal to the probability of committing a Type II error.
    c. equal to the probability of accepting H_1 when it is false.
    d. equal to the significance level.

___ 4. The condition or conditions under which H_0 is rejected is
    a. called the decision rule.
    b. the likelihood of a Type I error.
    c. called the test statistic.
    d. called the p-value.

___ 5. When the p-value is smaller than the significance level
    a. a Type I error is committed.
    b. a Type II error is committed.
    c. the null hypothesis is rejected.
    d. the critical value is correct.

___ 6. A Type II error is
    a. the same as the significance level.
    b. accepting a false H_0.
    c. reject H_0 when it is true.
    d. not rejecting a false H_0.

___ 7. In a test regarding a sample mean, σ is not known. Under which of the following conditions can s be substituted for σ and z used as the test statistic?
    a. when n is 30 or more
    b. when n is less than 30.
    c. when np and $n(1 - p)$ both exceed 5
    d. when μ is known.

___ 8. A proportion is
    a. a standard normal value.
    b. a test statistic.

c. the fraction of the sample that has a particular trait.
d. frequently negative.

___ 9. In a two–tailed test the rejection region is
    a. all in the upper tail of the standard normal distribution.
    b. all in the lower tail of the standard normal distribution.
    c. divided equally between the two tails.
    d. always equal to -1.96 or 1.96.

___ 10. To compare a single sample to a population proportion
    a. n must be less than 30.
    b. p must be less than 5.
    c. np and $n(1 - p)$ must both be greater than 5.
    d. σ must be given.

Part II Fill in the blank with the correct answer.

11. A_____is the likelihood of finding a value of the test statistic as large as or larger than the computed value.

12. The_____is a statement of the conditions when the null hypothesis is rejected.

13. List the five steps in hypothesis testing.
    a. _____
    b. _____
    c. _____
    d. _____
    e. _____

14. Rejecting the null hypothesis when it is true is call a_____error.

15. The four requirements of the_____distribution must be satisfied to conduct a test of proportions.

Part III Record your answer in the space provided. Show essential calculations.

16. A recent article in a computer magazine suggested that the mean time to fully learn a new software program is 30 hours. A sample of 40 first-time users of a new statistics program called *StatMagic* revealed the mean time to learn it was 28 hours and the standard deviation was 6.0 hours. At the .05 significance level, can we conclude that users learn the package in less than a mean of 30 hours?

    State the null and the alternate hypotheses.
    H_0:_____
    H_1:_____

    State the decision rule.

    Compute the value of the test statistic.

    Answer

    Compute the *p*-value.

    Answer

What is your decision regarding the null hypothesis? Interpret the result.

_____
_____
_____
_____

17. A financial planner wants to the compare the yield of income and growth oriented mutual funds. Five thousand dollars are invested in each of a sample of 35 income oriented and 40 growth oriented funds. The mean increase for a two year period for the income funds is $1100 with a standard deviation of $45. For the growth oriented funds the mean increase is $1090 with a standard deviation of $55. At the .01 significance level is there a difference in the mean yield of the two funds?

State the null and the alternate hypothesis.

H_0:_____

H_1:_____

State the decision rule.

Compute the value of the test statistic.

```
┌─────────────────┐
│                 │
└─────────────────┘
      Answer
```

Compute the p-value.

```
┌─────────────────┐
│                 │
└─────────────────┘
      Answer
```

What is your decision regarding the null hypothesis? Interpret the result.

_____
_____
_____
_____

18. Last year a survey in the Nashville TV viewing area showed that 20 percent of the viewers watched their news on WBEN, which is channel 13. In an effort to increase their rating, WBEN added several new reporters to cover local stories and events more thoroughly. A survey last week revealed that out of 400 viewers contacted, 94 watched the news on WBEN. Can we conclude that the percent of viewers has increased? Use the .05 significance level.

State the null and the alternate hypothesis.

H_0:_____

H_1:_____

State the decision rule.

Compute the value of the test statistic.

Compute the *p*-value.

What is your decision regarding the null hypothesis? Interpret the result.

_____

_____

_____

_____

19. The Human Resources Director for a large company is studying absenteeism among hourly workers. A sample of 120 day shift employees showed 15 were absent more than five days last year. A sample of 80 afternoon employees showed 18 to be absent five days or more. At the .01 significance level can we conclude that there is a higher proportion of absenteeism among afternoon employees?

State the null and the alternate hypothesis.

H_0:_____

H_1:_____

State the decision rule.

Compute the value of the test statistic.

```
┌──────────────┐
│              │
└──────────────┘
```
Answer

Compute the *p*-value.

```
┌──────────────┐
│              │
└──────────────┘
```
Answer

What is your decision regarding the null hypothesis? Interpret the result.

_____

_____

_____

_____

10

TESTS OF HYPOTHESES: SMALL SAMPLES

CHAPTER GOALS

After completing this chapter, you will be able to:

1. Discuss the characteristics of the t distribution.
2. Define the terms dependent and independent samples.
3. Understand the differences between the t and the z distributions.
4. Conduct a hypothesis test for a population mean when the population standard deviation is not known and the sample size is less than 30.
5. Conduct a hypothesis test for the difference between two population means when the population standard deviations are not known and both sample sizes are less than 30.
6. Conduct a hypothesis test for the difference between paired observations when the sample size is less than 30.

Introduction

In this chapter we continue our study of hypothesis testing. Recall that in Chapter 9 we considered hypothesis tests for means where the population standard deviation was known. If it was not known but we have a sample of more than 30 observations, then the sample standard deviation was substituted for the population standard deviation. The standard normal distribution was used as the test statistic.

What it the standard deviation of the population is not known and the sample size is less than 30? Under these conditions the standard normal distribution is *not* the appropriate test statistic. The appropriate test statistic is the **Student t distribution.** This distribution was first described by William S. Gosset, who wrote under the name ''Student'' in the early 1900s.

Characteristics of the t Distribution

The Student t distribution is similar to the standard normal distribution in some ways, but quite different in others. It has the following major characteristics:

1. It is a continuous distribution, like the standard normal distribution described in Chapter 7.
2. It is bell shaped and symmetrical, again similar to the standard normal distribution.
3. There is a ''family'' of t distributions. That is, each time the size of the sample changes, a new t distribution is created.
4. The t distribution is more spread out (that is ''flatter'') at the center than the standard normal distribution.

As noted above, the t distribution has a greater spread than the standard normal distribution. Thus, with a stated level of significance, the critical values for t are further removed from 0 than they are in the standard normal distribution. For a one-tailed test with a .05 significance level, the following graphs show that values of t are larger than those of z. Exactly how these values are obtained will be explained shortly. Note that when t is used as the test statistic instead of the standard normal: (1) the acceptance region will be wider, and (2) a larger value of t will be required to reject the null hypothesis. A further requirement is that the population from which the sample is obtained should be normal or approximately normal.

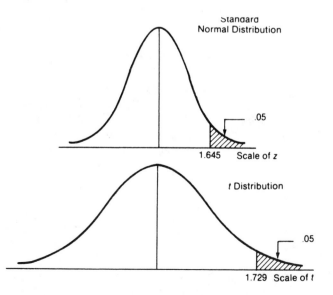

Degrees of Freedom

To locate the critical value of t, we need to know the number of degrees of freedom. For one sample, the number degrees of freedom is found by the number of sample observations minus one $(n - 1)$. Thus for a sample of three observations there are two degrees of freedom, $3 - 1 = 2$. Why is this so? Suppose the values of the three sample observations are 5, 7, and 9. The mean of the sample is 7. If any two of these values are changed, then the third is automatically fixed so the mean can remain 7. Suppose the first two are changed to 4 and 5, then the last must be changed to 12 for the three values to have a mean of 7, that is $(4 + 5 + 12)/3 = 7$. Hence, only two of the three values are free to vary and we say there are two degrees of freedom. For a sample of size 15, there are 14 degrees of freedom, found by $n - 1 = 15 - 1 = 14$.

The decision rule involving the t distribution is formulated from Appendix F. This table can be used for both one-tailed and two-tailed tests. To show how the table is used, suppose we have a sample of six, a one-tailed test, and the .05 significance level is to be used. First, determine the number of degrees of freedom. There are 5, found by $n - 1 = 6 - 1 = 5$. Next go down the left-hand column in Appendix F, labeled "df" to the row of 5. Find the column for a one-tailed test and the .05 significance level. The critical value is 2.015.

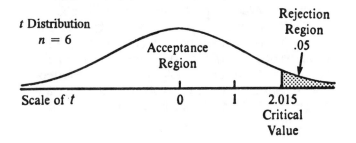

t Distribution
$n = 6$

Acceptance Region

Rejection Region
.05

Scale of *t*   0   1   2.015
Critical Value

One Sample Test for Means

In this chapter the t distribution is used as a test statistic for three tests: (1) for a single population mean, (2) for two population means, and (3) to test for the difference between paired observations.

The value of the t statistic for a one-sample test of means is computed by the formula 10–1, which is:

$$t = \frac{\bar{X} - \mu}{s/\sqrt{n}} \qquad 10\text{--}1$$

where $\bar{X}$ is the sample mean, s the sample standard

deviation, n the sample size, and μ the population mean. This formula is the same as the one presented in Chapter 9 for the standard normal distribution, except s is substituted for μ and the Student t distribution is used to locate the critical value.

Two Sample Test of Means

The t distribution may be employed as the test statistic for a test of hypothesis for the *difference* between two population means. The required assumptions are:

1. The observations in the two samples are unrelated—that is, independent.
2. The populations from which the samples were obtained are approximately normal.
3. The two populations have approximately equal variances.

To conduct the two-sample test, the first step is to pool the sample variances. This is accomplished by using the following formula.

$$s_p^2 = \frac{(n_1 - 1)s_1^2 + (n_2 - 1)s_2^2}{n_1 + n_2 - 2} \qquad 10\text{--}2$$

where s_1^2 and s_2^2 are the sample variances and n_1, and n_2 are the sample sizes. The value of t is then computed using formula 11–3.

$$t = \frac{\bar{X}_1 - \bar{X}_2}{\sqrt{s_p^2\left(\frac{1}{n_1} + \frac{1}{n_2}\right)}} \qquad 10\text{--}3$$

$\bar{X}_1$, and $\bar{X}_2$ refer to the sample means. The degrees of freedom for a two-sample test is found by $n_1 + n_2 - 2$.

The Test for Paired Differences

A third hypothesis testing situation occurs when we are concerned with the *difference* in a pair of related observations. Typically, this is a before-and-after situation, where we want to measure the difference. To illustrate, suppose we administer a reading test to a sample of ten students. Then we have them take a course in speed reading. Thus the test focuses on the reading improvements of each of the ten students. The distribution of the population of differences is assumed to be approximately normal. The test statistic is t, and the formula is:

$$t = \frac{\bar{d}}{s_d / \sqrt{n}}$$

10–4

where

d is the mean of the differences between paired observations.

S_d is the standard deviation of the differences in the paired observations.

n is the number of paired observations.

For a paired difference test there are $n - 1$ degrees of freedom.

GLOSSARY

Student's t distribution—A continuous symmetric probability distribution with a mean of 0. The distribution of t differs for each sample size, n. It is flatter and more spread out than the standard normal distribution, z.

Degrees of freedom—The number of observations in the samples that are free to vary. For a test of hypothesis involving one population mean it is found by $n - 1$, for two means $n_1 + n_2 - 2$, and for a paired difference test $n - 1$.

Independent samples—The sample selected from one population is not related to the sample selected from the second population. That is, the samples are selected from distinct populations.

Dependent samples—The sample selected from one population is related to the sample selected from the other population.

CHAPTER PROBLEMS

Problem 1

Suppose you drive your car to work. The mean driving time is 30 minutes. A fellow worker suggests a different, faster route. As an experiment you recorded these times: 29, 27, 30, 26, and 28 minutes, along the suggested route. You want to use the .05 significance level, to decide if the new route takes less driving time.

Solution

The null hypothesis is that the population mean is at least 30 minutes. The alternate hypothesis is that the mean driving time is less than 30 minutes. These hypotheses are written symbolically:

$$H_0: \mu \geqslant 30$$
$$H_1: \mu < 30$$

To determine the decision rule, we must first assume that the population is normally distributed. Because the population standard deviation is not known, and the sample size is small, the t distribution is used as the test statistic.

The value that will determine whether we should reject the null hypothesis is obtained from Appendix F. Note that in this problem there are 4 degrees of freedom ($n - 1 = 5 - 1 = 4$). We stipulated a .05 significance level and a one-tailed test. To obtain the critical value of t, move down the left-hand column of Appendix F to 4 degrees of freedom. Move across that row to the column headed by .05 and a one-tailed test. The value given is 2.132. Since the direction of the alternate hypothesis is negative, the critical value is -2.132. The null hypothesis is rejected if the computed t is to the left of -2.132; otherwise, it is not rejected. The decision rule is shown in the following diagram:

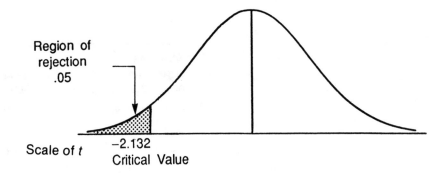

Region of
rejection
.05

Scale of t −2.132
Critical Value

Next the value of the test statistic is computed. Since the mean and standard deviation of the sample are not given they must be computed from the sample information. The sample mean is computed using formula 3–2, and the standard deviation by taking the square root of formula 4–7. (Formula 4–7 determines the sample variance).

Sample Times

X	X²
29	841
27	729
30	900
26	676
28	784
140	3,930

$$\bar{X} = \frac{\Sigma X}{n} = \frac{140}{5} = 28.0$$

$$s = \sqrt{\frac{\Sigma X^2 - \frac{(\Sigma X)^2}{n}}{n - 1}} = \sqrt{\frac{3,930 - \frac{(140)^2}{5}}{5 - 1}} = 1.58$$

These values are inserted into formula 11–1 and the value of the test statistic is computed.

$$t = \frac{\bar{X} - \mu}{s / \sqrt{n}} = \frac{28 - 30}{1.58 / \sqrt{5}} = -2.83$$

Since the computed value of −2.83 is to the left of −2.132, the null hypothesis is rejected and the alternate accepted. You conclude that the route suggested by your fellow worker is faster.

How can we determine the p-value for this test? We cannot get the exact p-value as we did in the previous chapters when the standard normal distribution was the test statistic. However, with Appendix F we can estimate the p-value. Go to Appendix F and find the row with 4 degrees of freedom (there were four degrees of freedom in this problem), and use the levels of significance for one-tailed tests (this test was one-tailed). Locate a value as close to 2.83, the value of the test statistic, as possible. At the .025 significance level the t value is 2.776 and at the .01 significance level it is 3.747. The p-value is between .025 and .010, so we can say that the p-value is less than .025.

Exercise 1

Check your answers against those in the ANSWER section.

A supervisor believes employees are taking longer than ten minutes for their breaks. A sample of six employees revealed the following times (in minutes) spent on a break: 9, 12, 14, 15, 10, and 12. At the .01 significance level, can it be concluded that employees are taking too long for their breaks? Estimate the p-value.

Problem 2

A study of recent graduates from your school revealed that for a sample of ten accounting majors the mean salary was $30,000 per year with a sample standard deviation of $2,000. A sample of eight general business majors revealed a mean salary of $29,000 per year with a standard deviation of $1,500. At the .05 significance level can we conclude accounting majors earn more?

Solution

The null hypothesis is that there is no difference in the mean salary of the two groups, or that accounting majors earn less. The alternate hypothesis is that accounting graduates earn more. They are written as follows:

$$H_0: \mu_1 \leqslant \mu_2$$
$$H_1: \mu_1 > \mu_2$$

where μ_1 refers to accounting graduates and μ_2 general business graduates.

   Assuming that the two populations follow the normal distribution and that their population variances are equal, then the t distribution is the test statistic. There are 16 degrees of freedom, found by $n_1 + n_2 - 2 = 10 + 8 - 2 = 16$. The alternate hypothesis is a one-tailed test with the rejection region in the upper tail. From Appendix F, the critical value is 1.746. Hence, H_0 is rejected if the computed value of the test statistic exceeds 1.746.

The first step is to pool the variances, using formula 10–2.

$$s_p^2 = \frac{(n_1 - 1)(s_1^2) + (n_2 - 1)(s_2^2)}{n_1 + n_2 - 2} = \frac{(10 - 1)(2,000)^2 + (8 - 1)(1,500)^2}{10 + 8 - 2} = 3,234,375$$

Next, the value of t is computed, using formula 10–3.

$$t = \frac{\$1,000}{\sqrt{(3,234,375)\left(\frac{1}{10} + \frac{1}{8}\right)}} = 1.17$$

Because the computed value of t (1.17) is less than the critical value of 1.746, H_0 is not rejected. The sample evidence does not suggest a difference in the mean salaries of the two groups. The p-value from Appendix F is greater than .100.

●

Exercise 2

Check your answers against those in the ANSWER section.

A large department store hired a researcher to compare the average purchase amounts for the downtown store with that of its mall store. The following information was obtained:

	Downtown Store	Mall Store
Average purchase amount	$36.00	$40.00
Sample standard deviation	$10.00	$12.00
Sample size	10	10

At the .01 significance level can it be concluded that the mean amount spent at the mall store is larger? Estimate the p-value.

Problem 3

The Dean of the College of Business at Kingsport University wants to determine if the Grade Point Average (GPA) of business college students decreases during the last semester of their senior year. A sample of six students is selected. Their GPAs for the fall and spring semesters of their senior year are:

Student	Fall Semester	Spring Semester
A	2.7	3.1
B	3.4	3.3
C	3.5	3.3
D	3.0	2.9
E	2.1	1.8
F	2.7	2.4

At the .05 significance level, can the Dean conclude that the GPA of graduating seniors declined during their last semester?

Solution

Let μ_d be the mean difference between the fall and spring semester grades for all business students at Kingsport U. in their senior year. Since we want to explore whether grades decrease, a one-tailed test is appropriate.

$$H_0: \mu_d \leqslant 0$$
$$H_1: \mu_d > 0$$

There are six paired observations; therefore, there are $n - 1 = 6 - 1 = 5$ degrees of freedom. Using Appendix F with 5 degrees of freedom, the .05 significance level and a one-tailed test, the critical value of t is 2.015. H_0 is rejected if the computed value of the test statistic exceeds 2.015.

The value of the test statistic is determined from formula 11–4 below.

$$t = \frac{\bar{d}}{s_d / \sqrt{n}}$$ 10–4

where $\bar{d}$ is the mean of the differences between fall and spring GPAs, s_d is the standard deviation of those differences, and n is the number of paired observations. First, subtract spring semester grades from fall semester grades. If this difference is positive then a *decline* has occurred.

The sample data is shown below and the values of $\bar{d}$ and s_d computed:

Student	Fall	Spring	d	d²
A	2.7	3.1	–.4	.16
B	3.4	3.3	.1	.01
C	3.5	3.3	.2	.04
D	3.0	2.9	.1	.01
E	2.1	1.8	.3	.09
F	2.7	2.4	.3	.09
			.6	.40

$$\bar{d} = \frac{\Sigma d}{n} = \frac{.6}{6} = .10$$

$$s_d = \sqrt{\frac{\Sigma d^2 - \frac{(\Sigma d)^2}{n}}{n - 1}} = \sqrt{\frac{.40 - \frac{(.6)^2}{6}}{6 - 1}} = .2608$$

The t statistic is computed by:

$$t = \frac{\bar{d}}{s_d / \sqrt{n}} = \frac{.10}{.2608/\sqrt{6}} = \frac{.10}{.1065} = 0.94$$

Since the computed value of t (.94) is less than the critical value of 2.015, H_0 is not rejected. The evidence does not suggest a reduction in grades from the fall to the spring semester. The decrease in GPAs can be attributed to chance. The p-value is greater than .100.

Exercise 3

Check your answers against those in the ANSWER section.

An independent government agency is interested in comparing the heating cost of all-electric homes and those of homes heated with natural gas. A sample of eight all-electric homes is matched with eight homes of similar size and other features that use natural gas. The heating costs for last January are obtained for each home.

Matched Pair	Electric Heat	Gas Heat
1	265	260
2	271	270
3	260	250
4	250	255
5	248	250
6	280	275
7	257	260
8	262	260

At the .05 significance level is there reason to believe there is a difference in heating costs?

CHAPTER ASSIGNMENT 10

Tests of Hypotheses: Small Samples

Name _____ Section _____ Score _____

Part I Select the correct answer and write the appropriate letter in the space provided.

___ 1. Which of the following statements are true regarding both the t distribution and the z distribution?
  a. both have a mean of 0.
  b. both are continuous
  c. both have standard deviations of 1.00
  d. all of the above

___ 2. As the degrees of freedom increase, the t distribution
  a. approaches the z distribution.
  b. becomes positively skewed.
  c. cannot be negative.
  d. becomes discrete.

___ 3. Which of the following statements is **not** true regarding the t distribution?
  a. It is a continuous distribution.
  b. Each time the degrees of freedom change the t distribution changes.
  c. The t distribution is flatter than the z distribution.
  d. It is positively skewed.

___ 4. In a two sample test of means for independent samples, $n_1 = 12$ and $n_2 = 10$. There are how many degrees of freedom in the test?
  a. 22
  b. 21
  c. 20
  d. none of the above.

___ 5. In the paired t-test, we assume in the null hypothesis that the distribution of the differences between the paired observation has a mean
  a. equal to 1.
  b. that is independent.
  c. equal to 0.
  d. none of the above

___ 6. For a particular significance level and sample size the value of t for a one-tailed test is
  a. always less that z
  b. always more the z.
  c. equal to 0.
  d. equal to t^2.

___ 7. Which of the following is **not** an assumption for the two-sample t-test?
  a. equal *sample* standard deviations
  b. independent samples
  c. normal populations
  d. equal *population* standard deviations

___ 8. Suppose in a one-sample test the sample mean was 10 and the sample size 15. The population standard deviation was 3. The appropriate test statistic is
  a. the binomial distribution.

b. the *t* distribution.

c. the *z* distribution.

d. none of the above

___ 9. For a test of hypothesis for a single sample mean, a one-tailed test (rejection region in the upper tail), using the .01 significance level, and with $n = 12$, the critical value is:

a. 2.718

b. 3.106

c. 2.681

d. 2.179

___ 10. To determine if a diet supplement is useful for increasing weight, patients are weighed at the start of the program and at the end of the program. This is an example of

a. dependent samples.

b. independent samples.

c. normal samples.

d. *t* samples.

Part II Fill in the blank with the correct answer.

11. List the three requirements for the two-sample *t*-test for independent samples.

a. _____

b. _____

c. _____

12. If the samples from the first population are not related to the samples from the second population the samples are_____.

13. List the four characteristics of the *t* distribution.

a. _____

b. _____

c. _____

d. _____

14. As the degrees of freedom are increased, the *t* distribution approaches the_____distribution.

15. In a two-sample test for means the sample variances are_____

Part III Record your answers in the space provided. Show essential calculations.

16. A retail management trade journal reported that the typical shopper spends an average of 1.80 hours per visit in a shopping mall. A sample of 8 shoppers at the Byrnwick Mall in south Toledo revealed the following times. At the .01 significance level, can we conclude that shoppers at the Byrnwick Mall spend less than a mean of 1.80 hours?

1.4   1.7   1.6   2.1   1.6   1.9   1.7   1.7

State the null and the alternate hypotheses.

H_0:_____

H_1:_____

State the decision rule.

Compute the value of the test statistic.

Answer

Compute the p-value.

Answer

What is your decision regarding the null hypothesis? Interpret the result.

_____

_____

_____

_____

17. Is the mean salary of accountants who have reached partnership status higher than that for accountants who are not partners? A sample 15 accountants who have the partnership status showed a mean salary of $62,000 with a standard deviation of $5500. A sample of 12 accountants who were not partners showed a mean of $58,000 with a standard deviation of $6500. At the .05 significance level can we conclude that accountants at the partnership level earn larger salaries?

State the null and the alternate hypotheses.

H_0:_____

H_1:_____

State the decision rule.

Compute the value of the test statistic.

Answer

Compute the p-value.

Answer

What is your decision regarding the null hypothesis. Interpret the result.

_____

_____

_____

_____

18. The President and CEO of Cliff Hanger International Airlines is concerned about the high cholesterol levels of the pilots. In an attempt to improve the situation a sample of seven pilots is selected to take part in a special program, in which each pilot is given a special diet by the company physician. After six months each pilot's cholesterol level is checked again. At the .01 significance level can we conclude that the program was effective in reducing the cholesterol levels?

Pilot	Before	After
1	255	210
2	230	225
3	290	215
4	242	215
5	300	240
6	250	235
7	215	190

State the null and the alternate hypotheses.

H_0:_____

H_1:_____

State the decision rule.

Compute the value of the test statistic.

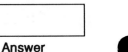

Answer

Compute the *p*-value.

Answer

What is your decision regarding the null hypothesis? Interpret the result.

_____

_____

_____

_____

11

ANALYSIS OF VARIANCE

CHAPTER GOALS

After completing this chapter, you will be able to:

1. List the characteristics of the F distribution.
2. Conduct a test of hypothesis to determine if two population variances are equal.
3. Set up an analysis of variance table.
4. Conduct a test for a difference among three or more treatment means.
5. Conduct a test to determine if there is a difference in block means.

Introduction

In Chapter 10 we developed a method to determine whether there is a difference between two population means, when the sample sizes are less than 30. What if we wanted to compare more than two populations? The two sample t test used in Chapter 10 requires that the populations be compared two at a time. This would be very time consuming, offers the possibility of errors in calculations, but most seriously there would be a build-up of Type I errors. That is, the total value of α would become large as the number of comparisons increased. In this chapter we will describe a technique that is efficient when simultaneously comparing more than two population means. This technique is known as **Analysis of Variance (ANOVA).**

A second test compares two sample variances to determine if they were obtained from the same or equal populations. This test is particularly useful in validating the requirement of the two sample t test that both populations have the same standard deviations.

The F Distribution

The test statistic used to compare the sample variances and to conduct the ANOVA test is the **F Distribution.** The major characteristics of the F distribution are:

1. The value of F is at least zero. That is, F cannot be negative.
2. The F distribution is continuous, is positively skewed, and its values may range from 0 to plus infinity.

3. The F distribution is based on two sets of degrees of freedom. One set is for the numerator and the other for the denominator.
4. There is a family of F distributions. Each time the number of degrees of freedom in either the numerator or the denominator change, a new F distribution is created.

Assumptions of ANOVA

To employ ANOVA, four conditions must be met:

1. The populations being studied must be approximately normally distributed.
2. The populations should have equal standard deviations.
3. The samples should be randomly selected and the populations independent.

The ANOVA Test

The same hypothesis-testing procedure used with the standard normal distribution (z) and Student's t is also employed with analysis of variance. The test statistic is the F distribution.

Step 1. The null hypothesis and the alternate hypothesis are stated.

When three populations means are compared, the null and alternate hypotheses are written:

$$H_0: \mu_1 = \mu_2 = \mu_3$$
$$H_1: \text{not all means are equal}$$

Note that rejection of the null hypothesis does not identify which populations differ significantly. It merely indicates that a difference *between at least one pair of means exists*.

Step 2. The level of significance is selected.

The most common values selected are .01 or .05.

Step 3. An appropriate test statistic is selected.

For an analysis of variance problem the appropriate test statistic is F. The F statistic is the ratio of two variance estimates and is computed by the formula:

$$F = \frac{\text{estimated population variance based on variance among the sample means}}{\text{estimated population variance based on variation within samples}}$$

There are $k - 1$ degrees of freedom associated with the numerator of the formula for F, and $N - k$ degrees of freedom associated with the denominator, where k is the number of populations and N is the total number of sample observations.

Step 4. Formulate the Decision Rule.

The critical value is determined from the F table found in Appendix G.

To illustrate how the decision rule is established, suppose a package delivery company purchased 14 trucks at the same time. Five trucks were purchased from Ford, four from General Motors, and five from Chrysler. All the trucks were used to deliver packages. The cost of maintaining the trucks for the first year is shown below. Is there a significant difference in the mean maintenance cost of the three manufacturers?

Maintenance Cost, By Manufacturer

Ford	Chrysler	General Motors
$ 914	$933	$1,004
1,000	874	1,114
1,127	927	1,044
988	983	1,100
947		1,139

The three different manufacturers are called **treatments**. A treatment is a specific source, or cause, of variation in a set of data. The term is borrowed from agricultural research, where much of the early development of the ANOVA technique took place. Crop yields were compared after different fertilizers (that is, treatments) had been applied to various plots of land.

In the study comparing truck manufacturers there are three treatments. Therefore there are two degrees of freedom in the numerator, found by $k - 1 = 3 - 1 = 2$. How is the number of degrees of freedom for the denominator determined? Note that in the three samples there is a total of 14 observations. Thus the total number of observations, designated by N, is 14. The number of degrees of freedom in the denominator is 11, found by $N - k = 14 - 3$.

The critical value of F can be found in Appendix G at the back of the study guide. There are tables for both the .01 and the .05 significance levels. Using the .05 significance level, the degrees of freedom for the numerator are at the top of the table and for the denominator in the left margin. To locate the critical value, move horizontally at the top of the table to 2 degrees of freedom in the numerator, then down that column to the number opposite 11 degrees of freedom in the left margin (denominator). That number is 3.98, which is the critical value of F.

The decision rule is to reject the null hypothesis if the computed value of F exceeds 3.98, otherwise it is not rejected. To reject the null hypothesis and accept the alternate hypothesis allows us to conclude that there is a significant difference between at least one pair of means. If the null hypothesis is not rejected this implies the differences between the sample means could have occurred by chance.

Portrayed graphically, the decision rule is:

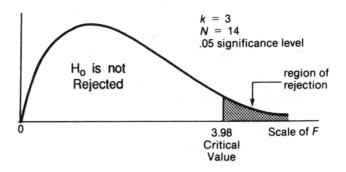

Step 5. Compute F and make a decision.

The value of F is computed from the sample information and a decision is made regarding the null hypothesis. If the computed value of F is 1.98, for example, the null hypothesis is not rejected. If it is greater than 3.98, say 4.26, then the null hypothesis is rejected and the alternate accepted.

144

The ANOVA Table

A convenient way of organizing the calculations for F is to put them in a table referred to as an ANOVA table. The meaning of SSTotal, SSE, SST, k, and N are explained in Problem 1.

ANOVA Table

Source of Variation	Sum of Squares	Degrees of Freedom	Mean Square
Treatments	SST	$k - 1$	SST/$(k - 1)$
Within	SSE	$N - k$	SSE/$(N - k)$
Total	SS Total		

The formula for computing F is:

$$F = \frac{\dfrac{SST}{k-1}}{\dfrac{SSE}{N-k}} \qquad 12\text{--}4$$

Comparing Two Population Variances

The F distribution can be used to determine if the sample variance from one normal population is the same as the variance obtained from another normal population. For example, if you were comparing the mean starting salaries for this year's marketing graduates to this year's computer science graduates, an assumption required of the two-sample t test is that both populations have the same standard deviation. Therefore, before conducting the test for means, it is essential to show that the two population variance are equal.

The idea behind the test for standard deviations is that if the null hypothesis is true that the two sample variances are equal, then their ratio will be approximately 1.00. If the null hypothesis is false, then the ratio will be much larger than 1.00. The F distribution provides a decision rule to let us know when the departure from 1.00 is too large to have happened by chance.

GLOSSARY

Analysis of variance (ANOVA)—A statistical technique for determining whether more than two populations have the same mean. This is accomplished by comparing the sample variances of the populations.

F distribution—A continuous probability distribution where F is always 0 or positive. The distribution is positively skewed. It is based on two parameters, the number of degrees of freedom in the numerator and the number of degrees of freedom in the denominator.

Treatment—A treatment is a specific source, or cause, of variation in the set of data.

CHAPTER PROBLEMS

Problem 1

Tiedke's Department accepts three types of credit cards—MasterCard, Visa, and their own store card. The sales manager is interested in finding out whether there is a difference in the mean amounts charged by customers on the three cards. A random sample of 18 credit card purchases (rounded to the nearest dollar) revealed these credit card amounts.

MasterCard	Visa	Store
$61	$85	$61
28	56	25
42	44	42
33	72	31
51	98	29
56	56	
	72	

At the .05 significance level, can we conclude there is a difference in the mean amounts charged per purchase on the three cards?

Solution

There are three populations involved—the three credit cards. The null and alternate hypotheses are:

$H_0: \mu_1 = \mu_2 = \mu_3$
$H_1:$ the means are not all equal

There are three "treatments" or columns. Hence, there are $k - 1 = 3 - 1 = 2$ degrees of freedom in the numerator. There are 18 observations, therefore $N = 18$. The number of degrees of freedom in the denominator is 15, found by $N - k = 18 - 3$. The critical value is found in Appendix G. Find the table for the .05 significance level and the column headed by 2 degrees of freedom. Then move down that column to the margin row with 15 degrees of freedom and read the value. It is 3.68. The decision rule is: reject the null hypothesis if the computed value of F exceeds 3.68, otherwise do not reject H_0. Shown graphically, the decision rule is:

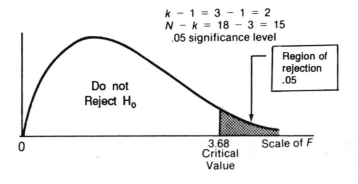

There are two sources of variation in an analysis of variance study. These sources occur between treatments (designated SST) and within treatments (designated SSE). The sum of SST and SSE is the total amount of variation, written SS Total; n_c refers to the number of observations in each column (treatments).

The calculations needed for SST, SSE, and SS Total are:

Amounts Charged

	MasterCard		Visa		Store		Total
	X	X²	X	X²	X	X²	
	$61	3,721	$85	7,225	$61	3,721	
	28	784	56	3,136	25	625	
	42	1,764	44	1,936	42	1,764	
	33	1,089	72	5,184	31	961	
	51	2,601	98	9,604	29	841	
	56	3,136	56	3,136			
			72	5,184			
Column Totals (T_c)	271		483		188		942
Sum of Squares X²		13,095		35,405		7,912	56,412
Sample Size: n_c	6		7		5		$N = 18$

146

The sum of squares total, SS total, is computed using formula 11–3.

$$SS\ Total = \Sigma X^2 - \frac{(\Sigma X)^2}{N} = 56,412 - \frac{(942)^2}{18} = 7,114$$

Recall that Σ refers to the sum of the squares of all observations. However, $(\Sigma X)^2$ is found by summing all the observations and then squaring that sum. The total number of observations is N, or 18.

The sum of squares due to treatment (SST) is computed using formula $11-1$ where T_c^2 is the square of the column (treatment) totals, and n_c is the number of sample in each treatment.

$$SST = \Sigma \frac{T_c^2}{n_c} - \frac{(\Sigma X)^2}{N}$$

$$= \left[\frac{(271)^2}{6} + \frac{(483)^2}{7} + \frac{(188)^2}{5}\right] - \frac{(942)^2}{18}$$

$$= 3,337.9667$$

The sum of squares error (SSE) is computed as follows:

$$SSE = \Sigma X^2 - \Sigma \frac{T_c^2}{n_c}$$

$$= 56,412 - \left[\frac{(271)^2}{6} + \frac{(483)^2}{7} + \frac{(188)^2}{5}\right]$$

$$= 3,776.0333$$

As a check, SST + SSE should equal SS Total:

$$SS\ Total = SST + SSE$$
$$= 3,337.9667 + 3,776.0333$$
$$= 7,114$$

which is the same as that computed above.

The next step is to insert these values into the ANOVA table.

Source Variation	Sum of Squares	Degrees of Freedom	Mean Squares	
Treatment	SST = 3,337.9667	$k - 1 = 3 - 1 = 2$	$\frac{3,337.9667}{2}$	= 1,668.9834
Within	SSE = 3,776.0333	$N - k = 18 - 3 = 15$	$\frac{3,776.0333}{15}$	= 251.7356
Total	SS Total = 7,114			

Computing F using 11–4:

$$F = \frac{\frac{SST}{k-1}}{\frac{SSE}{N-k}} = \frac{1,668.9834}{251.7356} = 6.63$$

147

Since the computed value of *F* (6.63) exceeds the critical value of 3.68, the null hypothesis is rejected at the .05 level and the alternate hypothesis is accepted. It is concluded that mean amounts charged by Tiedke's Department Store customers is not the same for the three credit cards.

There are many computer software packages that will perform the ANOVA calculations and output the results. MINITAB, SAS, SPSSX, and STATPACK are examples. The following output is from the MINITAB system. Notice that computed *F* is the same as determined previously.

```
ANALYSIS OF VARIANCE
SOURCE      DF          SS          MS          F          P
FACTOR      2           3338        1669        6.63       0.009
ERROR       15          3776        252
TOTAL       17          7114

                                    INDIVIDUAL 95 PCT CI'S FOR MEAN
                                    BASED ON POOLED STDEV
LEVEL       N           MEAN        STDEV   ----------+---------+---------+-------
master      6           45.17       13.08       (------*-----)
visa        7           69.00       18.61                   (------*-----)
store       5           37.60       14.52   (-------*------)
                                            ----------+---------+---------+-------
POOLED STDEV =          15.87               40        60        80
```

Exercise 1

Check your answers against those in the ANSWER section.

The accelerating cost of electricity and gas has caused the management at Arvco Electronics to lower the heat in the work areas. The instructor conducting night classes for employees is concerned that this may have an adverse effect on the employees' test scores. Management agreed to investigate. The employees taking the basic statistics course were randomly assigned to three groups. One group was in a classroom having a temperature of 60°, another group was placed in a room having a temperature of 70°, and the third group was in a room having a temperature of 80°. At the completion of the chapters on tests of hypotheses a common examination was given consisting of ten questions. The number correct for each of the 20 employees was:

Temperature		
60°	70°	80°
3	7	4
5	6	6
4	8	5
3	9	7
4	6	6
	8	5
	8	4
		3

At the .05 significance level can management conclude that there is a difference in achievement with respect to the three temperatures?

148

Problem 2

In Problem 1 it was concluded that there was a difference between the mean amounts charged for the three different credit cards, MasterCard, Visa, and the Tiedke's Store card. Between which credit cards is there a significant difference?

Solution

From the MINITAB output above note that the mean amount charged using the VISA card was $69.00 and $37.60 for the Department card. Since these means have the largest difference, let's determine if this pair of means differ significantly.

To determine if the means differ, a confidence interval for the difference between the two population means is developed. This confidence interval employs the t distribution and the mean square error (MSE) term. Recall that one of the assumptions for ANOVA is that the standard deviations (or variances) in the sampled populations must be the same. The MSE term is an estimate of this common variance. It is obtained from the MINITAB output. The formula is:

$$(\bar{X}_1 - \bar{X}_2) \pm t \sqrt{MSE\left(\frac{1}{n_1} + \frac{1}{n_2}\right)}$$ 11–5

where
  $\bar{X}_1$ is the mean of the first treatment.
  $\bar{X}_2$ is the mean of the second treatment.
   t is obtained from the t table. The degree of freedom is equal to $N - k$.
MSE is the mean square error term, which is obtained from the ANOVA table. It is equal to $SSE/(N - k)$ and is an estimate of the common population variance.
  n_1 is the number of observations in the first treatment.
  n_2 is the number of observations in the second treatment.

If the confidence interval includes 0, there is no difference in the treatment means. However, if both end points of the confidence interval are on the same side of 0 it indicates that pair of means differ.

$$(\bar{X}_1 - \bar{X}_2) \pm t \sqrt{MSE\left(\frac{1}{n_1} + \frac{1}{n_2}\right)}$$

$$(69.00 - 37.60) \pm 2.131 \sqrt{252\left(\frac{1}{7} + \frac{1}{5}\right)}$$

$$31.40 \pm 19.81$$

$$\$11.59 \text{ to } \$51.21$$

Where

$$\bar{X}_1 = 69.00 \qquad \bar{X}_2 = 37.60$$
$$n_1 = 7 \qquad n_2 = 5$$

   t is 2.131 from Appendix F with 15 degrees of freedom and the 95 percent level of confidence. MSE is 252, which is in the table constructed to calculate F.

Since both end points have the same sign, positive in this case, we conclude that there is a difference in the mean amount charged on VISA and the store card.

Similarly, approximate results can be obtained directly from the MINITAB output. In the lower right corner of the output a confidence interval was developed for each mean. The * indicates the mean of the treatment and the symbols (and) indicate the endpoints of the confidence interval. In comparing treatment means, if there is any common area between the two, they do *not* differ. If there is not any common area between the treatment means, they differ. For the credit card example, MasterCard and VISA have common area and do not differ. MasterCard and the store card do not differ, but the store and VISA do differ.

Problem 3

Lens Grinders, Inc. is an innovative company in terms of employee scheduling. Recently several employees have asked to take only one long break during the day, others have requested several short breaks. In addition, some workers have requested to work four day weeks, others flex time, and still others at random times. The Human Resources Department has decided to conduct a study to determine if the different schedule types and the number of breaks has an effect on output. A sample of 16 employees was obtained. Each employee was randomly assigned to one of the combinations of work schedules and number of breaks. The total output for each worker for a week was then recorded. At the .05 significance level is there a difference in the mean output for the various number of breaks and for the different schedules?

| | Number of Breaks | | | |
Schedule Type	1	2	3	4
Regular	94	105	96	98
Flex time	97	106	91	90
Four day	96	100	88	88
Random	92	104	86	84

Solution

This is an example of a two-factor ANOVA, often referred to as two-way ANOVA. We are considering variation from three sources: the number of breaks, the type of schedule, and random causes. Two sets of hypotheses are established, one regarding breaks and the other regarding the type of schedules. The breaks are the treatments and the second source of variation, type of schedule, is called the "blocking variable."

Breaks: H_0: The treatment means are the same.
$$\mu_1 = \mu_2 = \mu_3 = \mu_4$$

H_1: The treatment means are not the same.

Schedules: H_0: The block means are the same
$$\mu_1 = \mu_2 = \mu_3 = \mu_4$$

H_1: The block means are not the same.

The MINITAB system is used to perform the calculations. The output from this problem is as follows:

ANALYSIS OF VARIANCE output

SOURCE	DF	SS	MS	F
Breaks	3	495.19	165.06	17.16
Schedule	3	109.69	36.56	3.80
Error	9	86.56	9.62	
TOTAL	15	691.44		

There are four different schedules, so $n = 4$; there are also four different breaks so $k = 4$. Let's consider the treatments, or breaks, first. There are $k - 1 = 4 - 1 = 3$ degrees of freedom in the numerator and $(n - 1)(k - 1) = (4 - 1)(4 - 1) = 9$ degrees of freedom in the denominator. Using the .05 significance level, the critical value of 3.86 is obtained from Appendix G. That is, the null hypothesis that the mean output is the same for the number of breaks is rejected if the computed F exceeds 3.86. The value of F is computed as follows.

$$F = \frac{SST/(k - 1)}{SSE/(n - 1)(k - 1)} = \frac{495.19/3}{86.56/9} = 17.16$$

Since the computed value of 17.16 exceeds the critical value of 3.86 the null hypothesis is rejected. The mean output is not the same for the various number of breaks.

The hypothesis regarding the blocking variable, the schedules, is considered next. There are $n - 1 = 4 - 1 = 3$ degrees of freedom in the numerator and $(n - 1)(k - 1) = (4 - 1)(4 - 1) = 9$ degrees of freedom in the denominator. Using the .05 significance level and Appendix G, the critical value is 3.86. The computed value of F is 3.80.

$$F = \frac{SSB/(n - 1)}{SSE/(n - 1)(k - 1)} = \frac{109.69/3}{86.56/9} = 3.80$$

The decision is not to reject the null hypothesis. However, 3.80 is very close to the critical value of 3.86. The conclusion is that there is no difference in the output using the various schedules.

Exercise 2

Check your answers against those in the ANSWER section.

The following two-way ANOVA table was developed using the MINITAB system. Use the .05 significance level.

SOURCE	DF	SS	MS
TREATMENTS	3	45	15
BLOCKS	4	200	50
ERROR	12	144	12

a. How many treatments are there?
b. How many blocks are there?
c. What is the total sample size?
d. Is there a significant difference in the treatment means?
e. Is there a significant difference in the block means?

Problem 4

Teledko Associates is a marketing research firm that specializes in comparative shopping. Teledko is hired by General Motors to compare the selling price of the Pontiac Sunbird with the Chevy Cavalier. Posing as a potential customer, a representative of Teledko visited 8 Pontiac dealerships in Metro City and 6 Chevrolet dealerships and obtained quotes on comparable cars. The standard deviation for the selling prices of 8 Pontiac Sunbirds is $350 and on the six Cavaliers, $290. At the 0.02 significance level is there a difference in the variation in the quotes of the Pontiacs and Chevrolets?

Solution

Let the Sunbird be population 1 and the Cavalier population 2. A two-tailed test is appropriate because we are looking for a difference in the variances. We are not trying to show that one population has a larger variance than the other. The null and alternate hypotheses are:

$$H_0 : \sigma_1^2 = \sigma_2^2$$
$$H_1 : \sigma_1^2 \neq \sigma_2^2$$

The F distribution is the appropriate test statistic for comparing two sample variances. For a two-tailed test, the larger sample variance is placed in the numerator. The critical value of F is found by dividing the significance level in half and then referring to Appendix G and the appropriate degrees of freedom. There are $n - 1 = 8 - 1 = 7$ degrees of freedom in the numerator and $n - 1 = 6 - 1 = 5$ degrees of freedom in the denominator. From Appendix G, using the .01 significance level, the critical value of F is 10.5. If the ratio of the two variances exceeds 10.5, the null hypothesis is rejected and the alternate hypothesis is accepted. The computed value of the test statistic is determined by

$$F = \frac{s_1^2}{s_2^2} = \frac{(350)^2}{(290)^2} = 1.46$$

The null hypothesis is not rejected. There is no difference in the variation in the price quotes of Pontiac and Chevrolet, because the computed value of F (1.46) is less than the critical F value (10.5).

Exercise 3

Check your answers against those in the ANSWER section.

Thomas Economic Forecasting Inc., and Harmon Econometrics have the same mean error in forecasting the stock market over the last ten years. However, the standard deviation for Thomas is 30 points and 60 points for Harmon. At the .05 significance level can we conclude that there is more variation in the forecast given by Harmon Econometrics?

CHAPTER ASSIGNMENT 11

Analysis of Variance

Name _____ Section _____ Score _____

Part I Select the correct answer and write the appropriate letter in the space provided.

___ 1. The analysis of variance technique is a method for
    a. comparing three or more means.
    b. comparing F distributions.
    c. measuring sampling error.
    d. none of the above

___ 2. A treatment is
    a. a normal population.
    b. the explained variation.
    c. a source of variation.
    d. the amount of random error.

___ 3. In a one-way ANOVA k refers to the
    a. number of observations in each column.
    b. the number of treatments.
    c. the total number of observations.
    d. none of the above

___ 4. The F distribution is
    a. a continuous distribution.
    b. based on two sets of degrees of freedom.
    c. never negative.
    d. all of the above

___ 5. In an ANOVA test there are 5 observations in each of three treatments. The degrees of freedom in the numerator and denominator respectively are:
    a. 2, 4
    b. 3, 15
    c. 3, 12
    d. 2, 12

___ 6. Which of the following assumptions is **not** a requirement for ANOVA?
    a. dependent samples
    b. normal populations
    c. equal population variances.
    d. independent samples

___ 7. The mean square error term (MSE) is the
    a. estimate of the common population variance.
    b. estimate of the population means
    c. estimate of the sample standard deviation.
    d. treatment variation.

___ 8. In a one-way ANOVA, the null hypothesis indicates that the treatment means
    a. are all the same or from equal populations.

b. are not from the same populations.
c. are all different.
d. at least one pair of means are the same.

___ 9. The appropriate test statistic for comparing two sample variances to find out if they came from the same or equal populations is the
a. t distribution.
b. z distribution.
c. F distribution.
d. binomial distribution.

___ 10. What is the probability for an F of more than 6.55 with 3 degrees of freedom in the numerator and 10 in the denominator?
a. .025
b. .001
c. .01
d. .05

Part II Fill in the blank with the correct answer.

11. List the four characteristics of the F distribution.
a. _____
b. _____
c. _____
d. _____

12. A second source of variation is called a _____ variable.

13. Both endpoints for a confidence interval for the difference in a pair of treatment means were negative. This indicates that the treatment means _____.

14. List the assumptions necessary for ANOVA.
a. _____
b. _____
c. _____
d. _____

15. The _____ is an estimate of the common population variance in a one-way ANOVA.

Part III Record your answer in the space provided. Show essential calculations

16. The NPC, Inc. is a large mail order company that ships men's shirts all over the United States and Canada. They ship a large number of packages from their warehouse in Delta, Ohio. Their goal is to have 95 percent of the shipments delivered in 4 days. For many years they have used Brown Truck Inc., but recently there have been complaints about slow and inconsistent delivery. A sample of 10 recent shipments handled by Brown Truck showed a standard deviation in delivery time of 1.25 days. A sample of 16 shipments by Rapid Package Service showed a standard deviation in their delivery time of .45 days. At the .05 significance level is there more variation in the Brown Truck delivery time?

State the null and the alternate hypotheses.
H_0:_____
H_1:_____

State the decision rule.

Compute the value of the test statistic.

Answer

What is your decision regarding the null hypothesis? Interpret the result.

_____
_____
_____
_____

17. The County Executive for Monroe County is concerned about the response time for the three fire companies in the county. Samples of the response times (in minutes) for each company follow. At the .05 significance level is there a difference in the mean response time?

Youngsville	Northeast	Corry
2.2	2.3	0.9
1.2	1.5	0.8
1.9	1.2	1.1
3.1	1.4	1.2
1.8	2.2	0.7
1.5		

State the null and the alternate hypotheses.

H_0:_____

H_1:_____

State the decision rule.

Compute the value of the test statistic.

Answer

What is your decision regarding the null hypothesis? Interpret the result.

_____
_____
_____
_____

12

LINEAR REGRESSION AND CORRELATION

CHAPTER GOALS

After completing this chapter, you will be able to:

1. Draw a scatter diagram.
2. Define the terms dependent variable and independent variable.
3. Compute and interpret Pearson's coefficient of correlation.
4. Conduct a significance test for Pearson's coefficient of correlation.
5. Calculate and explain the meaning of the coefficient of determination.
6. Use the least squares method to determine the regression equation.
7. Determine the standard error of estimate.
8. Determine a confidence interval and a prediction interval for estimated values of the dependent variable.
9. Develop an ANOVA Table to display the regression output.

Introduction

We studied hypothesis testing concerning means and proportions where only a single feature of the sampled item was considered. For example, based on sample evidence we concluded that the beginning annual mean salary for accounting graduates is $26,000. With this chapter we begin our study of the relationship between two variables. We may want to determine if there is a relationship between the number of years of company service and the income of executives. Or we may want to explore the relationship between crime in the inner city and the unemployment rate.

Two techniques are used to study the relationship between two variables: (1) **correlation analysis,** a technique used to measure the strength of the relationship between two variables; and (2) **regression analysis**, which is concerned with estimating one variable based on another.

The variable used as the estimator is called the **independent variable.** The variable being estimated is called the **dependent variable.** Suppose we are attempting to estimate annual income based on years of service with the company. Years of service is the independent variable, income the dependent variable. In essence, we are suggesting that income is related to, or varies with, years of service.

The Scatter Diagram

A useful tool in correlation analysis and regression analysis is a **scatter diagram.** A scatter diagram portrays the relationship between the two variables. The values of the independent variable are portrayed on the horizontal axis (X-axis) and the dependent variable along the vertical axis (Y-axis). Note in Figure A that as the length of service increases so does income. In Figure B, as employment rises, the crime rate in the inner city declines.

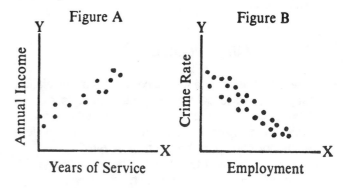

Correlation Coefficient

A measure of the linear (straight-line) strength of the association between two variables is given by the

coefficient of correlation. It is also called **Pearson's product-moment correlation coefficient** or **Pearson's** *r* after its founder Karl Pearson. The correlation coefficient is usually designated by the lower case *r* and may range from −1.0 to 1.0 inclusive. A value of −1.0 indicates perfect negative correlation and 1.0 perfect positive correlation. A correlation coefficient of 0.0 indicates there is no relationship between the two variables under consideration. This information is summarized in the charts below.

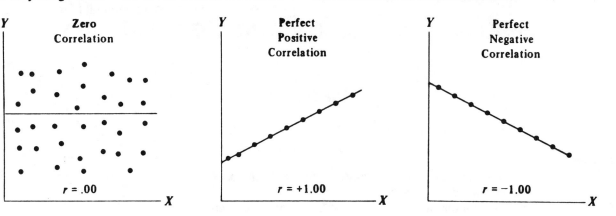

The coefficient of correlation requires that both variables be at least of interval scale.

The degree of strength of the relationship is not related to the sign (direction) of the coefficient of correlation. For example, an *r* value of −.60 represents the same degree of correlation as .60. An *r* of −.70 represents a stronger degree of correlation than .40. An *r* of −.90 represents a strong negative correlation and .15 a weak positive correlation.

The coefficient of correlation is computed by the following formula:

$$r = \frac{n(\Sigma XY) - (\Sigma X)(\Sigma Y)}{\sqrt{[n(\Sigma X^2) - (\Sigma X)^2][n(\Sigma Y^2) - (\Sigma Y)^2]}} \qquad 12\text{-}1$$

where ΣXY is the sum of the product of the variables, ΣX^2 and ΣY^2 the sum of the squares of the variables, ΣX and ΣY the sums of the variables, and *n* the sample size.

A Test of Significance

A test of significance for the coefficient of correlation may be used to determine if the computed *r* could have occurred in a population in which the two variables are not related. To put in the form of a question, is the correlation in the population zero?

For a two-tailed test the null hypothesis and the alternate hypothesis are written as follows:

$$H_0: \rho = 0$$
$$H_1: \rho \neq 0$$

The Greek lower case rho, ρ, represents the correlation in the population. The null hypothesis is that there is no association in the population, and the alternate that there is a correlation.

The alternate hypothesis can also be set up as a one-tailed test. It could read "the correlation coefficient is greater than zero."

The test statistic follows the *t* distribution with *n* −2 degrees of freedom.

$$t = \frac{r\sqrt{n-2}}{\sqrt{1-r^2}} \qquad 12\text{-}2$$

The Regression Equation

The linear relationship between two variables is given by the equation:

$$Y' = a + bX \qquad 12\text{-}3$$

where
Y' is the predicted value of *Y* for a selected value of *X*.
a is the *Y* intercept. It is the value of *Y* when *X* = 0.
b is the slope of the line. It measures the change in *Y'* for each unit change in *X*. It will always have the same sign as the coefficient of correlation discussed in Chapter 13.
X is the value of the independent variable.

The value of *a* is the **Y Intercept** and *b* is the **regression coefficient**. How do we get these values? They are developed mathematically using the **least squares principle**. This principle minimizes the sum of the squared vertical deviations between *Y* (the actual value) and *Y'* (the predicted value).

Computing and Interpreting the a and b Values

Suppose the least squares principle was used to develop an equation expressing the relationship between annual salary and years of work experience. The equation is:

$$Y' = a + bX = 20,000 + 500X \text{ (in dollars)}$$

In the example annual income is the dependent variable Y, and is being predicted on the basis of the employee's years of work experience, X, the independent variable. The value of 500 which is b, means that for each additional year of work experience the employee's salary increases by $500. Thus, we would expect an employee with 40 years of work experience to earn $5,000 more than one with 30 years of work experience.

What does the 20,000 dollars represent? It is the value for Y' when $X = 0$. Recall that this is the point where the line intersects the Y-axis. The formulas for computing a and b are:

$$b = \frac{n(\Sigma XY) - (\Sigma X)(\Sigma Y)}{n(\Sigma X^2) - (\Sigma X)^2} \qquad 12\text{–}4$$

$$a = \frac{\Sigma Y}{n} - b\left(\frac{\Sigma X}{n}\right) \qquad 12\text{–}5$$

where ΣXY is the sum of the products of the dependent variable and the independent variable; ΣX and ΣY the sum of the independent and dependent variables, ΣX^2 the sum of the squares of the independent variable, and n the size of the sample.

The Standard Error of Estimate

Rarely does the predicted value of Y' agree exactly with the actual Y value. That is, we expect some prediction error. One measure of this error is called the **standard error of estimate.** It is written $S_{y \cdot x}$. A small standard error of estimate indicates that the independent variable is a good predictor of the dependent variable.

The standard error, as it is often called, is similar to the standard deviation described in Chapter 4. Recall that the standard deviation was computed by squaring the difference between the actual value and the mean. This squaring was performed for all n observations. For the standard error of estimate, the difference between the predicted value Y' and the actual value of Y is obtained and that difference squared and summed over all n observations. The formula is:

$$s_{y \cdot x} = \sqrt{\frac{\Sigma(Y - Y')^2}{n - 2}} \qquad 12\text{–}6$$

A more convenient computational form is:

$$s_{y \cdot x} = \sqrt{\frac{\Sigma Y^2 - a\Sigma Y - b\Sigma XY}{n - 2}} \qquad 12\text{–}7$$

where a and b are the regression coefficients, ΣY^2 the sum of the squares of the dependent variable, ΣY the sum of the values of the dependent variables, ΣXY the sum of the products of the dependent and independent variable, and n the sample size.

Establishing a Confidence Interval for Y

The standard error is also used to set confidence intervals for the predicted value of Y'. When the sample size is large and the scatter about the regression line is approximately normally distributed, then the following relationships can be expected:

$Y' \pm 1s_{y \cdot x}$ encompasses about 68% of the points.
$Y' \pm 2s_{y \cdot x}$ encompasses about 95.5% of the points.
$Y' \pm 3s_{y \cdot x}$ encompasses about 99.7% of the points.

Two types of confidence intervals may be set—one for the mean value of Y' for a given value of X, and the other called a **prediction interval** for an *individual* value of Y', for a given value of X. To explain the difference between the mean predicted value and the individual prediction, suppose we are predicting the salary of management personnel who are 40 years old. In this case we are predicting the mean salary of all management personnel age 40. However, if we want to predict the salary of a particular manager who is 40, then we are making a prediction about a particular individual.

The formula for the confidence interval for the mean value of Y for a given X is:

$$Y' \pm t(s_{y \cdot x}) \sqrt{\frac{1}{n} + \frac{(X - \bar{X})^2}{\Sigma X^2 - \frac{(\Sigma X)^2}{n}}} \qquad 12\text{–}8$$

where Y' is the predicted value of Y for a given value of X; X is any selected value of the independent variable; $\bar{X}$ is the mean of the independent variable; n is the sample size; t is the value of the Student t distribution from Appendix F, with $n - 2$ degrees of freedom and the given level of significance for a two-tailed test.

The formula is modified slightly for a prediction interval. A 1 is placed under the radical and the formula becomes:

$$Y' \pm t(s_{y \cdot x}) \sqrt{1 + \frac{1}{n} + \frac{(X - \bar{X})^2}{\Sigma X^2 - \frac{(\Sigma X)^2}{n}}} \qquad 12\text{-}9$$

Regression Assumptions

Regression is based on four assumptions.

1. For a given value of X, there is a group of Y values and these values are normally distributed about Y'.
2. The standard deviation of each of these normal distributions is the same. The common standard deviation is estimated by $s_{y \cdot x}$.
3. The deviations from the regression line are independent. This means that if there is a large deviation from the regression line for a particular X, it does not necessarily mean that a large deviation must appear for other X values.
4. The relationship between the X and Y values is linear, i.e., a straight line.

The Relationship Among Various Measures of Association

The standard error of estimate measures how closely the actual values of Y are to the predicted values of Y'. When the values are close together the standard error is "small"; when they are spread out the standard error will be large. In the calculation of the standard error, the key term is $\Sigma(Y - Y')^2$. When this term is small, the standard error is also small.

Recall that the coefficient of correlation measured the strength of the association between two variables. When the points on a scatter diagram were close to a straight line the correlation coefficient tends to be "large." Thus the standard error and the coefficient of correlation reflect the same information, but use a different scale to report it. The standard error is in the same units as the dependent variable. The correlation coefficient has a range of -1.00 to 1.00.

The **coefficient of determination** also reports the strength of the association. It is the square of the correlation coefficient and has a range of .00 to 1.00.

A convenient means of showing the relationships among these measures is an ANOVA Table. This is similar to the table developed in the previous chapter. The total variation $\Sigma(Y - \bar{Y})^2$ is divided into two components: (1) that explained by the regression, and (2) the unexplained or random variation. These two categories are identified in the source column of the following ANOVA table. The column headed DF refers to the degrees of freedom associated with each category. The total degrees of freedom is $n - 1$. The degrees of freedom in the regression is 1, because there is one independent variable. The degrees of freedom associated with the error term is $n - 2$. The term SS, located in the middle of the table, refers to the variation. These terms are computed as follows:

Total variation $=$ SS total $= \Sigma(Y - \bar{Y})^2$

Error variation $=$ SSE $\quad = \Sigma(Y - Y')^2$

Regression $\quad =$ SSR $\quad = \Sigma(Y' - \bar{Y})^2$

Analysis of Variance Table

SOURCE	DF	SS	MS
Regression	1	SSR	SSR/1
Error	$n - 2$	SSE	SSE/$(n - 2)$
Total	$n - 1$	SS total*	

*SS total $=$ SSR $+$ SSE

The coefficient of determination, r^2, can be computed directly from the ANOVA table.

$$r^2 = \frac{\text{SSR}}{\text{SS total}} = 1 - \frac{\text{SSE}}{\text{SS total}}$$

Note that as SSE decreases r^2 increases. The coefficient of correlation is the square root of this value. Hence, both of these values are related to SSE. The standard error of estimate is obtained using the following equation.

$$s_{y \cdot x} = \sqrt{\frac{\text{SSE}}{n - 2}} \qquad 12\text{-}10$$

Note again the role played by the SSE term. A small value of SSE will result in a small standard error of estimate.

GLOSSARY

Coefficient of determination—It is the proportion of the variation in the dependent variable explained by the variation in the independent variable. It may range between 0 and 1, or 0 and 100 percent in terms of a percent. It is designated r^2.

Coefficient of correlation—It is a measure of the degree of linear association between two variables and written r. It is found by taking the square root of the coefficient of determination. It may range between -1.0 and $+1.0$.

Correlation analysis—A technique used to measure the strength or the degree of relationship between *two* variables.

Dependent variable—The variable that is to be predicted or estimated. It is denoted as Y.

Independent variable—The variable that provides the basis for estimation. It is the predictor variable and is denoted as X.

Scatter diagram—A graphic tool which visually portrays the relationship between the independent and dependent variables. The dependent variable is scaled on the Y-axis, the independent variable on the X-axis.

Regression analysis—A technique for predicting or estimating the value of one variable, called the dependent variable, based on the value of another variable, the independent variable.

Regression equation—A mathematical equation which defines the linear relationship between the dependent and independent variables. It has the form $Y' = a + bX$ where a is the Y intercept and b the slope of the line.

Least squares—It is a method for determining the regression equation by minimizing the sum of the squares of the vertical distances from the actual Y values to the predicted Y values.

Standard error of estimate—It is a measure of the accuracy of the prediction. It is the square root of the sum of the squared vertical deviations between the observed and predicted observations divided by the number of observations minus two.

CHAPTER PROBLEMS

Problem 1

It is believed that the annual repair cost for the sporty automobile Glockenspiel is related to its age. A sample of 10 automobiles revealed the following:

Repair Cost (in dollars) Y	Age (in years) X
$72	2
99	3
65	1
138	7
170	6
140	8
114	4
83	1
101	2
110	5

Plot these data in a scatter diagram. Does it appear there is a relationship between repair cost and age? Compute the coefficient of correlation. Determine at the .05 significance level whether the correlation in the population is greater than zero.

Solution

The repair cost is the dependent variable and is plotted along the Y-axis. Age is the independent variable and is plotted along the X-axis. To plot the first point move horizontally on the X-axis to 2 and then go vertically to 72 on the Y-axis and place a dot. This procedure is continued until all paired data are plotted. Note that it appears there is a positive relationship between the two variables. That is, as X, the age of the automobile increases, so does the repair cost. But, the relationship is not perfect as evidenced by the scatter of dots.

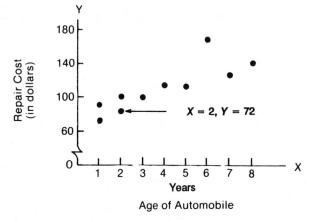

The degree of association between age and repair cost is measured by the coefficient of correlation. It is computed by formula 12.1.

$$r = \frac{n(\Sigma XY) - (\Sigma X)(\Sigma Y)}{\sqrt{[n(\Sigma X^2) - (\Sigma X)^2][n(\Sigma Y^2) - (\Sigma Y)^2]}}$$

The calculations in the following table are needed to compute the various totals and squared totals.

	Y	X	XY	X^2	Y^2
	72	2	144	4	5,184
	99	3	297	9	9,801
	65	1	65	1	4,225
	138	7	966	49	19,044
	170	6	1,020	36	28,900
	140	8	1,120	64	19,600
	114	4	456	16	12,996
	83	1	83	1	6,889
	101	2	202	4	10,201
	110	5	550	25	12,100
Total	1,092	39	4,903	209	128,940

The totals are inserted into the formula and the value of r computed:

$$r = \frac{10(4,903) - (39)(1,092)}{\sqrt{[10(209) - (39)^2][10(128,940) - (1,092)^2]}} = \frac{6,442}{\sqrt{[569][96,936]}} = .867$$

Recall that 0 indicates no correlation and 1.00 perfect correlation. The r of .867 suggests a strong positive correlation between the age of this sports car and annual repair costs. As the age of the car increases so does the annual repair cost.

162

The coefficient of determination is the square of the coefficient of correlation. It is .752, found by $(.867)^2$. This value indicates that 75.2 percent of the variation in repair costs can be explained by the age of the car.

A test of hypothesis is used to determine if the correlation in the population could be zero. In this instance, suppose we want to show that there is a positive association between the variables. Recall that the Greek letter ρ refers to the correlation in the population. The null and alternate hypotheses are written as follows:

$$H_0: \rho \leqslant 0$$
$$H_1: \rho > 0$$

If the null hypothesis is not rejected, it indicates that the correlation in the population could be zero. If the null hypothesis is rejected, the alternate is accepted. This indicates there is correlation in the population between the two variables and it is positive.

The test statistic follows the Student's t distribution with $n - 2$ degrees of freedom. The alternate hypothesis given above specifies a one-tailed test in the positive direction. There are 8 degrees of freedom, found by $n - 2 = 10 - 2$. The critical value for a one-tailed test using the .05 significance level is 1.860 (Appendix F). The decision rule is to reject the null hypothesis if the computed value of t exceeds 1.860. The computed value of t is 4.92, found by using formula 12–2.

$$t = \frac{r\sqrt{n-2}}{\sqrt{1-r^2}} = \frac{.867\sqrt{10-2}}{\sqrt{1-(.867)^2}} = 4.92$$

Since the computed value (4.92) exceeds the critical value of t, namely 1.860, the null hypothesis is rejected and the alternate accepted. It is concluded that there is a positive association between the age of the automobile and the annual repair cost.

Exercise 1

Check your answers against those in the ANSWER section.

A major oil company is studying the relationship between the daily traffic count and the number of gallons of gasoline pumped at company stations. A sample of eight company owned stations is selected and the following information obtained:

Location	Total Gallons of Gas Pumped (000)	Traffic count (hundreds of cars)
West St.	120	4
Willoughby St.	180	6
Mallard Rd.	140	5
Pheasant Rd.	150	5
I-75	210	8
Kinzua Rd.	100	3
Front St.	90	3
Indiana Ave.	80	2

(a) Develop a scatter diagram with the amount of gasoline pumped as the dependent variable. (b) Compute the coefficient of correlation and the coefficient of determination. (c) Interpret the meaning of the coefficient of determination. (d) Test to determine whether the correlation in the population is zero, versus the alternate hypothesis that the correlation is greater than zero. Use the .05 significance level.

Problem 2

In Problem 1 we examined the relationship between the annual repair cost of the Glockenspiel and its age. The correlation between the two variables was .867, which we considered to be a strong relationship. We conducted a test of hypothesis and concluded that the relationship between the two variables in the population was greater than zero. The same sample data is repeated below.

Repair Cost (in dollars) Y	Age (in years) X
$ 72	2
99	3
65	1
138	7
170	6
140	8
114	4
83	1
101	2
110	5

(a) Use the least squares principle to determine the regression equation. (b) Compute the standard error of estimate. (c) Develop a 95 percent confidence interval for the mean repair cost for all 4-year-old Glockenspiels, and (d) develop a 95 percent prediction interval for the repair cost for Ms. Paul's 4-year-old Glockenspiel.

Solution

(a) The first step is to compute the regression equation. The following calculations are needed.

Y	X	XY	X^2	Y^2
72	2	144	4	5,184
99	3	297	9	9,801
65	1	65	1	4,225
138	7	966	49	19,044
170	6	1,020	36	28,900
140	8	1,120	64	19,600
114	4	456	16	12,996
83	1	83	1	6,889
101	2	202	4	10,201
110	5	550	25	12,100
Total 1,092	39	4,903	209	128,940

Substituting these values into formula 12–4 for b and formula 12–5 for a:

$$b = \frac{n(\Sigma XY) - (\Sigma X)(\Sigma Y)}{n(\Sigma X^2) - (\Sigma X)^2} = \frac{10(4,903) - (39)(1,092)}{10(209) - (39)^2} = \frac{6,442}{569} = 11.32$$

$$a = \frac{\Sigma Y}{n} - b\left(\frac{\Sigma X}{n}\right) = \frac{1,092}{10} - 11.32\left(\frac{39}{10}\right) = 65.05$$

Thus, the regression equation is:

$$Y' = a + bX = 65.05 + 11.32X \text{ (in dollars)}$$

164

Interpreting, repair costs can be expected to increase $11.32 a year on the average. Stated differently, the repair cost of a 4-year-old Glockenspiel can be expected to cost $11.32 more a year than a 3-year-old Glockenspiel.

(b) The standard error of estimate is a measure of the dispersion about the regression line. It is similar to the standard deviation in that it uses squared differences. The differences between the value of Y' and Y are squared and summed over all n observations and then divided by $n - 2$. Then find the positive square root of this value. A small value for the standard error of estimate indicates a close association between the dependent and independent variable. The standard error is measured in the same units as the dependent variable. The symbol for the standard error of estimate is $s_{y \cdot x}$.

The standard error is computed using formula 12–7:

$$s_{y \cdot x} = \sqrt{\frac{\Sigma Y^2 - a\Sigma Y - b\Sigma XY}{n - 2}}$$

$$= \sqrt{\frac{128,940 - 65.05(1,092) - 11.32(4,903)}{10 - 2}} = 17.33$$

(c) The regression equation is used to estimate the repair cost of a 4-year-old Glockenspiel. The value of 4 is inserted for X in the equation.

$$Y' = 65.05 + 11.32X$$
$$= 65.05 + 11.32(4)$$
$$= 110.33 \text{ (in dollars)}$$

Thus the expected repair cost for a 4-year-old Glockenspiel is $110.33.

Formula 12–8 is used if we want to develop a 95 percent confidence interval for all four-year-old Glockenspiels.

$$Y' \pm t(s_{y \cdot x}) \sqrt{\frac{1}{n} + \frac{(X - \bar{X})^2}{\Sigma X^2 - \frac{(\Sigma X)^2}{n}}}$$

The necessary information for the formula is:

Y'	is 110.33 as previously computed.
t	is 2.306. There are $n - 2$ degrees of freedom, or $n - 2 = 10 - 2 = 8$. From Appendix F, using a two-tailed test and the .05 significance level, move down the .05 column to 8 df and read the value of t.
n	is 10. It is the sample size.
$s_{y \cdot x}$	is 17.33, as computed in an earlier section of this problem.
X	is 4, the age of the Glockenspiel.
$\bar{X}$	is the mean age of the sampled cars. It is 3.9, found by $\bar{X} = 39/10$.
ΣX	is 39, found from the earlier computation in part a.
ΣX^2	is 209, also used in earlier calculations in part a.

Solving for the 95 percent confidence interval:

$$Y' \pm t(s_{y \cdot x}) \sqrt{1 + \frac{1}{n} + \frac{(X - \bar{X})^2}{\Sigma X^2 - \frac{(\Sigma X)^2}{n}}} = \$110.33 \pm 2.306(\$17.33) \sqrt{\frac{1}{10} + \frac{(4 - 3.9)^2}{209 - \frac{(39)^2}{10}}}$$

$$= \$110.33 \pm \$12.65$$
$$= \$ 97.68 \text{ to } \$122.98$$

The 95 percent confidence interval for the mean amount spent on repairs to a 4-year-old Glockenspiel is between $97.68 and $122.98. About 95 percent of the similarly constructed intervals would include the population value.

Recall that Ms. Paul owns a 4-year-old Glockenspiel. The 95 percent prediction interval for her repair costs is computed as follows using formula 12–9.

$$Y' \pm t(s_{y \cdot x}) \sqrt{1 + \frac{1}{n} + \frac{(X - \bar{X})^2}{\Sigma X^2 - \frac{(\Sigma X)^2}{n}}} = \$110.33 \pm 2.306(\$17.33) \sqrt{1 + \frac{1}{10} + \frac{(4 - 3.9)^2}{209 - \frac{(39)^2}{10}}}$$

$$= \$110.33 \pm \$41.92$$
$$= \$ 68.41 \text{ to } \$152.25$$

Interpreting we would conclude that Ms. Paul will spend between $68.41 and $152.25 on repairs this year to her four-year-old Glockenspiel. About 95 percent of the similarly constructed intervals would include the population value.

Exercise 2

Check your answers against those in the ANSWER section.

In Exercise 1 we studied the relationship between the gasoline pumped in thousands of gallons, and the traffic count at eight company owned stations. The data are repeated below:

Location	Total Gallons of Gas Pumped (000)	Traffic Count (hundreds of cars)
	Y	X
West St.	120	4
Willoughby St.	180	6
Mallard Rd.	140	5
Pheasant Rd.	150	5
I-75	210	8
Kinzua Rd.	100	3
Front St.	90	3
Indiana Ave.	80	2

(a) Compute the regression equation and the standard error of estimate. (b) Develop a 95 percent confidence interval for the mean amount gasoline pumped for all stations where the traffic count is 4. (c) Develop a 95 percent prediction interval for the amount of gasoline pumped at the station at Dowling Rd. and I–60, which has a count of 4 (actually 400 cars).

Problem 3

Use the information from Problem 1 to develop an ANOVA Table. Compute the coefficient of determination, the coefficient of correlation, and the standard error of estimate from this table.

Solution

The MINITAB System was used to develop the following output.

Analysis of Variance

SOURCE	DF	SS	MS
Regression	1	7,293.4	7,293.4
Error	8	2,400.2	300.0
Total	9	9,693.6	

The coefficient of determination is computed as follows.

$$r^2 = \frac{SSR}{SS\ Total} = 1 - \frac{SSE}{SS\ Total} = 1 - \frac{2,400.2}{9,693.6} = 0.752$$

The correlation coefficient is .867, found by taking the square root of .752. These two coefficients (.867 and .752) are the same as computed earlier.

The standard error of estimate is computed by

$$s_{y \cdot x} = \sqrt{\frac{SSE}{n-2}} = \sqrt{\frac{2,400.2}{10-2}} = 17.32$$

Note again the role played by the SSE term. A small value of SSE will result in a small standard error of estimate.

Exercise 3

Check your answers against those in the ANSWER section.

Refer to Exercise 1, regarding the relationship between the amount of gasoline pumped and the traffic count. The following output was obtained from MINITAB.

Analysis of Variance

SOURCE	DF	SS	MS
Regression	1	14,078	14,078
Error	6	310	51.67
Total	7	14,388	

Compute the coefficient of determination, the coefficient of correlation, and the standard error of estimate.

CHAPTER ASSIGNMENT 12

Linear Regression and Correlation

Name _____ Section _____ Score _____

Part I Select the correct answer and write the appropriate letter in the space provided.

___ 1. Which of the following statements is **not** correct regarding the coefficient of correlation.
    a. It can range from -1 to 1.
    b. Its square is the coefficient of determination.
    c. It measures the percent of variation explained.
    d. It is a measure of the association between two variables.

___ 2. The variable plotted on the horizontal or X-axis in a scatter diagram is called the
    a. scatter variable.
    b. independent variable.
    c. dependent variable.
    d. correlation variable.

___ 3. A coefficient of correlation was computed to be $-.60$. This means
    a. the coefficient of determination is 0.7746.
    b. as X increases Y decreases.
    c. X and Y are both 0.
    d. none of the above.

___ 4. Which of the following is a stronger correlation than $-.54$?
    a. 0
    b. $-.45$
    c. .45
    d. .67

___ 5. A regression equation is used to
    a. measure the association between two variables.
    b. estimate the value of the dependent variable based on the independent variable.
    c. estimate the value of the independent variable based on the dependent variable.
    d. estimate the coefficient of determination.

___ 6. A regression equation was computed to be $Y' = 35 + 6X$. The value of 35 indicates that
    a. an increase of one unit in X will result in an increase of 35 in Y.
    b. the coefficient of correlation is 35.
    c. the coefficient of determination is 35.
    d. the regression line crosses the Y-axis at 35.

___ 7. The standard error of estimate
    a. is a measure of the variation around the regression line.
    b. cannot be negative.
    c. is in the same units as the dependent variable.
    d. all of the above.

___ 8. The coefficient of determination
    a. is usually written as r^2.
    b. cannot be negative.
    c. is the square of the coefficient of correlation.
    d. all of the above.

___ 9. The least squares principle means that
   a. $\Sigma(Y - Y')^2 = 0$.
   b. $\Sigma(Y - \overline{Y})^2$ is maximized.
   c. $\Sigma(Y - \overline{Y})^2$ is minimized.
   d. $\Sigma(Y - Y')^2$ is minimized.

___ 10. If all the points are on the regression line, then
   a. the value of b is 0.
   b. the value of a is 0.
   c. The correlation coefficient is 0.
   d. The standard error of estimate is 0.

Part II Fill in the blank with the correct answer.

11. The variable being estimated is called the _____ variable.

12. The slope of the regression line and the _____ always have the same sign.

13. The square root of the coefficient of determination is the _____.

14. Explain the difference between a confidence interval and a prediction interval._____

_____

15. List the major characteristics of the coefficient of correlation.

   a. _____

   b. _____

   c. _____

   d. _____

Part III Record your answers in the space provided. Show all essential work.

16. The correlation between the number of police on the street and the number of crimes committed, for a sample of 15 comparable sized cities, is 0.45. At the .05 significance level is there a positive association in the population between the two variables?

   State the null and the alternate hypothesis.
   H_0:_____
   H_1:_____

   State the decision rule.

   Compute the value of the test statistic.

   Compute the p-value.

170

What is your decision regarding the null hypothesis? Interpret the result.

_____

_____

_____

_____

17. Rob Whitmer, president of Whitmer Ford, believes there is a relationship between the number of new cars sold and the number of sales people on duty. To investigate he selects a sample of eight weeks and determines the number of new cars sold and the number of sales people on duty for that week.

Week	Sales staff	Cars sold
1	5	53
2	5	47
3	7	48
4	4	50
5	10	58
6	12	62
7	3	45
8	11	60

a. Determine the coefficient of correlation.

Answer

b. Determine the coefficient of determination. Comment on the strength of the association between the two variables.

_____

_____

_____

_____

c. Determine the regression equation.

Answer

d. Interpret the regression equation. Where does the equation cross the Y-axis. How many additional cars can the dealer expect to sell for each additional sales person employed?

_____

_____

_____

_____

_____

_____

e. Determine the standard error of estimate.

Answer

f. Develop a 95 percent confidence interval for all the mean car sales for weeks when the sales staff is at 10.

g. In checking the work schedules for next week, Rob finds there are 10 sales people scheduled. Develop a 95 percent prediction interval for the number of cars sold next week.

13

MULTIPLE REGRESSION AND CORRELATION

CHAPTER GOALS

After completing this chapter, you will be able to:

1. Describe the relationship between one dependent variable and two or more independent variables.
2. Interpret the MINITAB multiple regression computer output.
3. Understand and interpret terms such as correlation matrix, coefficient of multiple determination, net regression coefficient, and multiple standard error of estimate.
4. Conduct a global test of hypothesis to determine if any of the regression coefficients could be zero.
5. Conduct a test of hypothesis for each independent variable.
6. Conduct an evaluation of the residuals.

Introduction

In the last chapter we began our study of regression and correlation analysis. However, the methods presented considered only the relationship between one dependent variable and one independent variable. The possible effect of other independent variables was ignored. For example, we described how the repair cost of a car was related to the age of the car. Are there other factors that affect the repair cost? Does the size of the engine or the number of miles driven affect the repair cost? When several independent variables are used to estimate the value of the dependent variable it is called **multiple regression**.

The Multiple Regression Equation

Recall that for one independent variable the regression equation has the form:

$$Y' = a + bX$$

For more than one independent variable, the equation is extended to include the additional variables. For three independent variables is:

$$Y' = a + b_1X_1 + b_2X_2 + b_3X_3$$

The values of b_1, b_2, and b_3 are called the **net regression coefficients**. They indicate the change in the estimated value of the dependent variable for a unit change in one of the independent variables, when the other independent variables are held constant.

For example, suppose the National Sales Manager of General Motors wants to analyze regional sales using the number of autos registered in the region (X_1), the average age of the automobiles registered in the region (X_2), and the personal income in the region (X_3). Some of the sample information obtained is:

region	Sales ($ millions) Y	Number of autos in region (000) X_1	Average age of autos (years) X_2	Personal income in region (billions) X_3
I	$ 9.2	842	5.6	$ 29.5
II	46.8	2,051	5.1	182.6
III	26.2	1,010	5.8	190.7
etc.				

Suppose the multiple regression equation was computed to be:

$$Y' = a + b_1X_1 + b_2X_2 + b_3X_3$$
$$= 41.0 + .0071X_1 + (-3.19)X_2 + .01611X_3$$

In April of this year the automobile registration bureau announced that in a particular region 1,542,000 autos were registered, and their average age was 6.0 years. Another agency announced that personal income in the region was $150 billion. The sales manager could then estimate, as early as April, annual sales for this year by inserting the value of these independent variables in the equation and solving for Y':

$$Y' = 41.0 + .0071(1,542) - 3.19(6.0) + .01611(150)$$
$$= \$35.2 \text{ million}$$

What is the meaning of the regression coefficients? The .0071 associated with number of autos in the region (in thousands) indicates that for each additional 1,000 autos sold, sales will increase .0071 (million), if the other independent variables are held constant. That is, the regression coefficients show change in the dependent variable when the other independent variables are not allowed to change.

Measures of Association in Multiple Regression

It is likely that there is some error in the estimation. This can be measured by the **multiple standard error of estimate.** Like the standard error of estimate described in the previous chapter, it is based on the squared deviations between Y and Y'. The **coefficient of multiple determination,** written R^2, reports the proportion of the variation in Y which is explained by the variation in the set of independent variables. In the example, if the coefficient of multiple determination were .81, it would indicate that the three independent variables, considered jointly, explain 81 percent of the variation in millions of sales dollars.

Tests of Hypothesis for Multiple Regression

Two tests of hypotheses are considered in this chapter. The first tests the overall ability of the set of independent variables to explain differences in the dependent variable. This test is often referred to as the **global test.** The null hypothesis is that the net regression coefficients in the population are all zero. If accepted, it would imply that the set of coefficients is of no value in explaining differences in the dependent variable. The alternate hypothesis is that *at least one of the coefficients is not zero.* This test is written in symbolic form for three independent variables as:

$$H_0: \beta_1 = \beta_2 = \beta_3 = 0$$
$$H_1: \text{Not all the } \beta\text{'s are } 0$$

Rejecting H_0 and accepting H_1 implies that one or more of the independent variables is useful in explaining differences in the dependent variable. However, a word of caution, it does not suggest how many or identify which independent variables are not zero.

The test statistic used is the F distribution which was first described in Chapter 11, the ANOIA chapter.

To employ the F distribution, two sets of degrees of freedom are required. The degrees of freedom for the numerator is equal to k, the number of independent variables. The degrees of freedom in the denominator is equal to $n - (k + 1)$ where n refers, as usual, to the total number of observations.

The second test of hypothesis identifies which of the set of independent variables are significant predictors of the dependent variable. That is, it tests the independent variables individually rather than as a unit. This test is useful because unimportant variables can be eliminated. The test statistic is the t distribution with $n - (k + 1)$ degrees of freedom. For example, suppose we want to test whether the second independent variable was zero or greater, versus the alternate that it was less than zero. The null and alternate hypotheses would be written as follows:

$$H_0: \beta_2 \geqslant 0$$
$$H_1: \beta_2 < 0$$

Rejection of the null hypothesis and acceptance of the alternate hypothesis would imply that variable number two is significant and that its sign is negative.

Qualitative Variables

Variables used in regression analysis must be **quantitative.** That is, they must be numerical in nature. However, frequently we want to use variables that are not numeric. These variables are called **qualitative.** For example, we are interested in estimating the selling price of a used automobile based on its age. Selling price is the dependent variable and age is one independent variable. Another variable is whether or not the car was manufactured in the United States. Note that a particular car can assume only two conditions: either it was built in the U.S. or it was not. Qualitative variables are also called **dummy** or **indicator variables.** To employ a qualitative variable a 0 or 1 coding scheme is used. For example, in the study regarding estimated selling prices of used automobiles, those made in the U.S. are coded 1 and all others as 0.

Stepwise Regression

In an earlier section we mentioned that a global test can be used to determine whether any of a set of independent variables had regression coefficients different from zero. We also stated that the regression coefficients can be tested individually. If the null hypothesis is rejected, the variable is retained in the analysis. If the null hypothesis is not rejected, the variable can be dropped from the analysis.

The stepwise method provides a direct method of solution of multiple regression and correlation problems. The independent variables are brought into the regression equation in the order in which they will increase R-square the most. Only variables that have significant regression coefficients enter the regression equation.

A **correlation matrix** is developed first which gives all possible simple correlations between each independent variable and the dependent variable. Then the independent variable with the largest simple correlation with the dependent variable is entered. The independent variable that will yield the largest increase in R-square is entered into the multiple regression equation next.

The stepwise process continues until all the significant independent variables are entered into the regression equation. The stepwise method tests each independent variable to determine if the regression coefficient is different from zero before entering it into the regression equation. Hence, only independent variables with significant regression coefficients become a part of the final regression equation.

Assumptions for Multiple Regression and Correlation

There are six assumptions that must be met in multiple correlation.

1. The independent variable and the dependent variables must have a linear relationship.
2. The dependent variable must be continuous and on an interval scale.
3. The variation in the difference between the actual value of the dependent variable and the estimated value must be the same for all fitted values of Y. That is, $(Y - Y')$ must be the same for all values of Y'. For example, the $(Y - Y')$ term cannot have a tendency to be larger when Y' is large. The $(Y - Y')$ term is called the **residual.** When the differences are the same for all fitted values they exhibit **homoscedasticity**.
4. The residuals should be approximately normally distributed with a mean of zero. The standard error

of estimate is a measure of the dispersion of this distribution.
5. Successive observations of the dependent variable must be unrelated; that is, not correlated. Violation of this assumption is called **autocorrelation**. It frequently occurs when the data are collected over time.
6. The set of independent variables should not be highly correlated. When independent variables are correlated this condition is called **multicollinearity.**

Seldom in a real world example are all of the conditions fully met. However, the technique of regression still works effectively. If there is concern regarding the violation of one or more of the assumptions, it is suggested that a more advanced statistics book be consulted.

The ANOVA Table

A convenient means of showing the regression output is to use an ANOVA table. This table was first described in Chapter 11 and also mentioned in Chapter 12. The variation in the dependent variable is separated into two components: (1) that explained by the regression and (2) the unexplained variation. The categories are identified in the source column of the following ANOVA table. The column headed "DF" refers to the degrees of freedom associated with each category. The total degrees of freedom is $n - 1$. The degrees of freedom for regression is k, the number of independent variables. The degrees of freedom associated with the error term is $n - (k + 1)$. The MS column refers to the mean square and is obtained by dividing the SS by DF.

$$\text{Total variation} = \text{SS total} = \Sigma(Y - \bar{Y})^2$$
$$\text{Error variation} = \text{SSE} = \Sigma(Y - Y')^2$$
$$\text{Regression} = \text{SSR} = \Sigma(Y' - \bar{Y})^2$$

Analysis of Variance

SOURCE	DF	SS	MS
Regression	k	SSR	$MSR = SSR/k$
Error	$n - (k + 1)$	SSE	$MSE = SSE/(n - (k + 1))$
Total	$n - 1$	SS total	

GLOSSARY

Multiple regression and correlation analysis—A set of techniques used to analyze the relationship between two or more independent variables and a dependent variable.

Multiple regression equation—It defines the relationship between the dependent variable and the independent variables in the form of an equation. For two independent variables it is: $Y' = a + b_1X_1 + b_2X_2$.

Standard error of estimate—It measures the error in the predicted dependent variable.

Multiple coefficient of determination—The proportion of the variation in the dependent variable that is explained by the independent variables.

Quantitative variable—A numeric variable that is at least interval scale.

Dummy variable—A variable that assumes only certain categorical values (such as 0 and 1).

Stepwise regression—Independent variables enter the regression equation in the order in which they will increase R-square the most. Only independent variables that have significant regression coefficients are entered.

Correlation matrix—A matrix showing all possible simple coefficients of correlation among all the independent variables and the dependent variable.

Residual—The difference between the actual and the estimated value of the dependent variable.

Homoscedasticity—The residuals are the same for all estimated values of the dependent variable.

Autocorrelation—Successive observations of the dependent variable are correlated.

Multicollinearity—The correlation among the independent variables.

CHAPTER PROBLEMS

Problem 1

The Skaff Appliance Company currently has over 1,000 retail outlets throughout the United States and Canada. They sell name brand electronic products, such as TVs, stereos, and microwave ovens. Skaff Appliance is considering opening several additional stores in other large metropolitan areas. Paul Skaff, president, would like to study the relationship between the sales at existing locations and several factors regarding the existing store or its region. The factors are the population and the unemployment in the region, and the advertising expense of the store. Another variable considered is "mall." Mall refers to whether the existing store is located in an enclosed shopping mall or not. A "1" indicates a mall location; a "0" indicates the store is not located in a mall. A random sample of 30 stores is selected.

Sales ($000)	Population (000,000)	Percent Unemployed	Advertising Expense ($000)	Mall Location
5.17	7.50	5.1	59.0	0
5.78	8.71	6.3	62.5	0
4.84	10.00	4.7	61.0	0
6.00	7.45	5.4	61.0	1
6.00	8.67	5.4	61.0	1
6.12	11.00	7.2	12.5	0
6.40	13.18	5.8	35.8	0
7.10	13.81	5.8	59.9	0
8.50	14.43	6.2	57.2	1
7.50	10.00	5.5	35.8	0
9.30	13.21	6.8	27.9	0
8.80	17.10	6.2	24.1	1
9.96	15.12	6.3	27.7	1
9.83	18.70	0.5	24.0	0
10.12	20.20	5.5	57.2	1
10.70	15.00	5.8	44.3	0
10.45	17.60	7.1	49.2	0
11.32	19.80	7.5	23.0	0
11.87	14.40	8.2	62.7	1
11.91	20.35	7.8	55.8	0
12.60	18.90	6.2	50.0	0
12.60	21.60	7.1	47.6	1
14.24	25.25	0.4	43.5	0
14.41	27.50	4.2	55.9	0
13.73	21.00	0.7	51.2	1
13.73	19.70	6.4	76.6	1
13.80	24.15	0.5	63.0	1
14.92	17.65	8.5	68.1	0
15.28	22.30	7.1	74.4	1
14.41	24.00	0.8	70.1	0

Determine the regression equation using the MINITAB system. Conduct a test of hypothesis to determine if any of the regression coefficients are not equal to zero.

Solution

The first step is to determine the correlation matrix. It shows all possible simple coefficients of correlation. The MINITAB output is as follows:

```
          Sales    Popul    %-unemp    Adv
Popul     0.894
%-unemp  -0.198   -0.368
Adv       0.279    0.125    -0.030
Mall      0.155    0.085     0.017    0.259
```

Sales is the dependent variable. Of particular interest is which independent variable has the strongest correlation with sales. In this case it is population (.894). The negative sign between sales and %-unemp indicates that as the unemployment rate increases, sales decrease.

A second use of the correlation matrix is to check for multicollinearity. Multicollinearity can distort the standard error of estimate and lead to incorrect conclusions regarding which independent variables are significant. The strongest correlation among the independent variables is between %-unemp and popul (-0.368). A rule of thumb is that a correlation between -0.70 and 0.70 will not cause problems and can be ignored. At this point it does not appear there is a problem with multicollinearity.

We want to test the overall ability of the set of independent variables to explain the behavior of the dependent variable. Do the independent variables population, percent unemployed, advertising expense, and mall explain a significant amount of the variation in sales? This question can be answered by conducting a global test of the regression coefficients. The null and alternate hypotheses are:

$$H_0: \beta_1 = \beta_2 = \beta_3 = \beta_4 = 0$$
$$H_1: \text{At least one of the } \beta\text{'s is not zero.}$$

The null hypothesis states that the regression coefficients are all zero. If they are all zero, this indicates they are of no value in explaining differences in the sales of the various stores. If the null hypothesis is rejected and the alternate accepted the conclusion is that at least one of the regression coefficients is not zero. Hence, we would conclude that at least one of the variables is significant in terms of explaining difference in sales.

The F distribution introduced in Chapter 11 is used as the test statistic. The F distribution is based on the degrees of freedom in the numerator and in the denominator. The degrees of freedom associated with the regression, which is the numerator, is equal to the number of independent variables. In this case there are four independent variables, so there are 4 degrees of freedom in the numerator. The degrees of freedom in the error row is $n - (k + 1) = 30 - (4 + 1) = 25$. There are 25 degrees of freedom in the denominator. The critical value of F is obtained from Appendix G. Find the column with 4 degrees of freedom and the row with 25 degrees if freedom in the table for the .05 significance level. The value is 2.76. The null hypothesis is rejected if the computed F is greater than 2.76.

The output from MINITAB is as follows.

```
Analysis of Variance
SOURCE          DF        SS        MS         F         p
Regression       4   270.461    67.615     34.71     0.000
Error           25    48.705     1.948
Total           29   319.166
```

The computed value of F is 34.71 as shown above. It is also computed as follows.

$$F = \frac{\dfrac{SSR}{k}}{\dfrac{SSE}{n-(k+1)}} = \frac{\dfrac{270.461}{4}}{\dfrac{48.705}{30-(4+1)}} = \frac{67.615}{1.948} = 34.71$$

Since the computed value of 34.71 exceeds the critical value of 2.76, the null hypothesis is rejected and the alternate accepted. The conclusion is that at least one of the regression coefficients does not equal zero.

Exercise 1

Check your answers against those in the ANSWER section.

Todd Heffren, President of Heffren Manufacturing Co., is studying the power usage at his Vanengo Plant. He believes that the amount of electrical power used is a function of the outside temperature during the day and the number of units produced that day. A random sample of ten days is selected. The power usage in thousands of kilowatt hours of electricity and the production on that date is obtained. The National Weather Service is contacted for the high temperature on the selected dates.

Power Used	Temperature (F)	Units Produced
12	83	120
11	79	110
13	85	128
9	75	101
14	87	105
10	81	108
12	84	110
11	77	107
14	85	112
11	84	119

The MINITAB system was used to compute a correlation matrix and ANOVA table for the Heffren Manufacturing Co. data. Do you see any problems with multicollinearity? Test the hypothesis that all the regression equations are zero. Use the .05 significance level.

	Usage	Temp
Temp	0.838	
Output	0.361	0.506

Analysis of Variance

SOURCE	DF	SS	MS
Regression	2	17.069	8.534
Error	7	7.031	1.004
Total	9	24.100	

Problem 2

In Problem 1 we found that at least one of the four independent variables had a regression coefficient different from zero. Use the MINITAB system to aid in determining which of the regression coefficients is not equal to zero. Would you consider deleting any of the independent variables?

Solution

The following output is from MINITAB.

The regression equation is
Sales = − 1.67 + 0.552 Popul + 0.203 %-unemp + 0.0314 Adv + 0.220 Mall

Predictor	Coef	Stdev	t-ratio	p
Constant	− 1.669	1.408	− 1-18	0.247
Popul	0.55191	0.05063	10.90	0.000
%-unemp	0.2032	0.1171	1.74	0.095
Adv	0.03135	0.01606	1.95	0.062
Mall	0.2198	0.5400	0.41	0.687

s = 1.396   R-sq = 84.7%   R-sq(adj) = 82.3%

The four independent variables explain 84.7% of the variation in sales. For those coefficients where the null hypothesis that the regression coefficients are equal to zero cannot be rejected, we will consider eliminating them from the regression equation. We are actually conducting four tests of hypotheses.

For Population	For % Unemployed	For Advertising	For Mall
H_0: $\beta_1 = 0$	H_0: $\beta_2 = 0$	H_0: $\beta_3 = 0$	H_0: $\beta_4 = 0$
H_1: $\beta_1 \neq 0$	H_1: $\beta_2 \neq 0$	H_1: $\beta_3 \neq 0$	H_1: $\beta_4 \neq 0$

We will use the .05 significance level and a two-tailed test. The test statistic is the t distribution with $n - (k + 1) = 30 - (4 + 1) = 25$ degrees of freedom. The decision rule is to reject the null hypothesis if the computed value of t is less than − 2.060 or greater than 2.060.

From the MINITAB output, the column labeled "Coef" reports the regression coefficients. The "Stdev" column reports the standard deviation of the slope coefficients. The "t-ratio" column reports the computed value of the test statistic. The t-ratio for population exceeds the critical value, but the computed values for percent unemployed, advertising expense, and mall are not in the rejection region. This indicates that the independent variable population should be retained and the other three dropped.

However, there is a problem that occurs in many real situations. Note that both percent unemployed and advertising expense are close to being significant. In fact, advertising expense would be significant if we increased the level of significances to .10. (The critical value would be − 1.708 and 1.708, and − 1.95 is outside the critical region.) Another indicator of trouble is a reversal of a sign of the regression coefficient. Earlier in Problem 1, in the correlation matrix, the correlation between percent unemployed and sales was negative. Note in the above regression equation the sign of the coefficient is positive. (The regression coefficient is 0.203). A reversal of sign such as this is often an indication of multicollinearity. The earlier conclusion that there was not a problem in this area should be reviewed. Perhaps one or both of the independent variables—either advertising expense or percent unemployment—should be included in the regression equation.

An effective method for determining the optimum set of independent variables is to employ the stepwise procedure. In the stepwise procedure variables enter the regression equation in the order in which they will increase the R-square term the most. In addition, tests of significance are conducted at each step to insure that only independent variables that have significant regression coefficients are entered and retained in the regression equation.

The following output is from MINITAB's stepwise procedure.

STEPWISE REGRESSION OF Sales ON 4 PREDICTORS, WITH $N = 30$

STEP	1	2
CONSTANT	1.38697	−0.07874
Popul	0.533	0.521
T-RATIO	10.56	10.83
Adv		0.033
T-RATIO		2.10
s	1.51	1.43
R-sq	79.92	82.75

This procedure indicates that both population and advertising expense should be included in the regression equation.

How does the stepwise procedure work? As noted before, it starts with the correlation matrix. It examines the simple correlations between each of the independent variables and the dependent variable. The variable population has the strongest correlation with sales (.894) so it enters the equation first. In the first step, 79.92% of the variation in sales is explained by the independent variable population. This variable is tested to insure that its regression coefficient is significant.

The next step is to look at the remaining variables. The independent variable, from those not currently in the regression equation, that will result in the largest increase to R-square is selected. The regression equation is recomputed including this new variable and the newly entered variable is tested to determine if its regression coefficient is significant. This process continues until all possible independent variables with significant regression coefficients are entered into the regression equation. If all the proposed set of independent variables have significant regression coefficients, they are all entered into the regression equation.

In our example the next variable to enter the equation is advertising expense. When advertising expense is added to the regression equation the R-square term is increased from 79.92% to 82.75%. In the column headed "2" in the stepwise output the complete regression equation is given as well as the "T-RATIO." The T-RATIO is the value computed for the test of individual regression coefficients. Can we show these regression coefficients to be significant? To answer this question we employ the test of individual regression coefficients.

For Population	For Advertising
$H_0: \beta_1 = 0$	$H_0: \beta_3 = 0$
$H_1: \beta_1 \neq 0$	$H_1: \beta_3 \neq 0$

There are 2 independent variables in the equation, so the degrees of freedom is 27, found by 30 − (2 + 1). The critical values of t are −2.052 and 2.052. The computed t-ratio is 10.83 for population and 2.10 for advertising expense. Both of these values cause the rejection of the hypothesis that the regression coefficient is zero. We conclude that both of these independent variables have significant regression coefficients. Note that the stepwise method did not introduce the variables mall or percent unemployment, because neither has a significant regression coefficient.

The regression equation with the four independent variables had an R-square term of 84.7% but the stepwise method produced an equation with only two independent variables and that regression equation explained 82.8% of the variation in sales. The stepwise method leads to a simpler equation, with two significant variables, that explains nearly the same amount of variation. Thus by using the stepwise method we were able to obtain nearly the same R-square value with only two variables. Advertising expense and population should be included in the equation and the percent unemployment and mall should be dropped. Using advertising expense and population also removes the sign reversal problem and hence there is no multicollinearity.

●

Exercise 2

Check you answers against those in the ANSWER section.

Refer to **Exercise 1.** The following output is for the Heffren Manufacturing problem. Conduct a test of hypothesis to determine which of the independent variables have regression coefficients not equal to zero. Use the .05 significance level.

The regression equation is

Usage = − 16.8 + 0.37 Temp − 0.0171 Output

Predictor	Coef	Stdev	t-ratio
Constant	−16.801	7.162	−2.35
Temp	0.37089	0.09962	3.72
Output	−0.01707	0.04791	−0.36

Problem 3

Verify the regression equation developed in Problem 2 where the stepwise method was used meets the required assumptions. Use the MINITAB System to aid in the computation.

Solution

●

The regression equation developed in **Problem 2** was:

$$Y' = -.079 + 0.521X_1 + .033X_3$$

The MINITAB system was used to develop the fitted values of Y' and the residuals. The fitted values are obtained by substituting the actual values of population and advertising expense in the regression equation. For example, the first store was in a city having 7.5 million population and advertising expense of 59.0 thousand dollars. These values are substituted in the regression equation and the estimated, or "fitted" value of Y' obtained.

$$Y' = -0.079 + 0.521(7.5) + 0.033(59.0) = 5.7755$$

The residual is the difference between the actual and the predicted value. For the first store it is −0.6055, found by $(Y - Y') = (5.17 - 5.7755)$. The residuals are computed for the other 29 stores in a similar fashion. The MINITAB system will perform these time-consuming calculations for us, however the results are slightly different, due to rounding. For example, MINITAB estimates 5.8017 for the first store compared to our estimate of 5.7755.

●

Sales Y	Fitted Y'	Residual (Y − Y')
5.17	5.8017	−0.63169
5.78	6.5489	−0.76894
4.84	7.1705	−2.33050
6.00	5.8426	0.15741
6.00	6.4779	−0.47790
6.12	6.0679	0.05213
6.40	7.9830	−1.58299
7.10	9.1177	−2.01773
8.50	9.3502	−0.85022
7.50	6.3270	1.17299
9.30	7.7342	1.56581
8.80	9.6327	−0.83270
9.96	8.7221	1.23788
9.83	10.4625	−0.63255
10.12	12.3549	−2.23493
10.70	9.2153	1.48474
10.45	10.7332	−0.28321
11.32	11.0019	0.31810
11.87	9.5187	2.35131
11.91	12.3862	−0.47618
12.60	11.4370	1.16304
12.60	12.7626	−0.16265
14.24	14.5261	−0.28614
14.41	16.1129	−1.70287
13.73	12.5707	1.15930
13.73	12.7439	0.98610
13.80	14.6060	−0.80601
14.92	11.3919	3.52814
15.28	14.0242	1.25579
14.41	14.7655	−0.35555

The residuals should approximate a normal distribution. The residuals from the right hand column above are organized into the following histogram. The shape seems to approximate the normal distribution.

```
        Histogram of RESI1   N = 30

Midpoint    Count
    -2.5      1   *
    -2.0      2   **
    -1.5      2   **
    -1.0      4   ****
    -0.5      7   *******
     0.0      3   ***
     0.5      1   *
     1.0      5   *****
     1.5      3   ***
     2.0      0
     2.5      1   *
     3.0      0
     3.5      1   *
```

Another assumption, called **homoscedasticity**, requires that the residuals remain constant for all fitted values of Y'. This means the variation around the regression line should be the same for all values of Y'. A scatter diagram can be used to investigate. The horizontal axis is the fitted values, i.e., Y', and the vertical axis reflects the residuals. This assumption seems to be met, according to the following plot.

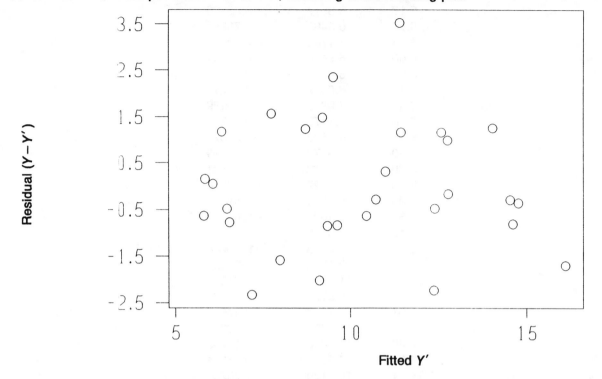

In summary, Mr. Skaff wants to open new stores. The two variables that are the most effective in explaining differences in sales are the population in the surrounding area and the amount spent on advertising. The basic requirements for the use of regression analysis are met when these variables are used. The unemployment rate and whether or not the store is located in a mall are not important.

Exercise

Check your answers against those in the ANSWER section.

Refer to exercises 1 and 2. Using the independent variable temperature, the following regression equation was developed. What is the R-Square value. Is the independent variable temperature significant?

The regression equation is
Power = − 17.2 + 0.353 Temp

Predictor	Coef	Stdev	t-ratio	p
Constant	−17.241	6.658	−2.59	0.032
Temp	0.35294	0.08112	4.35	0.002

s = 0.9460　　　　R−sq = 70.3%　　　　R−sq(adj) = 66.6%

Analysis of Variance

SOURCE	DF	SS	MS	F	p
Regression	1	16.941	16.941	18.93	0.002
Error	8	7.159	0.895		
Total	9	24.100			

The following two plots were obtained. Comment on the normality assumption and the condition of homoscedasticity.

```
Histogram of RESI1   N = 10

Midpoint    Count
   -1.6       1    *
   -1.2       1    *
   -0.8       0
   -0.4       2    **
    0.0       1    *
    0.4       3    ***
    0.8       0
    1.2       2    **


  RESI1   -
          -
          -
     1.0+            x                              x
          -
          -
          -                  x                                   x
          -                                            x
     0.0+                                    x
          -  x
          -                                      x
          -
          -
    -1.0+
          -
          -                            x           x
          -
          ------+---------+---------+---------+---------+---------+FITS1
              9.60     10.40     11.20     12.00     12.80     13.60
```

CHAPTER ASSIGNMENT 13

Multiple Regression and Correlation

Name _____ Section _____ Score _____

Part I Select the correct answer and write the appropriate letter in the space provided.

___ 1. In a multiple regression equation there is more than one
    a. independent variable.
    b. dependent variable.
    c. coefficient of correlation.
    d. R^2 value.

___ 2. If the multiple coefficient of determination is 1, then the
    a. net regression coefficients are 0.
    b. standard error of estimate is 0.
    c. X values are also equal to 0.
    d. standard error of estimate is also 1.

___ 3. A dummy variable
    a. is also called an indicator variable.
    b. can only assume values of 0 or 1.
    c. is used as an independent variable.
    d. all of the above.

___ 4. In the global test of hypothesis
    a. we use the t distribution as the test statistic.
    b. we test to see if all of the net regression coefficients are 0.
    c. we test to insure that each of the independent variables is 0.
    d. all of the above.

___ 5. A residual is
    a. the independent variable.
    b. the dependent variable.
    c. equal to R^2.
    d. the difference between the actual value and the fitted value.

___ 6. In stepwise regression
    a. the value of R^2 is always 1.00.
    b. only significant independent variables are reported in the final equation.
    c. all the coefficients of correlation are computed.
    d. Y' is greater than 0.

___ 7. A correlation matrix shows the
    a. coefficients of correlation among all the variables.
    b. net regression coefficients.
    c. stepwise regression coefficients.
    d. residuals.

___ 8. Homoscedasticity refers to
    a. residuals that are correlated.
    b. independent variables that are correlated.
    c. a nonlinear relationship.
    d. residuals that are the same for all fitted values of Y'.

___ 9. Multicollinearity means that
   a. the independent variables are correlated.
   b. time is involved with one of the independent variables.
   c. the dependent variable is correlated with the independent variables.
   d. the residuals do not have a constant variance.

___ 10. When successive residuals are correlated we refer to this as
   a. multicollinearity.
   b. a dummy variable.
   c. homoscedasticity.
   d. autocorrelation.

Part II Fill in the blank with the correct answer.

11. The proportion of variation explained by the set of independent variables is called_____.

12. When we test the net regression coefficients as a group, the test statistic follows which distribution?_____

13. The difference between the actual and the fitted value is called a_____.

14. When the independent variables are correlated we call this condition_____.

15. When successive observations of the dependent variable are correlated we call this condition_____.

Part III Record your answer in the space provided.

16. William Clegg is the owner and CEO of Clegg QC Consulting. Mr. Clegg is concerned about the salary structure of his company and has asked the Human Relations Department to conduct a study. Mr. Stan Hire, an analyst in the department, is assigned the project. Stan selects a random sample of 15 employees and gathers information on the salary, the number of years with Clegg Consulting, the employee's performance rating for the previous year, and the number of days absent last year.

Salary ($000)	Years with Firm	Performance Rating	Days Absent
50.3	6	60	8
69.0	9	85	3
50.7	7	60	8
46.9	4	78	12
44.2	5	70	6
50.3	6	73	6
49.2	6	83	6
54.6	5	74	5
52.1	5	85	5
58.3	6	85	4
54.8	4	88	5
63.0	8	78	5
50.1	5	61	6
52.1	4	74	5
36.5	3	65	7

a. The following correlation matrix was developed from the MINITAB System. Do you see any problems? Which independent variable has the strongest correlation with salary?

	Salary	Years	Perform
Years	0.768		
Perform	0.514	0.130	
Absent	−0.587	−0.370	−0.435

_____

_____

_____

_____

_____

b. Conduct a test of hypothesis to determine if any of the regression coefficients are not equal to 0. This analysis of variance table was computed as part of the output. Use the .05 significance level.

Analysis of Variance

SOURCE	DF	SS	MS	F	p
Regression	3	641.10	213.70	13.91	0.000
Error	11	168.94	15.36		
Total	14	810.04			

H_0: _____

H_1: _____

The decision rule is to reject H_0 if _____.

What is your decision. Interpret.

_____

_____

Determine the R-square value. _____

Interpret it. _____

_____

_____

c. Additonal information was obtained from MINITAB. Conduct a test of hypothesis to determine if any of the regression coefficients do not equal 0. Use the .05 significance level.

The regression equation is
Salary = 19.2 + 3.10 Years + 0.269 Perform − 0.704 Absent

Predictor	Coef	Stdev	t-ratio	p
Constant	19.19	12.15	1.58	0.143
Years	3.0962	0.7061	4.38	0.001
Perform	0.2694	0.1196	2.25	0.046
Absent	−0.7043	0.5859	−1.20	0.255

H_0: _____ H_0: _____ H_0: _____

H_1: _____ H_1: _____ H_1: _____

The decision rules are to reject H_0 if _____.

What is your decision? Interpret.

_____

_____

14

NONPARAMETRIC METHODS: CHI-SQUARE APPLICATIONS

CHAPTER GOALS

After completing this chapter, you will be able to:

1. Explain the characteristics of the chi-square distribution.
2. Test a hypothesis regarding the difference between an observed and an expected set of frequencies.
3. Test whether two criteria of classification in a contingency table are related.
4. Conduct a test for normality.

Introduction

Recall that in Chapters 9, 10, and 11 the level of measurement was assumed to be at least of interval scale and the population from which the sample was drawn was assumed to be normal. What if these conditions cannot be met? In such instances **nonparametric** or **distribution-free tests** are used. These tests do not require any assumptions about the shape of the population, thus tests of hypothesis can be performed on nominal and ordinal scale data. Recall that the nominal level of measurement requires only that the sample information be categorized, with no order implied. As an example, students are classified by major: business, history, political science, etc.

This chapter considers tests where only the nominal level of measurement is required, although these tests may be used at a higher level of measurement. In Chapter 15 you will be introduced to tests where at least the ordinal scale of measurement is assumed.

The Chi-Square Distribution

In the previous chapters the standard normal, t and F distributions were used as the test statistics. Recall that a test statistic is a quantity, determined from the sample information, used as a basis for deciding whether to reject the null hypothesis. In this chapter another distribution, called chi-square and designated χ^2, is used as the test statistic. It is similar to the t and F distributions in that there is a family of χ^2 distributions, each with a different shape, depending on the number of degrees of freedom. When the num-

ber of degrees of freedom is small the distribution is positively skewed, but as the number of degrees of freedom increases it becomes symmetrical and approaches the normal distribution. Chi-square is based on squared deviations between an observed frequency and an expected frequency, the therefore is always positive.

Goodness-of-Fit Tests

In the **goodness-of-fit** test the χ^2 distribution is used to determine how well an "observed" set of observations "fits" an "expected" set of observations. For example, an instructor told his class that his grading system would be "uniform." That is, that he would give the same number of A's, B's, C's, D's and F's. Suppose that these grades were recorded at the end of the quarter:

Grade	Number
A	12
B	24
C	23
D	30
F	11
	100

The question to be answered is: Do these final grades depart significantly from those that could be expected if the instructor had in fact graded uniformly? The null and alternate hypotheses are:

H_0: The distribution is uniform.
H_1: The distribution is not uniform.

The sampling distribution follows the χ^2 distribution and the value of the test statistic is computed by:

$$\chi^2 = \sum \left[\frac{(f_0 - f_e)^2}{f_e} \right]$$ 14–1

where f_o is the observed frequency and f_e is the expected frequency.

It is not necessary that the expected frequencies be equal to apply the goodness-of-fit test. For example, at Scandia Technical Institute, over the years 50 percent of the students were classified as freshmen, 40 percent sophomores, and 10 percent unclassified. A sample of 200 students this past semester revealed that 90 were freshmen, 80 were sophomores, and 30 were unclassified. The null and alternate hypotheses are:

H_0: The distribution of students has not changed.
H_1: The distribution of students has changed.

Contingency Tables

The χ^2 distribution is also applicable if we want to determine if there is a relationship between two criteria of classification. As an example, we are interested in whether there is a relationship between job advancement within a company and the gender of the employee. A sample of 100 employees is selected. The survey results revealed:

Gender	No Advancement	Slow Advancement	Rapid Advancement	Total
Male	7	13	30	50
Female	13	17	20	50
Total	20	30	50	100

Note that an employee is classified two ways: by gender and by advancement. When an individual or item is classified according to two criteria, the resulting table is called a **contingency table**. The null and alternate hypotheses are expressed as follows:

H_0: There is no relationship between gender and advancement.
H_1: There is a relationship between gender and advancement.

Formula 14–1 is used to compute the value of the test statistics. The expected frequency, f_e, is computed by noting that 50/100 or 50 percent of the sam-

ple is male. If the null hypothesis is true and advancement is unrelated to the gender of the employee, then it is expected that 50 percent of those who have not advanced will be male. The expected frequency f_e for males who have not advanced is 10, found by .50(20). The other expected frequencies are computed similarly. If the difference between the observed and the expected value is too large to have occurred by chance, the null hypothesis is rejected.

There is a limitation to the use of the χ^2 distribution. The value of f_e should be at least 5 for each cell (box). This requirement is to prevent any cell from carrying an inordinate amount of weight, and causing the null hypothesis to be rejected.

A Test of Normality

As we mentioned several times, the normal probability distribution plays a key role in statistical analysis. In Chapter 7 we devoted an entire chapter to its study. In several other chapters, such as Chapter 9, 10 and 11, we assumed the sampled populations were normally distributed. How can we verify the normality assumption? The chi-square distribution offers a method.

The procedure uses the goodness-of-fit test and formula 14–1. With the goodness-of-fit procedure the data are already in categories. When we want to test for normality the usual first step is to organize the data into a frequency distribution. Next, we transform the class limits to a z value by subtracting the class limits from the population mean and dividing by the standard deviation. Thus, we transform the categories of the frequency distribution into deviations from the mean and use the areas in the standard normal distribution to determine the f_e values. For example, we have the following frequency distribution of bi-weekly salaries. Assume that $\mu = \$1,200$ and $\sigma = \$200$. The frequency distribution of salaries is converted to a z value by $z = (X - \mu)/\sigma$.

Category	Salaries	z values
1	below $800	below −2.00
2	$ 800 to 1,000	−2.00 to −1.00
3	1,000 to 1,200	−1.00 to 0.00
4	1,200 to 1,400	0.00 to. 1.00
5	1,400 to 1,600	1.00 to 2.00
6	above 1,600	above 2.00

The expected frequencies are computed by determining the area between the z values and multiplying by the sample size. The null hypothesis is that the sampled population is normal, the alternate is that the sampled population is not normal. The degrees of freedom is the number of categories minus 1. Further details are of the steps are given in **Problem 4**.

GLOSSARY

Nonparametric tests of hypotheses—Also called distribution-free tests. These tests do not require the population to be normally distributed. Appropriate for nominal and ordinal data.

Goodness-of-fit test—A nonparametric test involving a set of observed frequencies and a corresponding set of expected frequencies. The fundamental purpose of the test is to determine if there is a statistical difference between the two sets of data one of which is observed, the other expected.

Contingency table—A two-way classification of a particular observation in table form.

CHAPTER PROBLEMS

Problem 1

A distributor of personal computers has five locations in the city of Ashland. The sales in units for the first quarter of the year were as follows. At the .01 significance level do the records suggest that sales are uniformly distributed among the five locations?

Location	Sales (Units)
North Side	70
Pleasant Township	75
Southwyck	70
I-90	50
Venice Ave.	35
	300

Solution

The first step is to state the null hypothesis and the alternate hypothesis. The null hypothesis is that sales are uniformly distributed. The alternate is that there has been a change and the sales pattern is not uniformly distributed among the five stores. These hypotheses are written as follows:

H_0: Sales are uniformly distributed among the five locations
H_1: Sales are not uniformly distributed among the five locations

The appropriate test statistic is the χ^2 distribution. The critical value is obtained from Appendix I. The number of degrees of freedom is equal to the number of categories minus 1. There are five categories (locations), therefore there are four degrees of freedom found by $k - 1 = 5 - 1 = 4$. The problem states beforehand that the .01 significance level is to be used. To locate the critical value, find the column headed .01 and the row where *df*, the degrees of freedom, is 4. The value at the intersection of this row and column is 13.277. Therefore, the decision rule is: Reject H_0 if the computed value of the test statistic exceeds 13.277, otherwise do not reject the null hypothesis. Graphically, the decision rule is:

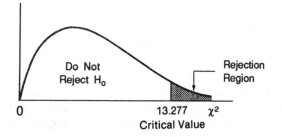

The observed frequencies, f_o, are in Col. 1 of the following table. The expected frequencies are in Col. 2. How are the expected frequencies determined? If the null hypothesis is true (that sales are uniformly distributed among the five locations), then 1/5 of 300, or 60 computers should have been sold at each location.

Location	Col. 1 f_o	Col. 2 f_e	Col. 3 $f_o - f_e$	Col. 4 $(f_o - f_e)^2$	Col. 5 $\dfrac{(f_o - f_e)^2}{f_e}$
North Side	70	60	10	100	1.67
Pleasant Township	75	60	15	225	3.75
Southwyck	70	60	10	100	1.67
I-90	50	60	−10	100	1.67
Venice Ave.	35	60	−25	625	10.42
	300	300	0		19.18

Recall that the value of the test statistic is computed by formula 14–1.

$$\chi^2 = \sum \left[\frac{(f_0 - f_e)^2}{f_e} \right]$$

The value of the test statistic is determined by first taking the difference between the observed frequency and the expected frequency (Col. 3). Next these differences are squared (Col. 4). Then the result is divided by the expected frequency (Col. 5). This result is then summed over the five locations. The total is 19.18. The value of 19.18 is compared to the critical value of 13.277. Since 19.18 is greater than the critical value, H_0 is rejected and H_1 accepted. We conclude that sales are not uniformly distributed among the five locations.

Exercise 1

Check your answers against those in the ANSWER section.

A tire manufacturer is studying the position of tires in blowouts. It seems logical that the tire blowouts will be uniformly distributed among the four positions. For a sample of 100 tire failures, is there any significant difference in that tire's position on the car? Use the .05 significance level.

Location of tire on the car

Left Front	Left Rear	Right Front	Right Rear
28	20	29	23

Problem 2

From past experience the manager of the parking facilities at a major airport knows that 58 percent of the customers stay less than one hour, 23 percent between one and two hours, 10 percent between two and three hours, and nine percent three hours or more.

The manager wants to update this study. A sample of 500 stamped parking tickets is selected. The results showed 300 stayed less than one hour, 100 from one to two hours, 60 from two to three hours, and 40 parked three hours or more. At the .01 significance level does the data suggest there has been a change in the length of time customers use the parking facilities?

194

Solution

The first step is to state the null hypothesis and alternate hypothesis.

H_0: There has been no change in the distribution of parking times.
H_1: There has been a change in the distribution of parking times.

The next step is to determine the decision rule. Note in the table below that there are four categories. The number of degrees of freedom is the number of categories minus 1. In this problem it is $4 - 1 = 3$ degrees of freedom. Referring to Appendix I, the .01 level and 3 degrees of freedom, the critical value of chi-square is 11.345, so H_0 is rejected if χ^2 is greater than 11.345.

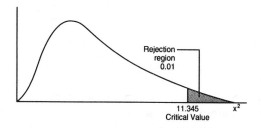

The value of the test statistic is computed as follows:

The observed frequencies from the sample are shown in Column 2 of the following table. Recall that based on past experience 58 percent of the customers parked their car less than one hour. If the null hypothesis is true, then $58\% \times 500$ (in the sample) $= 290$, the expected frequency. Likewise, 23 percent stayed from one to two hours. Thus, $23\% \times 500$ gives the expected frequency of 115. The complete set of expected frequencies are given in Column 3. Chi-square is computed to be 4.86.

Time in Parking Lot	Col. 1 Percent of Total	Col. 2 Number in Sample f_o	Col. 3 f_e	Col. 4 $f_o - f_e$	Col. 5 $(f_o - f_e)^2$	Col. 6 $\dfrac{(f_o - f_e)^2}{f_e}$
Less than 1 hour	58%	300	290	10	100	$100/290 = 0.34$
1 up to 2 hours	23%	100	115	−15	225	$225/115 = 1.96$
2 up to 3 hours	10%	60	50	10	100	$100/50 = 2.00$
3 hours or more	9%	40	45	− 5	25	$25/45 = 0.56$
Total	100%	500	500	0		$\chi^2 = 4.86$

Since the computed value of chi-square (4.86) is less than the critical value (11.345), the null hypothesis is not rejected. There has been no change in the lengths of parking time at the airport.

Exercise 2

Check your answers against those in the ANSWER section.

In recent years, 42 percent of the American-made automobiles sold in the United States were manufactured by General Motors, 33 percent by Ford, 22 percent by Chrysler, and 3 percent by all others.

A sample of the sales of American-made automobiles conducted last week revealed that 174 were manufactured by Chrysler, 275 by Ford, 330 by GM, and 21 by all others.

Test the hypothesis at the .05 level that there has been no change in the sales pattern.

Problem 3

A study is made by an auto insurance company to determine if there is a relationship between the driver's age and the number of automobile accident claims submitted during a one year period. From a sample of 300 claims, the following sample information was recorded.

No. of Accidents	Age (Years) Less than 25	25-50	Over 50	Total
0	37	101	74	212
1	16	15	28	59
2 or more	7	9	13	29
Total	60	125	115	300

Use the .05 significance level to find out if there is any relationship between the driver's age and the number of accidents.

Solution

The question under investigation is whether the number of auto accidents is related to the driver's age. The null and alternate hypotheses are:

H_0: There is no relationship between age and the number of accidents.
H_1: There is a relationship between age and the number of accidents.

The critical value is obtained from the chi-square distribution in Appendix I. The number of degrees of freedom is equal to the number of rows minus one times the number of columns minus one. Hence, the degrees of freedom is $(3 - 1)(3 - 1) = 4$. The significance level, as stated in the problem, is .05. The critical value from Appendix I is 9.488. The null hypothesis is not rejected if the computed value of χ^2 is equal to or less than 9.488.

Formula 14–1, as cited earlier, is used to determine χ^2.

$$\chi^2 = \sum \left[\frac{(f_0 - f_e)^2}{f_e} \right]$$

where f_o is the frequency observed and f_e is the expected frequency. The first step is to determine the expected frequency for each corresponding observed frequency. If the null hypothesis is true (the number of accidents is not related to age) we can expect 212 out of the 300 sampled, or 70.67 percent of the drivers to have had no accidents. Thus, we can expect 70.67 percent of the 60 drivers under 25 years, or 42.40 drivers, to have had no accidents.

Likewise, if the null hypothesis is true, 70.67 percent of the 125 drivers in the 25 to 50 age bracket, or 88.33 drivers, should have had no accidents.

The table below shows the complete set of observed and expected frequences.

No. of Accidents	Age						
	Less than 25		25-50		Over 50		
	f_o	f_e	f_o	f_e	f_o	f_e	Total
0	37	42.40	101	88.33	74	81.27	212
1	16	11.80	15	24.58	28	22.62	59
2 or more	7	5.80	9	12.08	13	11.12	29
	60	60.00	125	125.00	115	115.00	300

The expected frequency for any category is found by:

$$f_e = \frac{(\text{row total})(\text{column total})}{\text{grand total}}$$

The value for the first row and column is used as an example. There are 212 people who did not have any accidents, 60 persons are less than 25 years old, and there is a total of 300 people. These values are inserted into the formula:

$$f_e = \frac{(\text{row total})(\text{column total})}{\text{grand total}} = \frac{(212)(60)}{300} = 42.40$$

which is the same value computed previously.

The computed value of x^2 is 11.03.

$$x^2 = \sum \left[\frac{(f_o - f_e)^2}{f_e} \right] = \frac{(37.00 - 42.40)^2}{42.40} + \frac{(101.00 - 88.33)^2}{88.33} + \ldots + \frac{(13 - 11.12)^2}{11.12} = 11.03$$

Since the computed value of x^2 is greater than the critical value of 9.488, the null hypothesis is rejected and the alternate accepted. We conclude that there is a relationship between age and the number of accidents.

Exercise 3

Check your answers against those in the ANSWER section.

A random sample of 480 male and female adults was asked the amount of time each person spent watching TV last week. Their responses are shown below. At the .05 significance level, does it appear that the amount of time spent watching TV is related to the gender of the viewer?

Hours	Sex of viewer		
	Male	Female	Total
Under 8	75	90	160
8 to 15	100	60	160
15 or more	55	105	160
	225	255	480

Problem 4

The following is the distribution of the number of outpatients surgeries per day for the last 100 days at St. Luke's Hospital, Maumee, Ohio. Assume the population mean is 24 patients per day and the standard deviation is 4 patients per day.

Number of Patients	Number of Days
Less than 18	12
18 up to 22	19
22 up to 26	39
26 up to 30	21
30 or more	9
Total	100

Is it reasonable to assume that the population of the number of patients per day is normally distributed? Use the .05 significance level.

Solution

The null hypothesis and the alternate hypothesis are:

H_0: The population is normal.
H_1: The population is not normal.

There are 5 categories, so there are $5 - 1 = 4$ degrees of freedom. From Appendix I, H_0 is rejected if the computed value of chi-square is greater than 9.488.

Next, we compute the expected values. To do this we determine the areas under a normal curve with $\mu = 24$ and $\sigma = 4$. Recall from Chapter 7, to determine the areas we convert from a normal distribution to the standard normal distribution by $z = (X - \mu)/\sigma$. To find the area below 18 patients:

1. The z value corresponding to 18 is -1.50, found by $(18 - 24)/4$.
2. The area between $z = 0.00$ and 1.50 is .4332, from Appendix D.
3. The area between -1.50 and 0.00 is also .4332, because of symmetry.
4. The area below -1.50 is .0668 found by $.5000 - .4332$.
5. If the distribution is normal with $\mu = 24$ and $\sigma = 4$, then we expect $100 (.0668) = 6.68$ days during which there were less than 18 patients.

To determine the expected frequency for 18 up to 22 patients, first find the z value for 22 patients. It is -0.50, found by $(22 - 24)/4 = -0.50$. The area between a z value of -0.50 and -1.50 is $.4332 - .1915 = .2417$. We therefore expect $100(.2417) = 24.17$ days to have between 18 and 22 patients.

The remaining expected frequencies are determined similarly.

Number of Patients	z values	f_o	f_e
Less than 18	less than −1.50	12	6.68
18 up to 22	−1.50 up to −0.50	19	24.17
22 up to 26	−0.50 up to 0.50	39	38.30
26 up to 30	0.50 up to 1.50	21	24.17
30 or more	1.50 or more	9	6.68
Total		100	100.00

To determine the value of chi-square we use formula 14–1. The computations are as follows:

Number of Patients	f_o	f_e	$\dfrac{(f_o - f_e)^2}{f_e}$
Less than 18	12	6.68	4.2369
18 up to 22	19	24.17	1.1059
22 up to 26	39	38.30	0.0128
26 up to 30	21	24.17	0.4158
30 or more	9	6.68	0.8057
Total	100	100.00	6.5771

The computed value of chi-square is 6.5771, which is less than the critical value of 9.488. Hence, the null hypothesis is not rejected. We conclude that the sample could have been obtained from a normal population. It is reasonable to conclude that the distribution of days is normal with a mean of 24 and a standard deviation of 4.

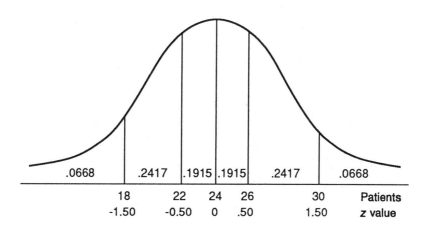

CHAPTER ASSIGNMENT 14

Nonparametric Methods: Chi-Square Applications

Name _____ Section _____ Score _____

Part I Select the correct answer and write the appropriate letter in the space provided.

___ 1. The level of measurement required for the goodness-of-fit test is
    a. nominal.
    b. ordinal.
    c. interval.
    d. ratio.

___ 2. In a nonparametric test
    a. no assumption is made regarding the shape of the population.
    b. the sample size must be at least 30.
    c. σ is always known.
    d. the population follows the normal distribution.

___ 3. A two-way classification of the data is called a
    a. chi-square distribution.
    b. normal distribution.
    c. contingency table.
    d. none of the above.

___ 4. The chi-square distribution is
    a. positively skewed.
    b. a continuous distribution.
    c. based on the number of categories.
    d. all of the above.

___ 5. In a goodness-of-fit test where the f_e values are the same in all four categories
    a. the degrees of freedom is 3.
    b. $k = 4$.
    c. the null hypothesis is that the proportion in each category is the same.
    d. all of the above.

___ 6. A sample of 100 undergraduate students is classified by major (3 groups) and gender. How many degrees of freedom are there in the test?
    a. 99.
    b. 3.
    c. 2.
    d. none of the above.

___ 7. In a chi-square test the $df = 4$. At the .05 significance level the critical value of chi-square is
    a. 9.488.
    b. 7.815.
    c. 7.779.
    d. 13.388.

___ 8. The shape of the chi-square distribution is
    a. based on the degrees of freedom.
    b. based on the sample size.
    c. based on the shape of the population.
    d. based on at least 30 observations.

___ 9. In a test to find out if the two criteria of classification are related, the expected cell frequencies should be
    a. all less than 5.
    b. at least one less than 5.
    c. at least 5 percent of the population.
    d. at least 5.

___ 10. The sum of the observed and the expected frequencies are
    a. always at least 30.
    b. always less than 5.
    c. always less than 5 percent.
    d. always the same.

Part II Fill in the blank with the correct answer.

11. When each sampled observation is classified according to two criteria, this is called a _____.

12. In _____ tests no assumption is necessary regarding the shape of the population.

13. Only the _____ scale of measurement is required for a goodness-of-fit test.

14. We are testing the null hypothesis that the proportion of accidents is the same for each day of the work week. H_0 is rejected. This means that _____.

15. List the characteristics of the chi-square distribution.
    a. _____
    b. _____
    c. _____

Part III Record your answer in the space provided. Show essential work.

16. Walter Churchill, owner of Churchill's Super Market, would like to know if there is a preference for the day of the week on which customers do their shopping. A sample of 420 families revealed the following. At the .05 significance level, is there a difference in the proportion of customers that prefer the each day of the week?

Day of the week	Number of persons
Monday	20
Tuesday	30
Wednesday	20
Thursday	60
Friday	80
Saturday	130
Sunday	80

State the null and the alternate hypotheses.
    H_0:_____

    H_1:_____

State the decision rule.

Compute the value of the test statistic.

$$\boxed{}$$

Answer

What is your decision regarding the null hypothesis? Interpret the result.

_____

_____

_____

_____

17. A charity solicits donations by phone. From long experience the charity's director reports that 60 percent of the calls will result in refusal to donate, 30 percent will request more information via the mail, and 10 percent will result in an immediate credit card donation. For a sample of 200 calls last week, 140 refused to donate, 50 requested additional information, and 10 made an immediate donation. At the .10 significance level was the sample result different from the usual pattern?

State the null and the alternate hypotheses.

H_0:_____

H_1:_____

State the decision rule.

Compute the value of the test statistic.

$$\boxed{}$$

Answer

What is your decision regarding the null hypothesis? Interpret the result.

_____

_____

_____

_____

18. There are three loan officers at the Post National Bank. All decisions on mortgage loans are made by one of these officers. The president of the bank would like to be sure that the rejection rate is about the same for the three officers. A sample of 200 recent applications yielded the following results. Is the rejection rate related to the officer that processes the loan? Use the .05 significance level.

	Hercher	Officer Korosa	Black
Approved	50	70	55
Rejected	10	10	5
Total	60	80	60

State the null and the alternate hypothesis.

H_0:_____

H_1:_____

State the decision rule.

Compute the value of the test statistic.

```
┌─────────────────┐
│                 │
└─────────────────┘
       Answer
```

What is your decision regarding the null hypothesis? Interpret the result.

_____

_____

_____

_____

15

NONPARAMETRIC METHODS: ANALYSIS OF RANKED DATA

CHAPTER GOALS

After completing this chapter, you will be able to:

1. Calculate and describe applications of the sign test.
2. Conduct a test of hypothesis about a median.
3. Describe and apply the Wilcoxon matched-pairs signed-rank test.
4. Describe and apply the Wilcoxon rank-sum test.
5. Describe and apply the Kruskal-Wallis test.
6. Measure the relationship between sets of ranked data using Spearman's coefficient of rank correlation.

Introduction

This chapter continues our study of nonparametric tests of hypotheses. Recall that for nonparametric tests no assumption regarding the shape of the population is required. The data can be either the nominal or ordinal scale. In Chapter 14, applications of the chi-square distribution, which requires only the nominal scale of measurement, were presented. In this chapter several tests based on the ordinal scale of measurement are examined. The first two tests require paired or dependent samples. The sign test is based on only the *sign of the difference between paired observations*. The Wilcoxon matched-pair signed rank test considers both the sign of the difference and also the magnitude of the difference. The Wilcoxon rank-sum test and the Kruskal-Wallis test are applied to independent samples. Also we look at a coefficient of correlation especially designed for ranked data.

Sign Test

The sign test is based on the sign of the difference between paired observations. The difference is either positive ($+$) or negative ($-$). It is an alternative to the paired t test presented in Chapter 10. The paired t test requires that the distribution of the differences in paired observations be normally distributed. If this normality assumption cannot be met, the sign test is employed as an alternative.

The underlying assumption for the sign test is that the number of positive differences should be about the same as the number of negative differences, assuming the treatment or pairing has no effect. The null hypothesis is that the pairing has no effect. If H_0 is true, then any difference in the number of positive and negative differences is due to chance. If the treatment has an effect, then there will be significantly more positive (or negative) differences.

We have concentrated so far on testing a hypothesis about a mean or means. We can also apply the ideas of the sign test to conduct a hypothesis test about the *median* of a population. Recall that the median is a value above which half of the observations lie and the other half below it. For example, we might want to find out whether the median annual salary of quality assurance managers is $52,000, meaning that half the managers earn more than $52,000 and the other half of the managers earn less. In our sample if an annual salary more than $52,000 is assigned a plus sign, a salary below $52,000 a minus sign. A salary exactly equal to $52,000 is omitted from further analysis.

The human relations director wants to explore the annual salary of quality assurance managers further. So she first sets up the following null and alternate hypotheses.

H_0: Median salary is $52,000
H_1: Median salary is not $52,000

The way the alternate hypothesis is stated signifies that a two-tailed test is being applied. The solution to this problem is presented in the Problem/Solution section.

The binomial distribution, discussed in Chapter 6, is the test statistic. Recall that there are four conditions for the binomial: only two outcomes, independent trials, a constant probability of success, and a fixed sample size. The null hypothesis, stated in terms of the binomial, is that $p = .50$. p is the probability of a success. The normal approximation to the binomial is used if both np and $n(1 - p)$ are greater than 5.

The Wilcoxon Signed-Rank Test

The sign test considers only the sign of the difference between paired observations. Any information regarding the magnitude of the difference is not used. The Wilcoxon signed-rank test not only considers the sign of the difference but also the magnitude of the difference. It is also a replacement for the paired t test, when the normality assumption cannot be met. When information on the magnitude of the paired difference is available, the Wilcoxon test is a stronger or a more powerful test because it makes more effective use of the data.

The Wilcoxon Rank-Sum Test

This test is the nonparametric alternative to the Student t test described in Chapter 10. The purpose of Student's t was to determine if two independent populations had the same mean. Recall we assumed that the two independent random samples were selected from normally distributed populations with equal standard deviations. What if the equal standard deviation or the normality assumption cannot be met? The Student t is not appropriate and a nonparametric alternative, the **Wilcoxon rank-sum test**, is used.

The Wilcoxon rank-sum test is based on the sum of the ranks of independent samples. If the populations are the same, then the combined rankings of the two samples will be nearly evenly divided between the two samples and the total of the ranks will be about the same. If the populations are not the same, one of the samples will have a predominance of the larger ranks and its total (rank-sum) will be larger. When *both samples are at least 8*, the standard normal distribution is used as the test statistic. The formula is:

$$z = \frac{W - \frac{n_1(n_1 + n_2 + 1)}{2}}{\sqrt{\frac{n_1 n_2(n_1 + n_2 + 1)}{12}}} \qquad 15\text{-}4$$

W is the sum of the ranks in the first population, n_1 is the number of observations in the sample from the first population, and n_2 the number of observations in the sample from the second population.

The Kruskal-Wallis Test

The Wilcoxon rank-sum test compares *two* independent populations. The **Kruskal-Wallis** test allows for the simultaneous comparison of *more* than two independent populations. It is an alternative to the ANOVA, described in Chapter 11, for comparing more than two population means. Recall from Chapter 11 that to apply ANOVA it was necessary that, (1) the samples be independent, (2) the populations be normally distributed, and (3) the populations have equal standard deviations. The Kruskal-Wallis test should be used if one or more of these cannot be met. It requires at least five observations in each sample.

To employ the Kruskal-Wallis test, we substitute the rankings of the sampled items for the actual values. The test statistic, designated by H is computed using formula 15–5, below.

$$H = \frac{12}{N(N + 1)} \left(\frac{\Sigma R_1^2}{n_1} + \frac{\Sigma R_2^2}{n_2} + \ldots + \frac{\Sigma R_k^2}{n_k} \right) - 3(N + 1) \qquad 15\text{-}5$$

where
ΣR_1 is the sum of the ranks for the sample designated 1, ΣR_2 is the sum of the ranks for the sample designated 2, and so on.
n_1 is the number in the sample designated 1, n_2 is the number in the sample designated 2, and so on.
N is the combined number of observations for all samples.
k is the number of populations.

Spearman's Rank Order Correlation

Pearson's coefficient of correlation assumes the data to be of at least interval scale. What if the data are only ranked? **Spearman's rank-order correlation coefficient**, designated r_s, is used to express the relationship. Its value may range between -1.0 and 1.0 inclusive with -1.0 and 1.0 representing perfect rank correlation. Zero indicates no rank correlation.

The formula is:

$$r_s = 1 - \frac{6(\Sigma d^2)}{n(n^2 - 1)} \qquad 15\text{-}6$$

where n is the number of paired observations and d is the difference between the ranks for each pair.

The value of r_s is tested to rule out the possibility that the association was due to chance. For a two-tailed test, the null and alternate hypotheses are stated as follows:

H_0: The rank correlation in the population is zero.
H_1: The rank correlation in the population is not zero.

For large samples where n is 10 or more, the Student's t distribution can be used as the test statistic.

There are $n - 2$ degrees of freedom and the computed t value is found by:

$$t = r_s \sqrt{\frac{n - 2}{1 - r_s^2}} \qquad 15\text{--}7$$

GLOSSARY

Wilcoxon rank-sum test—A test to determine whether there is a difference between two independent populations. No assumption is made regarding the normality of the populations.

Kruskal-Wallis test—A test to determine whether there is a difference among more than two populations. No assumption regarding the shape of the populations is necessary.

Wilcoxon signed rank test—A test for determining whether there is a difference between two sets of data, one of which is based on a ''before'' situation and the other an ''after'' situation. The two sets of data must be related dependent or paired.

Sign test—A test to determine whether there is a difference in paired observations. Uses only the sign, + or −, of the difference between observations.

Median test—A test to determine whether the median of a set of sample data is equal to a hypothesized value.

Coefficient of rank correlation—A measure of the relationship between two sets of ranked data.

CHAPTER PROBLEMS

Problem 1

A sample of ten Army recruits was given a test to determine how well they liked the Army. Later that same day they were taken on a march—very long and very strenuous. On their return they were given a similar test to again measure how well they liked the Army. The scores are shown below. At the .05 significance level, can we conclude that the recruits liked the Army less after the march?

| | Test Score | |
Recruit	Before	After
Barrett	132	122
Bier	150	165
Spitler	139	127
Contact	108	101
Walker	106	99
Stasiak	105	92
Soto	133	110
Lopez	157	139
Kies	114	99
Landrum	122	113

Solution

First, note that the samples are dependent. That is, we have a score for Barrett before the march and after the march. We are concerned with the distribution of the differences and are not willing to assume that the differences are normally distributed. Thus the paired t test, described in Chapter 10, which requires the normality assumption, cannot be used.

The null hypothesis and the alternate hypothesis are as follows:

H_0: There was no change in how well the recruits liked the Army ($p \leqslant .50$)
H_1: The recruits liked the Army less after the march. ($p > .50$)

Why is the alternate hypothesis $p > .50$? We subtract the score after the march from the score before the march. Hence, a positive difference indicates that the recruits liked the Army less after the march.

If the null hypothesis is true that there is no change in the view of the recruits toward the Army, then there should be about as many positive differences in the scores as negative. If the recruits liked the Army less after the march, then there should be significantly more positive differences.

The binomial distribution is used as the test statistic. Recall that to apply the binomial:

1. Each outcome is classified into one of two possible outcomes. A difference can only be positive or negative. (If a difference is 0, that observation is dropped from the study.)
2. There is a fixed number of trials. In this case "trials" refers to the sample size. There are ten recruits (trials).
3. Each trial is independent. This means, for example, the scores obtained by Barrett are not related to Landrum's scores.
4. The probability of a success remains the same from trial to trial. If the null hypothesis is true—that the march had no effect—the probability of the positive difference is .50.

The following table shows that of the ten recruits, 9 out of 10 liked the Army better before the march.

Test Score

Recruit	X Before March	Y After March	X–Y Sign of Difference
Barrett	132	122	+
Bier	150	165	–
Spitler	139	127	+
Contact	108	101	+
Walker	106	99	+
Stasiak	105	92	+
Soto	133	110	+
Lopez	157	139	+
Kies	114	99	+
Landrum	122	113	+

The normal approximation to the binomial can be used when both np and $n(1 - p)$ are greater than 5. In this case both are equal to five ($10(.5) = 5$ and $10(1 - .5) = 5$), so the binomial distribution will be used as the test statistic. The binomial table is found in Appendix A.

How is the critical value determined? Recall that the alternate hypothesis indicated a one-tailed test. The binomial probability distribution, when $n = 10$ and $p = .50$, is shown below.

Binomial Probabilities when $n = 10$, $p = .50$, alpha = .05

Number of Success	Probability of Success	Cumulative Probability
0	.001	
1	.010	
2	.044	
3	.117	
4	.205	
5	.246	
6	.205	
7	.117	
8	.044	.055
9	.010	.011
10	.001	.001

The decision rule is formulated by adding the probability starting with ten successes (+ signs) in ten trials, then nine successes, and so on, until we come as close to the significance level as possible without exceeding it. In this instance the probability of ten successes in ten trials is .001, the probability of nine successes is .010, and so on.

The cumulative probabilities are shown in the right-hand column. The probability of nine or more successes is .011, and the probability of eight or more successes is .055. Since .055 is greater than the significance level, of .05, the decision rule is to reject the null hypothesis if nine or more plus signs are obtained in the sample.

There are nine plus signs, indicating that nine of the ten recruits liked the Army better before the march. So the null hypothesis is rejected. It is concluded that the recruits liked the Army less after the march.

Exercise 1

Check your answers against those in the ANSWER section.

Twelve persons whose IQs were measured in college between 1960 and 1965 volunteered recently to be retested with an equivalent IQ test. The information is given below.

Student	Recent Score	Original Score
John Barr	119	112
Bill Sedwick	103	108
Marcia Elmquist	115	115
Ginger Thealine	109	100
Larry Clark	131	120
Jim Redding	110	108
Carol Papalia	109	113
Victor Suppa	113	126
Dallas Paul	94	95
Carol Kozoloski	119	110
Joe Sass	118	117
P. S. Sundar	112	102

At the .05 significance level can we conclude that the IQ scores have increased?

Problem 2

After reviewing the results in Problem 1, the Army ordered an additional study involving a larger number of Army recruits. A sample of 70 recruits were given the test to determine how well they liked the Army and then taken on the long and strenuous march. Then the second test was administered. A total of 50 of the recruits were found to like the Army better before the march. At the .05 significance level can we conclude that recruits liked the Army better before the march?

Solution

The null hypothesis and the alternate hypothesis are stated as follows:

$$H_0: p \leqslant .50$$
$$H_1: p > .50$$

Rejection of the null hypothesis and acceptance of the alternate hypothesis allows us to conclude that the recruits like the Army better before the march.

The normal approximation to the binomial is used as the test statistic. Recall that this approximation is used as the test statistic when np and $n(1 - p)$ both exceed 5. In this instance $np = 70(.50) = 35$ and $n(1 - p) = 70(1 - .50) = 35$.

The continuity correction, described in Chapter 7, is appropriate when a continuous distribution, such as the normal, is used to describe a discrete distribution (the binomial). The continuity correction factor includes a value of .50 which is either added to or subtracted from X. If the number of plus signs is greater than $n/2$, .50 is subtracted from X. If the number of plus signs is less than $n/2$, then .50 is added. The formula for the test statistic, 15–1 is:

$$z = \frac{(X \pm .5) - \mu}{.5\sqrt{n}} \qquad \qquad 15\text{–}1$$

where

      X is the number of plus (or minus) signs
      n is the number of paired observations (disregarding ties)
      μ is the population mean, found by np
      z is the z value

The decision rule is to reject the null hypothesis if the computed value of z exceeds 1.645. This decision rule is based on a one-tailed test, the standard normal distribution, and the .05 significance level.

The value of z is computed to be 3.47.

$$z = \frac{(X \pm .5) - \mu}{n\sqrt{n}} = \frac{(50 - .5) - 70(.50)}{.5\sqrt{70}} = 3.47$$

Since the computed value of 3.47 exceeds the critical value of 1.645, the null hypothesis is rejected. It is concluded that the recruits liked the Army less after the march.

Exercise 2

Check your answers against those in the ANSWER section.

Refer to Exercise 1. A sample of 50 adults who were in college between 1960 and 1965 were recently given an IQ test and the scores compared. Thirty of those tested showed an increase in their scores and 20 a decrease. At the .05 significance level can we conclude that the scores have increased?

Problem 3

The human relations director at ARCO is wondering whether the median age of executives is 45 years. She selects a sample of 228 executives at random. Of the 228 selected, 3 were exactly 45 years old, 120 were over 45 years, and 105 were less than 45 years of age. At the .10 significance level, can we conclude that the median age is different from 45 years?

Solution

The null and the alternate hypotheses are:

$$H_0: \text{Median} = 45$$
$$H_1: \text{Median} \neq 45$$

The three executives who were exactly 45 years old were omitted from the analysis, so the sample size is reduced from 228 to 225. Using a two-tailed test, the .10 significance level, and the standard normal distribution (Appendix D) as the test statistic, the decision rule is to reject H_0 if the computed value of z is less than -1.645 or greater than 1.645.

We will conduct the test for the number of observations greater than 45 years of age. Because the number of observation above the median is more than $n/2$ we use formula 15–1. There are 120 observations larger than the hypothesized median and $n/2 = 225/2 = 112.5$. The value of z is 0.933, found by

$$z = \frac{(X - .50) - .50n}{.50 \sqrt{n}} = \frac{120 - .50 - .50(225)}{.5 \sqrt{225}} = 0.933$$

Because 0.933 is not in the region beyond 1.645, the null hypothesis is not rejected. We cannot reject the hypothesis that the median age of ARCO executives is 45 years.

Problem 4

Use the Wilcoxon signed-rank test and the sample data in Problem 1, regarding the Army march, to determine if recruits liked the Army better before the march. Again, use the .05 significance level.

Solution

The sign test considers only the sign of the difference between paired observations. The Wilcoxon signed-rank test not only considers the sign of the difference between paired observations but also the magnitude of the difference. The null and alternate hypotheses are stated as follows.

H_0: There was no change in how the recruits liked the Army.
H_1: The recruits liked the Army better before the march.

The steps to complete the Wilcoxon signed-rank test are as follows.

1. The difference between each paired observations is found. If any difference is 0, it is eliminated and the size of the sample is reduced by the number of 0 differences.
2. These differences are ranked from highest to lowest, without regard to their signs. If ties occur, the ranks involved are averaged and each tied observation is awarded the mean value.
3. The ranks with a positive difference are assigned to one column and those with a negative difference to another.
4. The sums of the positive (R^+) and negative (R^-) ranks are determined.
5. The smaller of the two sums (R^+ and R^-) is compared with the critical values found in Appendix J. This critical value is called T.

Appendix J is used to formulate the decision rule. First locate the column headed by .05 using a one-tailed test. Next move down that column to the row where N = 10. The critical value is 10. The decision is to reject H_0 if the smaller of R^+ and R^- is 10 or less.

The values for R^+ and R^- as follows:

Recruit	Before	After	Difference	Rank	R+	R-
Barrett	132	122	10	4	4	
Bier	150	165	−15	7.5		7.5
Spitler	139	127	12	5	5	
Contact	108	101	7	1.5	1.5	
Walker	106	99	7	1.5	1.5	
Stasiak	105	92	13	6	6	
Soto	133	110	23	10	10	
Lopez	157	139	18	9	9	
Kies	114	99	15	7.5	7.5	
Landrum	122	113	9	3	3	
					47.5	7.5

Since $R^- = 7.5$, H_0 is rejected and H_1 accepted. It is concluded that recruits liked the Army better before the march.

Exercise 3

Check your answers against those in the ANSWER section.

Refer to Exercise 1. Twelve persons whose IQs were measured in college between 1960 and 1965 were located recently and retested with an equivalent IQ test. The information is given below.

Student	Recent Score	Original Score
John Barr	119	112
Bill Sedwick	103	108
Marcia Elmquist	115	115
Ginger Thealine	109	100
Larry Clark	131	120
Jim Redding	110	108
Carol Papalia	109	113
Victor Suppa	113	126
Dallas Paul	94	95
Carol Kozoloski	119	110
Joe Sass	118	117
P. S. Sundar	112	102

At the .05 significance level can we conclude that the IQ scores have increased in over 20 years? Use the Wilcoxon signed-rank test.

Problem 5

A manufacturer of candy, gum and other snacks wants to compare the daily amounts spent by men and women in vending machines. To investigate, samples of eight men and nine women are selected. Each person is asked to keep a record of the amount they spend in vending machines for a week. The results are as follows:

Amount Spent by Men	Amount Spent by Women
$ 4.32	$ 2.81
6.05	3.45
7.21	4.16
8.57	4.32
9.80	5.54
10.10	6.93
12.76	7.54
13.65	8.32
15.87	10.76
	11.21

Assume that the distribution of the amounts spent for men and women is not normally distributed. At the .05 significance level can we conclude that men spend more?

Solution

The first step is to determine which test to use. Because the populations are not normally distributed the *t* test for independent samples is not appropriate. The Wilcoxon rank-sum test allows for two independent samples and does not require any assumptions regarding the shape of the population, so it is appropriate.

The next step is to state the null and the alternate hypotheses. A one-tailed test is used because we want to show that the distribution of the amounts spent by the men is larger, or to the right of, that of the women. To put it another way, the median amount spent by the men is larger than the median amount spent by the women.

H_0: The distributions are the same
H_1: The distribution of the men is located to
the right of that of the women.

When the two independent samples both have at least eight observations the test statistic is the standard normal distribution. The formula for *z* is:

$$z = \frac{W - \dfrac{n_1(n_1 + n_2 + 1)}{2}}{\sqrt{\dfrac{n_1 n_2(n_1 + n_2 + 1)}{12}}}$$

Where n_1 is the number of observations in the first sample, n_2 the number of observations in the second sample, and *W* the sum of the ranks in one of the samples.

At the .05 significance level the null hypothesis is rejected if *z* is greater than 1.645.

The test is based on the sum of the ranks. The two samples are ranked as if they belonged to a single sample. If the null hypothesis is true—that the two populations are the same—then the sum of the ranks for the two groups would be about the same. If the null hypothesis is not true, then there will be a disparity in the rank sums.

The data on the amounts spent by both the men and the women are ranked in the following table and the rank sums determined.

Amount Spent by Men		Amount Spent by Women	
Dollars	Rank	Dollars	Rank
4.32	4.5	2.81	1.0
6.05	7.0	3.45	2.0
7.21	9.0	4.16	3.0
8.57	12.0	4.32	4.5
9.80	13.0	5.54	6.0
10.10	14.0	6.93	8.0
12.76	17.0	7.54	10.0
13.65	18.0	8.32	11.0
15.87	19.0	10.76	15.0
		11.21	16.0
	113.5		76.5

The value of *z* is computed where $W = 113.5$, $n_1 = 9$ and $n_2 = 10$. Note that there was a man and a woman who each spent $4.32. That is, there is a tie for this position. To resolve the tie, the ranks involved are averaged. That is, the ranks of 4 and 5 are averaged and the value of 4.5 is assigned to those involved.

214

$$z = \frac{W - \dfrac{n_1\,(n_1 + n_2 + 1)}{2}}{\sqrt{\dfrac{n_1 n_2\,(n_1 + n_2 + 1)}{12}}}$$

$$z = \frac{113.5 - \dfrac{9(9 + 10 + 1)}{2}}{\sqrt{\dfrac{9(10)(9 + 10 + 1)}{12}}} = 1.919$$

Because the computed value of z (1.919) is greater than the critical value of 1.645, the null hypothesis is rejected. The distribution of the amounts spent by men is to the right of that of women. The median of the distribution of the amounts spent by men is larger than the median of the amounts spent by women.

Exercise 4

Check your answers against those in the ANSWER section.

The Continental Muffler Company manufactures two different mufflers, the Tough Muffler and the Long Last Muffler. As an experiment, they installed Tough Mufflers on eight of their employees' automobiles and the Long Last on nine cars. The number of miles driven before a muffler needed replacing is recorded below (in thousands of miles).

Tough Muffler	Long Last Muffler
24	35
31	46
37	49
44	52
36	41
30	40
28	32
21	29
	27

Assume the distributions of miles driven are not normal. Does the evidence suggest a difference in the number of miles driven using the two mufflers before replacement? Use the .05 significance level.

Problem 6

A study is made regarding the reaction time (in seconds) to danger among four groups of professional drivers: cab drivers, bus drivers, truck drivers, and race car drivers. The results are as follows:

Reaction Time (seconds)

Cab Drivers	Bus Drivers	Truck Drivers	Race Car Drivers
3.4	4.5	3.7	2.8
3.3	4.0	3.0	2.7
1.9	2.9	2.1	3.8
3.1	3.1	2.9	2.2
2.5	3.7	1.8	1.7
	4.4	3.6	

Assume that the reaction times are not normally distributed. At the .05 significance level, is there a difference in reaction times?

Solution

The ANOVA technique described in Chapter 11 for comparing several population means assumed that the populations are normally distributed. In this case the normality assumption cannot be made. Hence a nonparametric alternative, the Kruskal-Wallis test, is used. The null and alternate hypotheses are:

H_0: The distributions of reaction times are the same.
H_1: The distributions of reaction times are not the same.

The χ^2 distribution is the test statistic. For this test there are $k - 1$ degrees of freedom, where $k = 4$ is the number of treatments (groups of professional drivers), so the degrees of freedom is $k - 1 = 4 - 1 = 3$. The critical value from Appendix I is 7.815 given a significance level of .05.

The value of the test statistic is computed using formula 15–5.

$$ H = \frac{12}{N(N + 1)} \left(\frac{\Sigma R_1^2}{n_1} + \frac{\Sigma R_2^2}{n_2} + \ldots + \frac{\Sigma R_k^2}{n_k} \right) - 3 (N + 1) \qquad \text{15–5} $$

where N refers to the total number sampled (22 in this instance), ΣR_1^2 to the square of the sum of the ranks in the first sample, n_1 to the number of observations in the first sample, ΣR_2^2 to the square of the sum of the ranks of the second sample, and so on.

The value of the test statistic is computed by first ranking the reaction times of the four groups as though they were a single group. Note that there are several instances involving tied ranks. The third bus driver and the fourth truck driver each had a reaction time of 2.9 seconds. These two drivers involve the 9th and 10th rank. To resolve the tie the ranks involved are averaged and the average rank assigned to each. Hence both drivers are assigned the rank of 9.5, found by $(9 + 10)/2$. The other ties are resolved in a similar fashion.

Reaction Times and Ranks for Professional Drivers

Cab Drivers		Bus Drivers		Truck Drivers		Race Car Drivers	
Time	Rank	Time	Rank	Time	Rank	Time	Rank
3.4	15	4.5	22	3.7	17.5	2.8	8
3.3	14	4.0	20	3.0	11	2.7	7
1.9	3	2.9	9.5	2.1	4	3.8	19
3.1	12.5	3.1	12.5	2.9	9.5	2.2	5
2.5	6	3.7	17.5	1.8	2	1.7	1
		4.4	21	3.6	16		
Totals	50.5		102.5		60		40

Next, these results are substituted into the formula for H and its value is computed:

$$H = \frac{12}{N(N+1)} \left(\frac{\Sigma R_1^2}{n_1} + \frac{\Sigma R_2^2}{n_2} + \frac{\Sigma R_3^2}{n_3} + \frac{\Sigma R_4^2}{n_4} \right) - 3(N+1)$$

$$= \frac{12}{22(22+1)} \left(\frac{(50.5)^2}{5} + \frac{(102.5)^2}{6} + \frac{(60)^2}{6} + \frac{(40)^2}{5} \right) - 3(22+1)$$

$$= 6.44$$

Since the computed value (6.44) is less than the critical value of 7.815, the null hypothesis cannot be rejected. The evidence does not suggest a difference in the distribution of reaction times to emergency situations among various types of professional drivers.

Exercise 5

Check your answers against those in the ANSWER section.

A travel agency selected samples of hotels from each of three major chains and recorded the occupancy rate for each hotel on a specific date. The occupancy rate is the percentage of the total number of rooms that were occupied the previous night. The results are as follows:

Best Eastern	Comfort Inn	Quality Court
58%	69%	72%
57	67	80
67	62	84
63	69	94
61	77	86
64		

Do these data suggest any difference in the occupancy rates? Use the .05 significance level. Assume that the percentages of occupancy rates are not normally distributed.

Problem 7

A sample of 12 auto mechanics was ranked by the supervisor regarding their mechanical ability and their social compatibility. The results are as follows:

Worker	Mechanical Ability	Social Compatibility
1	1	4
2	2	3
3	3	2
4	4	6
5	5	1
6	6	5
7	7	8
8	8	12
9	9	11
10	10	9
11	11	7
12	12	10

Compute the coefficient of rank correlation. Can we conclude that there is a positive association in the population between the ranks of mechanical ability and social compatibility? Use the .05 significance level.

Solution

The first steps in finding the coefficient of rank correlation are (1) compute the difference between each set of ranks and then (2) square these differences. The difference is designated d.

Worker	Mechanical Ability	Social Compatibility	d	d^2
1	1	4	-3	9
2	2	3	-1	1
3	3	2	1	1
4	4	6	-2	4
5	5	1	4	16
6	6	5	1	1
7	7	8	-1	1
8	8	12	-4	16
9	9	11	-2	4
10	10	9	1	1
11	11	7	4	16
12	12	10	2	4
			0	74

Applying formula 15–6:

$$r_s = 1 - \frac{6(\Sigma d^2)}{n(n^2 - 1)} = 1 - \frac{6(74)}{12(12^2 - 1)} = .74$$

The value .74 indicates a fairly strong positive association between the ranks of mechanical ability and social compatibility. It appears those workers with more mechanical ability also show more social compatibility.

Could this association be due to chance? Use the .05 significance level. To answer this question we first state the null and alternate hypotheses.

H_0: The rank correlation in the population is zero.
H_1: The rank correlation in the population is positive.

Note the alternate hypothesis suggests a one-tailed test. There are ten degrees of freedom, found by $n - 2 = 12 - 2 = 10$. To locate the critical value refer to Appendix F. For the .05 level the critical value of t is 1.812. H_0 is rejected if the computed value of t is greater than 1.812. Using formula 15–7, the computed t is 3.48.

$$t = r_s \sqrt{\frac{n - 2}{1 - r_s^2}} = .74 \sqrt{\frac{12 - 2}{1 - (.74)^2}} = 3.48$$

Since the computed value of 3.48 exceeds the critical value of 1.812, H_0 is rejected and H_1 accepted. It is concluded that there is a positive association between the ranks of social compatibility and mechanical ability among auto mechanics.

Exercise 6

Check your answers against those in the ANSWER section.

The sports editors of the two daily Detroit newspapers predicted the order of finish for the upcoming Big Ten football season.

Team	News	Free Press
Penn State	1	2
Ohio State	2	1
Michigan	3	5
Iowa	4	6
Wisconsin	5	3
Michigan State	6	7
Indiana	7	8
Minnesota	8	9
Purdue	9	10
Illinois	10	4
Northwestern	11	11

Compute the coefficient of rank correlation. Interpret.

CHAPTER ASSIGNMENT 15

Nonparametric Methods: Analysis of Ranked Data

Name _____ Section _____ Score _____

Part I Select the correct answer and write the appropriate letter in the space provided.

___ 1. For nonparametric tests
    a. the population must be normal.
    b. there cannot be more than two populations.
    c. the populations must be independent.
    d. assumptions regarding the shape of the population are not necessary.

___ 2. Which of the following is **not** an example of a nonparametric test?
    a. sign test.
    b. median test.
    c. one-way ANOVA.
    d. Kruskal-Wallis test.

___ 3. Which of the following tests require paired observations or dependent samples?
    a. sign test and Kruskal-Wallis.
    b. Wilcoxon's rank-sum and signed-rank tests.
    c. coefficient of rank correlation and Wilcoxon rank-sum test.
    d. sign test and Wilcoxon signed-rank test.

___ 4. The Wilcoxon signed-rank test is stronger than the sign test because the
    a. Wilcoxon uses interval scale.
    b. sign test actually uses independent observations.
    c. sign test has fewer observations.
    d. Wilcoxon considers the magnitude of the differences.

___ 5. Which of the following conditions must be met for the sign test?
    a. independent samples.
    b. at least 30 observations.
    c. dependent samples.
    d. all of the above.

___ 6. The *z* distribution is used as the test statistic for the Wilcoxon rank-sum test when
    a. each sample has at least 8 observations.
    b. the populations are normal.
    c. the populations have equal standard deviations.
    d. the samples are dependent.

___ 7. The binomial distribution is used as the test statistic for which of the following tests?
    a. sign test.
    b. Wilcoxon signed-rank test.
    c. Wilcoxon rank-sum test.
    d. Kruskal-Wallis test.

___ 8. Which of the following nonparametric tests can be used when comparing more than two populations?
    a. sign test.
    b. Kruskal-Wallis test.
    c. median test.
    d. Wilcoxon signed-rank test.

9. What is the difference between Pearson's and Spearman's coefficients of correlation.
    a. Spearman cannot be negative.
    b. Pearson requires that n be at least 10.
    c. Spearman uses ranked data.
    d. Pearson uses nominal data.

10. The Kruskal-Wallis is a nonparametric alternative to
    a. the chi-square tests.
    b. the paired t test.
    c. the independent t test.
    d. ANOVA.

Part II Fill in the blank with the correct answer.

11. What test is a nonparametric alternative to the paired t test? _____

12. What test is a nonparametric alternative to the one-way ANOVA? _____

13. The Wilcoxon rank-sum test requires that each of the samples contain at least how many observations? _____

14. Spearman's coefficient of rank correlation can range between what two values?_____

15. Under what conditions can the standard normal distribution be used as the test statistic for the sign test?
_____

Part III Record your answer in the space provided. Show essential work.

16. The National Association of Certified Public Accountants selected a sample of taxpayers with gross incomes of more than $100,000. They asked two major accounting firms to compute the income tax liability for each sampled taxpayer. Use the sign test and the .10 significance level to determine if there is a difference in the liability.

Taxpayer	Sheet Tax Service	Square Deal
Schwind	18.9	28.0
Gankowski	33.1	24.8
Virost	38.2	28.0
Williamson	30.2	38.0
Govito	30.7	31.7
Trares	30.9	25.7
Willbond	28.1	30.7
Fowler	27.2	29.9
Hawley	30.2	31.0
Hall	26.2	34.5
Sanchez	33.4	35.3
Naymik	33.6	28.2

State the null and the alternate hypotheses.

H_0:_____

H_1:_____

State the decision rule.

Compute the value of the test statistic.

What is your decision regarding the null hypothesis. Interpret the result.

_____

_____

_____

_____

17. Refer to Problem 16. Rework the problem using the Wilcoxon signed-rank test.

State the null and the alternate hypotheses.

H_0:_____

H_1:_____

State the decision rule.

Compute the value of the test statistic.

What is your decision regarding the null hypothesis? Interpret the result.

_____

_____

_____

_____

18. A large Publishing Company wants to compare the annual operating costs of two brands of copying machines. The chief accountant gathered the following information. At the .05 significance level is there a difference in the operating costs of the two machines? The distributions of costs are not normally distributed.

Copier A	Copier B
12,965	4,462
13,145	4,990
13,504	5,106
13,603	5,844
13,727	7,470
13,833	7,740
13,925	8,429
14,438	9,954
14,948	10,975
15,202	12,532
	13,338
	14,828
	21,641
	23,045
	28,110

State the null and the alternate hypotheses.

H_0:_____

H_1:_____

State the decision rule.

Compute the value of the test statistic.

What is your decision regarding the null hypothesis? Interpret the result.

_____
_____
_____
_____

19. A retired husband and wife were asked to rate their favorite day-time soaps on a scale of 1 to 20. Their ratings are:

Soap	Husband	Wife
Mother Knows Best	1	3
Parlor Games	20	18
Teddy	3	2
Sam's Other Sister	5	7
Time Elapses	4	5
Sands in the Ocean	16	19
Laugh, Laugh	10	11
Hurry Home	3	4
Stall No More	9	9
Tidlie, Toodle	6	4

a. Rank each of the shows for the husband and the wife.

b. Compute the coefficient of rank correlation.

16

STATISTICAL QUALITY CONTROL

CHAPTER GOALS

After completing this chapter, you will be able to:

1. Discuss the role of statistical quality control in evaluating the quality of production in a manufacturing or service operation.
2. Define the quality control terms chance causes, in control, and out of control.
3. Distinguish between variable and attribute control charts.
4. Construct two charts for variables—a mean chart and a range chart.
5. Construct two charts for attributes—a percent defective chart and a chart for the number of defects per unit.
6. Construct an operating characteristic curve for various sampling plans.

Introduction

Prior to the Industrial Revolution, a craftsman was in complete charge of the quality of the finished product. Before selling a buggy, the craftsman made sure the wheels were round, all the bolts were tight, etc. The Industrial Revolution changed the way clothing, furniture, farm implements, shoes, and other consumer items were manufactured. Employees were organized in assembly lines and each employee performed one or two tasks. To control the quality of the output, all of the finished products were inspected, that is, there was 100 percent inspection after the manufacturing operation was completed.

During the 1930s and 1940s the concept of **statistical quality control** was developed. Instead of 100 percent inspection, a sample of the parts produced is selected and inspected during production and a decision made regarding the quality of the production. The goal was to minimize the amount of defective material produced.

Causes of Variation

On a production line there is no such thing as two identical parts. The difference between two parts may be very small but they are different. The tensile strength of a roll of steel wire varies throughout the length of wire, and not every McDonald's Quarter Pounder has exactly 0.25 lbs. of meat. There are two general categories of variation in a process: chance causes and assignable causes. **Chance causes** are large in number and random in nature and usually cannot be eliminated. The amount of material or "shot" of plastic used in the injection molding of a plastic product varies due to many conditions. Conditions such as temperature, dust and dirt, etc. are not always constant causing the amount of plastic to vary slightly. An **assignable cause** of variation is nonrandom variation which can be eliminated or greatly reduced. Suppose the sample boxes of breakfast cereal are significantly overweight. An investigation revealed that the lever controlling the weight of the cereal had become loose. Thus, the assignable cause is a loose lever, and it can be easily reset and tightened.

In recent years competition from foreign manufacturers, especially in the automotive industry, has caused American firms to revamp and strengthen their quality control programs.

Control Charts

A useful tool for insuring that a product is manufactured properly is a **statistical control chart**. Control charts are based on the theory of sampling. We select random samples of the product during the production process portray the results and in chart form. These control charts are useful for separating random causes of variation from those that are assignable to some particular condition.

On a chart there is an *in control* area and an *out of control* area. If the plot on the chart representing production is in the "in control" area, it is assumed that the production is satisfactory. If the plot on the chart is in the "out of control" area, it is assumed that the production is unsatisfactory. There is an **upper control limit** (UCL), and a **lower control limit** (LCL). A typical chart before any plots are made appears as:

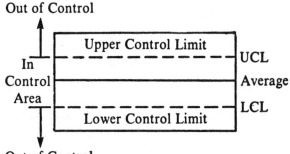

If we are concerned with the mean outside diameter of a pipe and if the manufacturing process is "in control," the sample mean will fall between the UCL and LCL 99.73 percent of time by chance. This is the same as ± three standard deviations from the arithmetic mean.

Types of Control Charts

There are two basic types of control charts. We use control charts for **variables** when the characteristic under investigation can be measured, such as the outside diameter of a pipe or the weight of the contents of a bottle of cola. Two types of control charts for variables are the **mean chart** and the **range chart**. The mean chart shows management, production, engineers, machine operators, and others whether the arithmetic mean weight, length, outside diameter, inside diameter, etc., is in control (satisfactory), or out of control (unsatisfactory).

A **range chart** has a similar purpose, that is, to depict graphically whether the ranges are in control or out of control. As examples, the two charts for variables might appear as:

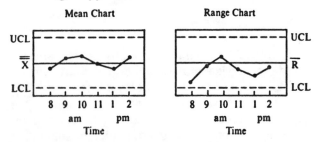

An analysis of the two charts reveals that both the arithmetic mean length of a piece of steel and the range of the lengths of the pieces are satisfactory (in control).

Some products can only be classified as being "acceptable" or "unacceptable." Charts developed for these products are called **attribute charts**. For example, a light bulb is either defective or not defective. When this type of classification is used, control charts for these attributes include the **percent defective chart** and **c chart**. The **percent defective chart** drawn to control the percent defective for a ball bearing might appear as:

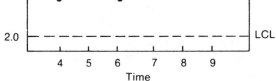

Percent Defective Chart

The process was in control from 4 p.m. until 8 p.m. The 9 p.m. check revealed that the percent defective exceeded the upper control limit of 4 percent. The quality control engineer would no doubt take steps to bring the process back into control (below 4 percent).

It is difficult for many processes to manufacture all the units without a defect appearing. For example, the exterior of an automobile being manufactured might have a paint glob on the hood, the trunk lid might not be centered correctly, and there might be a steel sliver protruding on the left front door. In that case, there would be three defects per unit. A chart designed to portray the number of defects per unit is called a **c-bar chart**. For this problem it might appear as:

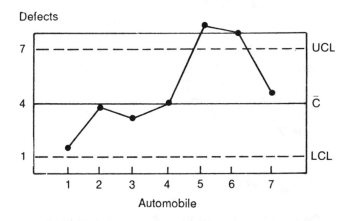

Based on the above chart, between 1 and 7 defects per car is expected. The average is 4. However, the number of defects in car 5 and car 6 exceeded the upper control limit and the process would be declared "out of control." It was brought under control for car 7. That is, the process was back "in control."

Acceptance Sampling

In any business situation there is concern over the quality of an incoming shipment of a product. For example, a cola manufacturer purchases plastic 2 liter bottles from a blow molding supplier. The plastic bottles are received in lots of 2,400. The manufacturer does not expect each bottle to be perfect, but he has an agreement with the supplier regarding the percent of the bottles that are defective. The usual procedure is to check the quality of the incoming product using a statistical sampling plan. A random sample of n units is selected from the lot of N units. The inspection will determine the number of defective parts in the sample. This number is compared to the predetermined number called the **acceptance number**. If the number of defects exceeds the acceptance number, the lot is rejected and returned to the supplier. As an example, the cola manufacturer selects a random sample of 30 bottles and inspect each. If 3 or less are defective the entire lot of bottles is accepted. Otherwise, the shipment is returned to the supplier.

Acceptance sampling is a decision-making process. According to the specific sampling plan, the lot is either acceptable or unacceptable. So there are two decisions that can be made. In addition, there are two states of nature. If the lot is acceptable and the sampling process reveals it to be good, or the lot is unacceptable and the sampling process shows the lot to be unacceptable, then a correct decision has been made. However, there are two additional possibilities. The lot may actually contain more defects than it should, but the sampling process reveals it to be acceptable. This is called a **beta error** or **consumer's risk**. If the lot is actually within agreed upon limits, but the sampling process reveals that it should be rejected, this is called the **producer's risk**.

An **operating characteristic** curve is developed to show the probabilities of accepting incoming lots with various quality levels. The binomial distribution is used to determine the probabilities corresponding to the various quality levels.

GLOSSARY

Statistical quality control—Developed in the 1930s and 1940s, it was a new concept for controlling the quality of mass-produced items. Instead of inspecting each item, a sample of the production is taken and a decision regarding all the production during a given period is made.

Quality control charts—They portray graphically the results of samples taken during the production period. They have two areas—an area of "in control" and an area of "out of control." If the sample result falls in the "in control" area it means that production is satisfactory. Otherwise, it is "out of control" (unsatisfactory).

Upper control limit and lower control limit—The two points which separate the in control area from the out of control area.

Attributes—A product or service is classified as acceptable or unacceptable. No reading or measurement is obtained.

Variable—A reading or measurement on the product or service is obtained.

Acceptance sampling—A random sample of n units is selected from a lot of N units. If c or less units are found defective among the n sampled units the lot is accepted, otherwise it is rejected.

Acceptance number—The maximum number of defective units allowed in a sample before the lot will be rejected. The number is usually designated as c.

Operating characteristic curve—A graph developed to show the probability of accepting lots of various quality levels. The horizontal axis shows the proportion of defective units in the population and the vertical axis the probability that a lot of that quality is accepted.

Producer's risk—The likelihood that an acceptable lot is rejected.

Consumer's risk—The likelihood that a lot that should not be accepted is actually accepted.

CHAPTER PROBLEMS

Problem 1

A machine set to fill a bottle with 60.0 grams of liquid was started at 7 a.m. today. Slight variations (called chance variations) were expected. The quality control inspector made her initial check of the weights at 8 a.m. She selected five bottles from the first hour of production and weighed the contents of each bottle. The results of the first seven inspections follow:

			Sample		
Time	1	2	3	4	5
8 a.m.	60.0	59.9	60.0	60.0	60.1
9 a.m.	60.0	60.2	60.1	60.2	60.0
10 a.m.	60.1	60.1	60.0	59.8	60.0
11 a.m.	60.0	59.8	60.0	60.0	60.2
12 noon	60.2	60.0	59.8	60.1	59.8
1 p.m.	60.3	60.1	59.9	60.1	59.8
2 p.m.	60.1	59.8	59.7	59.9	59.8

Develop a control chart for (a) the sample means and (b) the sample ranges.

Solution

a. The upper and lower control limits for the mean are determined using formula 16–2

$$\text{UCL and LCL} = \overline{\overline{X}} \pm A_2 \overline{R} \qquad\qquad 16\text{–}2$$

$\overline{\overline{X}}$ is the mean of the sample means, $\overline{R}$ is the mean of the ranges, and A_2 is a factor which is related to the standard deviation. A_2 is based on the number of observations taken each hour, that is the sample size.

Statistical theory has shown that there is a constant relationship between the range and the standard deviation, for a given sample size. A_2 expresses this constant relationship. To obtain the specific value for A_2 refer to Appendix B where the number of items in the sample is 5. The value is 0.577 in this example.

Refer to the table below. The sample values for 8 a.m. are 60.0, 59.9, 60.0, 60.0 and 60.1 grams respectively. The sum of those five values is 300.0, so the mean is 60.0 grams (found by 300.0/5). The means for all remaining hours are computed. The sum of the seven means is 419.98, and the mean of these seven means ($\overline{\overline{X}}$) is 59.997, found by 419.98/7.

For the 8 a.m. check the highest weight is 60.1 grams, the lowest 59.9. The difference between the highest and lowest (the range) is 0.2. The sum of the seven ranges is 2.4 and the mean 0.343, found by 2.4/7. This information is summarized in the following table.

Time	Sample 1	2	3	4	5	ΣX	$\overline{X}$	R
8 a.m.	60.0	59.9	60.0	60.0	60.1	300.0	60.00	0.2
9 a.m.	60.0	60.2	60.1	60.2	60.0	300.5	60.10	0.2
10 a.m.	60.1	60.1	60.0	59.8	60.0	300.0	60.00	0.3
11 a.m.	60.0	59.8	60.0	60.0	60.2	300.0	60.00	0.4
12 noon	60.2	60.0	59.8	60.1	59.8	299.9	59.98	0.4
1 p.m.	60.3	60.1	59.9	60.1	59.8	300.2	60.04	0.5
2 p.m.	60.1	59.8	59.7	59.9	59.8	299.3	59.86	0.4
							419.98	2.4

As noted, the control limits for the hourly sample means are determined using formula 16–2.

$$\text{UCL and LCL} = \overline{\overline{X}} \pm A_2\overline{R}$$
$$= 59.997 \pm 0.577(0.343)$$
$$= 59.997 \pm 0.198$$

So the lower control limit is set at 59.799 and the upper control limit is set at 60.195. The MINITAB software system was used to generate the following control charts. There is a small difference in the limits due to rounding, but it is clear that the process is in control until 2 p.m. At that time the sample mean drops to 59.86 grams. This is still greater than the lower limit on the chart of 59.80 grams. However, this rather dramatic downward shift is likely an indicator of trouble and should be investigated.

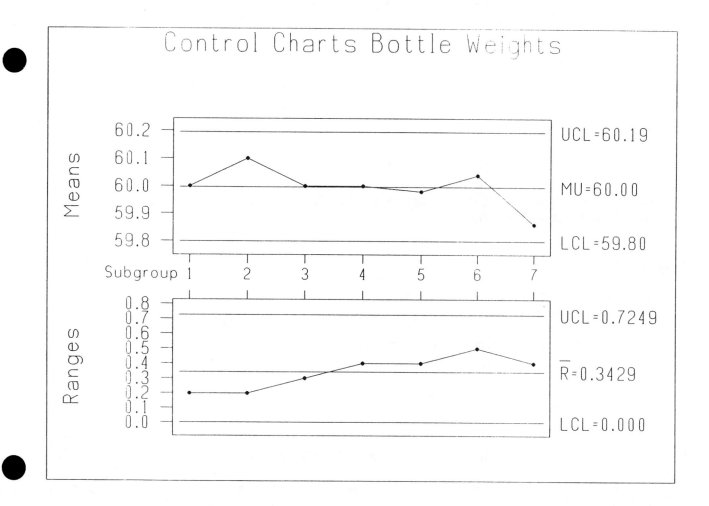

b. The LCL and UCL of the control chart for ranges is constructed using formula 16–3.

$$\text{Upper control limit UCL} = D_4 \bar{R}$$
$$\text{Lower control limit LCL} = D_3 \bar{R}$$

The factors D_3 and D_4 (like A_2) are developed from the constant relationship between the range and the standard deviation. The factors D_3 and D_4 are also obtained from Appendix B. To obtain the values go down the left column to the number in the sample (5) and then go across to the columns headed D_3 and D_4. The factor D_4 = 2.115 and D_3 = 0. To determine the UCL and LCL for the range chart:

$$\text{UCL} = D_4 \bar{R} = 2.115 \ (0.343) = 0.725$$
$$\text{LCL} = D_3 \bar{R} = 0 \ (0.343) = 0$$

The process appears to be in control for variability.

Problem 2

The Administration of Rossford General Hospital is investigating the quality of meals served to patients. A ten-day survey is conducted by submitting a questionnaire to 50 patients with the noon meal each day. The patients are required only to indicate whether the meal was satisfactory or unsatisfactory. The results are as follows:

Date		Sample Size	Number of Unsatisfactory Meals
May	1	50	2
	2	50	3
	3	50	1
	4	50	4
	5	50	8
	6	50	2
	7	50	5
	8	50	4
	9	50	7
	10	50	4

Construct a control chart for the proportion defective. In this case, the chart is really measuring the proportion of the patients dissatisfied with the meal.

Solution

This problem requires the use of an attribute chart because a meal is classified only as satisfactory or unsatisfactory. No "measurement" is obtained.

The upper and lower control limits are determined using formula 16–5

$$\text{UCL AND LCL} = \bar{p} \pm 3 \sqrt{\frac{\bar{p}\ (1 - \bar{p})}{n}} \qquad \text{16–5}$$

where $\bar{p}$ is the proportion defective over all the samples and n is the number in each sample.

The value of p, the proportion unsatisfactory, is computed by first determining the proportion of unsatisfactory meals for each sample.

Date	Sample Size	Number of Unsatisfactory Meals	Proportion of Unsatisfactory Meals
May 1	50	2	.04
2	50	3	.06
3	50	1	.02
4	50	4	.08
5	50	8	.16
6	50	2	.04
7	50	5	.10
8	50	4	.08
9	50	7	.14
10	50	4	.08
			.80

Then, to compute the mean percent defective:

$$\bar{p} = \frac{\text{Sum of proportion drive}}{\text{Number of samples}} = \frac{0.80}{10} = 0.08$$

$$\text{UCL AND LCL} = \bar{p} \pm 3 \sqrt{\frac{\bar{p}(1-\bar{p})}{n}}$$

$$= .08 \pm 3 \sqrt{\frac{.08(1-.08)}{50}}$$

$$= .08 \pm .115$$

$$= 0 \text{ and } .195$$

Thus, the control limits for the proportion of unsatisfactory meals are set at 0 and .195. The lower control limit could not logically be a negative number. The following MINITAB chart indicates that the proportion of unsatisfactory meals is well within the control limit.

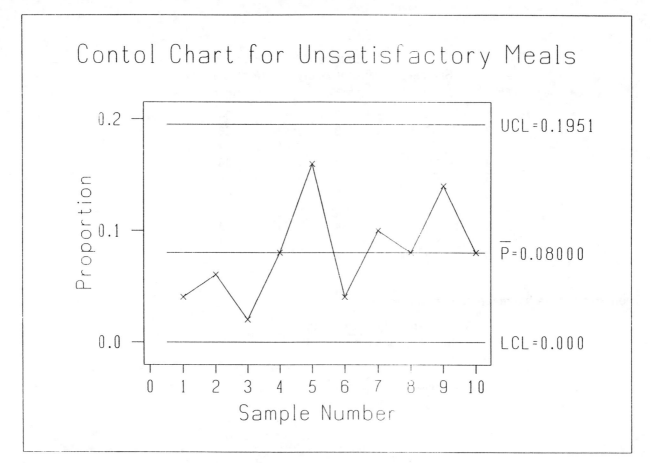

Contol Chart for Unsatisfactory Meals

Proportion

0.2 — UCL=0.1951

0.1 — $\bar{P}$=0.08000

0.0 — LCL=0.000

0 1 2 3 4 5 6 7 8 9 10

Sample Number

Problem 3

A new automobile assembly line was put into operation. The number of defects on the exterior of the first ten cars off the assembly line were: 3, 5, 4, 6, 2, 3, 5, 4, 2, and 4. Construct a $\bar{c}$ chart for the number of defects per unit.

Solution

the formula for the upper and lower limits for a $\bar{c}$ chart are determined using Formula 16–6

$$\text{UCL and LCL} = \bar{c} \pm 3\sqrt{\bar{c}}$$

The total number of defects in the first ten cars is 38, found by 3 + 5 + 4 + 6 + 2 + 3 + 5 + 4 + 2 + 4. The mean number of defects per car $(\bar{c})$ is:

$$\bar{c} = \frac{\Sigma \text{ of the number of defects}}{\text{Total number of cars}}$$

$$= \frac{38}{10} = 3.8$$

The upper and lower control limits are:

$$\text{UCL and LCL} = \bar{c} \pm 3\sqrt{\bar{c}}$$

$$= 3.8 \pm 3\sqrt{3.8}$$

$$= 3.8 \pm 5.848$$

$$\text{UCL} = 9.648$$

$$\text{LCL} = 0 \text{ (since the number of defects cannot be less than 0)}$$

232

Based on the sample data for the $\bar{c}$ bar chart, more than 99 percent (99.73% to be more precise) of the cars will have between 0 and 9.648 defects.

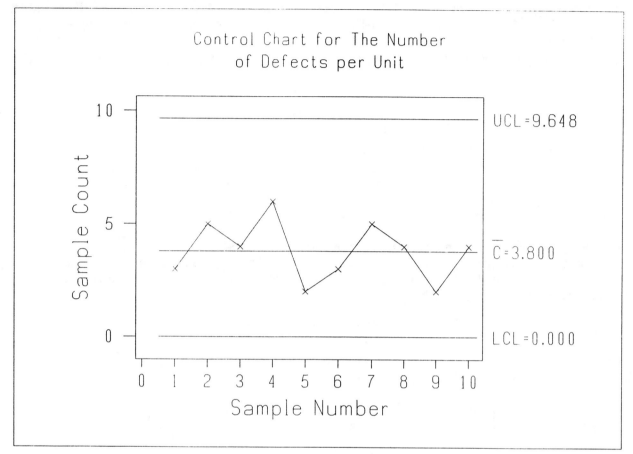

Problem 4

The Berry Cola Company processes a soft drink with a blueberry flavor added to the cola. It is packaged in 2-liter plastic bottles. The bottles are purchased from Persall Plastics in lots of 2,400. Berry Cola has agreed to select a sample of 25 incoming bottles and inspect them for all quality characteristics. If 2 or less defective bottles are found in the sample, the lot is considered acceptable. Suppose we want to develop an operating characteristic curve showing the likelihood that lots will be accepted that are 5%, 10%, or 20% defective.

Solution

This is an example of attribute sampling, because each bottle sampled is classified as either acceptable or not acceptable. No measurement or "reading" is obtained on the bottle.

The binomial distribution is used to compute the various probabilities. Recall that to employ the binomial distribution four requirements must be met.

1. There are only two possible outcomes. A bottle is either acceptable or not acceptable.
2. There is a fixed number of trials. The number of trials is the sample size, 25 in this case.
3. There is a constant probability of success. A success is the probability of finding a defective part. In this case, Berry Cola is concerned about lots that are 5 percent, 10 percent and 20 percent defective.
4. The trials are independent. The probability the fifth bottle is defective is not related to the probability the eighth bottle is defective.

The binomial probabilities are given in Appendix A. First, let's assume the lot is actually 5% defective, so $p =$ .05, n, the size of the sample, is 25, and the acceptance number is 2. We usually let c refer to the acceptance number, so here $c = 2$. To find the probability turn to Appendix A, an n of 25, and the column where $p = .05$. Berry Cola will allow 0, 1, or 2 defects in the sample of 25. Find the row where r, the number of defects, is 0 and read the probability. It is .277. The probability of 1 defect in a sample of 25 where $p = .05$ is .365. The probability of 2 defects is .231. Adding these three probabilities (0, 1 and 2) give the probability of accepting a lot that is actually 5 percent defective. The result is .873, found by .277 + .365 + .231. Hence, the probability of accepting a lot that is actually 5 percent defective is .873. This is often written in the following shorthand form.

$$P(X \leqslant 2 \mid p = .05 \text{ and } n = 25) = .873$$

where X is the number of defects and the slash | means "given that."

To find the probability of 2 or fewer defects, when $p = .10$:

$$P(X \leqslant 2 \mid p = .10, n = 25) = .072 + .199 + .266 = .537$$

The probability of 2 or fewer defects when $p = .20$ is .099, found by .004 + .024 + .071.

The following OC curve shows the various values of p and their corresponding probability of accepting a lot of that quality. The management of Berry Cola will be able to quickly evaluate the acceptance probabilities for the various quality levels. Other probabilities can be developed by using the normal approximation to the binomial distribution (not discussed here).

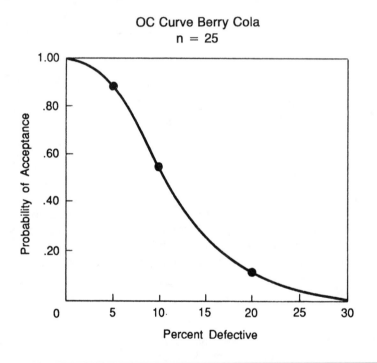

OC Curve Berry Cola
n = 25

Exercise 1

Check your answers against those in the ANSWER section.

Use the sampling plan developed above and compute the probability that a lot which is 30% defective is accepted.

CHAPTER ASSIGNMENT 16

Statistical Quality Control

Name _____ Section _____ Score _____

Part I Select the correct answer and write the appropriate letter in the space provided.

___ 1. Statistical quality control was developed
   a. in the dark ages.
   b. during the industrial revolution.
   c. in the 1930s and the 1940s.
   d. in the 1960s.

___ 2. Chance causes are
   a. random in nature.
   b. due to some specific cause, like a worn tool.
   c. the result of the use of control charts.
   d. used in hypothesis testing.

___ 3. A variable control chart is
   a. based on a measurement or a reading.
   b. used to estimate the probability of acceptance.
   c. based on whether the product is acceptable or unacceptable.
   d. used to estimate the standard deviation.

___ 4. Which of the following is a variable control chart?
   a. *c*-bar chart.
   b. percent defective chart.
   c. mean and range chart.
   d. all of the above.

___ 5. The upper and lower control limits are how far away from the mean?
   a. 99.73 percent.
   b. plus or minus two standard deviations.
   c. plus or minus three standard deviations.
   d. half the range.

___ 6. In acceptance sampling
   a. the sample size is *n*.
   b. the binomial distribution is used.
   c. the letter *c* is the acceptance number.
   d. all of the above.

___ 7. A particular sampling plan consists of 20 items. The lot is considered acceptable if there are 0 or 1 defects found in the sample.
   a. *c* is equal to 1.
   b. the probability of accepting a lot 20 percent defective is .070.
   c. *n* is equal to 20.
   d. all of the above.

___ 8. Refer to Question 7. If the acceptance number is increased from 1 to 2, the probability of accepting a lot 20 percent defective will
   a. stay the same.
   b. increase.
   c. decrease.
   d. cannot tell from the information given.

___ 9. An operating characteristic curve shows the probability of
   a. finding a particular sample size.
   b. finding a particular value for c.
   c. rejecting a lot.
   d. accepting a lot with a given percent defective.

___ 10. The producer's risk is
   a. the likelihood an acceptable lot is rejected.
   b. the likelihood an acceptable lot is accepted.
   c. a new value for c.
   d. the size of the sample.

Part II Fill in the blank with the correct answer.

11. A _____ is a graph that shows the probability of accepting a lot at various quality levels.

12. Which probability distribution underlies the percent defective chart? _____

13. List two attribute charts.
   a. _____
   b. _____

14. What probability distribution is the basis for an OC curve? _____

15. What type of variable classifies the product service as acceptable or not acceptable? _____

Part III Record the answers in the space provided. Show essential calculations.

16. The North Central Insurance Company is studying recent claim history. A sample of 5 claims for each of the last 5 months is obtained. Develop a control chart for the mean and the range of the amount (in $000) of settled claims for each month. Does it appear that any of the months are unusual?

Month	Samples					Total	Mean	Range
	1	2	3	4	5			
January	1.1	0.9	1.3	1.5	1.2			
February	0.5	1.4	1.4	1.3	1.1			
March	0.4	0.3	0.9	0.9	1.0			
April	1.3	1.6	1.6	1.5	0.6			
May	1.2	0.3	1.1	0.7	0.6			

a. Determine the upper and lower control limits for the mean.

b. Determine the upper and lower control limits for the range.

17. A high speed machine produces a small plastic spacer. To check on the machine's performance, a sample of 30 spacers is selected each hour and the number of defects in the sample determined. On the basis of the samples taken yesterday determine the control limits for a percent defective chart.

Sample Number	Number in Sample	Number of Defects	Proportion Defective
1	30	1	
2	30	5	
3	30	5	
4	30	1	
5	30	5	
6	30	9	
7	30	5	
8	30	10	
9	30	7	
10	30	3	

18. Dr. Sundar is chairman of the Sociology Department at Southeast State University. He is studying the number of students who drop a sociology course after they initially registered. The following is the number of drops per section for the 15 courses offered last semester in the department:

4, 9, 3, 4, 4, 4, 8, 6, 8, 2, 1, 2, 2, 3, 5

What are the control limits for a c-bar chart of the number of drops?

19. The Mills Hardware Company purchases various types of pliers, in lots of 5,000, for sale in the Home Improvement Department. The Purchasing Department inspects 20 pliers at random before accepting each lot. If 2 or less of the pliers are defective the lot is accepted. If 3 or more of the sample are defective the lot is returned to the manufacturer. Determine the probability of accepting a lot that is 10 percent defective. Determine the probability of finding a lot that is 20 percent defective.

17

INDEX NUMBERS

CHAPTER GOALS

After completing this chapter, you will be able to:

1. Cite the reasons why index numbers are constructed and published on a regular basis.
2. Construct weighted and unweighted indexes.
3. Understand how the Consumer Price Index is constructed and its applications in determining real income, deflating sales and the purchasing power of the dollar.

Introduction

There are thousands of indexes published on a regular basis by the federal government, foreign governments, the United Nations, magazines devoted to business such as *Forbes,* universities, and so on. The main use of index numbers is to describe the percent change in price, quantity, or value from one time period (called the **base period**) to another time period. The **base** of most indexes is 100. At this writing, the base period for the Consumer Price Index (CPI) and most other indexes is the period 1982–84, written 1982–84 = 100. If the CPI for this month is 149.2 it indicates that the overall price of goods and services purchased by American consumers increased 49.2 percent from the 1982–84 base to the present month. Likewise, if the index measuring the quantity of pig iron exported is presently 90.0 (1986 = 100), it indicates that the quantity of exports decreased 10 percent from 1986 to the present.

Simple Index

Unweighted, or **simple indexes**, are calculated by dividing the number in the *given period* by the number in the *base period*. For a price index, an unweighted index of price P is found by formula 17–1.

$$P = \frac{p_t}{p_o}(100) \qquad\qquad 17\text{--}1$$

where p_t is the price in the given period (any period other than the base period), and p_o is the price in the base period. As an example, suppose the wholesale price of tomatoes in 1988 (selected as the base period

and written 1988 = 100), was 32¢ a pound, and currently they are 69¢ a pound. The index of tomato prices for the given period is 215.6, found by (69¢/32¢)(100). This reveals that the price of tomatoes increased 115.6 percent from 1988 to the present time.

Simple Aggregate Index

A slightly more complex problem would be to compute the **aggregate index** for several commodities. To illustrate, suppose the prices of several items for 1985 and 1995 are:

		Prices	
Commodity	Unit	1985	1995
Battery	Each	$ 60.00	$ 70.00
Tires	Set of 4	240.00	280.00
Gasoline	gallon	1.23	1.05

A simple price index could be computed by summing the three items for 1985 ($60 + $240 + $1.23 = $301.23), and for 1995 ($70 + $280.00 + 1.05 = 351.05). Using 1985 as the base, this index gives a measure of change in price of this group, or aggregate, of items over the 10-year period.

Inserting the 1995 and 1985 totals in the following formula results in an index of 116.5.

$$P = \frac{\Sigma p_t}{\Sigma p_o}(100) = \frac{\$351.05}{\$301.23}(100) = 116.5$$

This indicates there has been a 16.5 percent increase in the prices over the 10 year period from 1985 to 1995.

This method of computing a price index has two major disadvantages. It fails to consider the relative importance (weights) of the items, and it does not take into account the differing units. The index would be different, for example, if we considered one tire instead of a set of four tires.

Weighted Price Index

There are two common methods of computing a weighted index. The most commonly used is the **Laspeyres** method named after its originator. It uses *base-year* quantities as weights. In essence, it assumes that consumption of the items selected for the index do not change from the base period to the current period. Thus, only price is allowed to change and the index for the current period reflects this price change.

The formula is:

$$P = \frac{\Sigma p_t q_o}{\Sigma p_o q_o}(100) \qquad \qquad 17\text{--}2$$

where p_t is the price in the current period, p_o is the price in the base period, and q_o the quantity consumed in the base period. The Laspeyres method—with some modification—is the method used for most weighted price indexes.

The **Paasche** method uses the *current quantity* weights and adjusts the base each time a new period is considered. The formula is:

$$P = \frac{\Sigma p_t q_t}{\Sigma p_o q_t}(100) \qquad \qquad 17\text{--}4$$

A **value index** measures the change in value of a group of items from one time period to another. The formula is:

$$V = \frac{\Sigma p_t q_t}{\Sigma p_o q_o}(100) \qquad \qquad 17\text{--}5$$

The Consumer Price Index

The **Consumer Price Index** (CPI) is the most well known price index. Actually there are currently two consumer price indexes being published by the federal government every month. The Consumer Price Index for all consumers is applicable for about 80 percent of all households. The other CPI, the Consumer Price Index for City Wage Earners and Clerical Worker Families covers about 40 percent of the households in the United States.

They are designed to measure the price changes in a fixed "market basket" of goods and services purchased by most American consumers using the base period 1982–84. Included are such diverse items as the price of gasoline, bread, dental fees, taxes, and soft drinks. It has been published regularly since 1921.

The CPI is not just one index. Separate indexes are published for food and beverages, transportation, medical care, entertainment, rent, and apparel. In addition, there are CPIs for most large cities, such as Dallas, Detroit, and Seattle.

Real Income

Both consumer price indexes have a number of other applications. The CPI can be used to determine **real income**. The computation of real income allows a person to evaluate whether his or her take-home pay has been keeping up with price increases. If prices are rising faster than the increase in take-home pay (called money income) a person's standard of living is decreasing, meaning that she or he cannot purchase the same amount of goods and services as in the base period. Formula 17–6 for real income is:

$$\text{Real income} = \frac{\text{Money income}}{\text{CPI}}(100) \qquad 17\text{--}6$$

Purchasing Power of a Dollar

The **purchasing power of the dollar**, as the name implies, shows how much purchasing power the dollar has today compared with the base period. For a particular time period it is computed by:

$$\text{Purchasing power of dollar} = \frac{\$1}{\text{CPI}}(100) \qquad 17\text{--}8$$

GLOSSARY

Index number—It is a number which measures the change in price, quantity, or value from one time period (called the base period) to another time period (called the given period).

Base period—It is usually one year, such as 1982, which is used as a reference period. Changes in price, quantity or value are measured from the base period to another period, called the given period.

Base—It is the number in the denominator used to compute the index. Most indexes have the base of 100.

Laspeyres Price Index—A weighted aggregate price index that uses the quantities in the base period as weights.

Paasche Price Index—A weighted aggregate price index that uses the quantities in the current year as the weights.

Consumer Price Index—One of the most used indexes. It measures the change in the price consumers pay for goods and services from the base period of 1982–84 to the present month, or some other given period.

Given period—A period other than the base period.

Real income—A person's income adjusted for changes in price. It allows a person to determine whether his or her standard of living has increased, stayed the same, or decreased since the base period.

Purchasing power of the dollar—It is the value of one dollar in a given period compared with the value of a dollar in the base period.

CHAPTER PROBLEMS

Problem 1

The hourly earnings for registered nurses at St. Luke's Hospital for selected years between 1986 and 1992 is shown below. Using 1986 as the base period, develop an index that shows the changes in hourly earnings during the period. Interpret.

Year	Hourly Earnings
1986	$10.45
1988	12.66
1990	14.22
1992	15.91
1995	17.02

Solution

The wage in a selected period is divided by the wage in the base period and the result is multiplied by 100 (formula 17–1). The calculations are shown below. The usual practice is to report the index either to the nearest tenth or the nearest hundredth.

Year	Hourly Earnings	Index	Found by
1986	$10.45	100.0	($10.45/$10.45)(100)
1988	12.66	121.1	($12.66/$10.45)(100)
1990	14.22	136.1	($14.22/$10.45)(100)
1992	15.91	152.2	($15.91/$10.45)(100)
1995	17.02	162.9	($17.02/$10.45)(100)

The hourly earnings of the nurses increased by 62.9 percent from 1986 to 1995, found by 162.9 − 100.0.

Problem 2

An index is to be constructed to show the changes in the price of selected hardware items sold from 1986 to 1995. The prices and quantities consumed in the two periods are shown below.

	1986		1995	
	Price	Quantity	Price	Quantity
Hammer (each)	$ 6.00	100	$ 8.00	120
Linseed oil (qt.)	2.00	1,000	2.00	1,100
Sandpaper (sheet)	0.10	800	0.07	900
1/2 hp. motor (each)	30.00	10	35.00	15

Compute a simple aggregate price index, the Laspeyres price index, and the Paasche price index, using 1986 as the base period.

Solution

First the simple aggregate price index is computed. The prices of the four items for the base year (1986) and the current year are totaled.

	1986 Price	1995 Price
Hammer	$ 6.00	$ 8.00
Linseed oil	2.00	2.00
Sandpaper	0.10	0.07
1/2 hp. motor	30.00	35.00
Total	$38.10	$45.07

The formula for the simple price index is:

$$P = \frac{\Sigma p_i}{\Sigma p_o}(100) = \frac{\$45.07}{\$38.10}(100) = 118.3$$

The simple aggregate index shows the price has increased 18.3 percent in the six year period.

The simple, or unweighted index, does not take into account any of the quantities involved. For example, the price of sandpaper decreased by $0.03, but this will have little impact compare to the $2.00 increase in hammers or the $5.00 increase in the motor. A more meaningful measure is to consider the quantities consumed. The

Laspeyres index assumes that the quantities in the base period are still representative in the current period and uses them as weights. Recall that the formula 17–2 for the Laspeyres price index is:

$$P = \frac{\Sigma p_t q_o}{\Sigma p_o q_o}(100)$$

The calculations for the Laspeyres weighted-price index are shown below:

| | 1986 | | | 1995 | |
| | Price | Quantity | | Price | |
	p_o	q_o	$p_o q_o$	p_t	$p_t q_o$
Hammer	$6	100	$ 600	$8	$ 800
Linseed oil (qt.)	2	1,000	2,000	2	2,000
Sandpaper (sheet)	0.10	800	80	0.07	56
½ hp. motor (each)	30	10	300	35	350
			$2,980		$3,206

Applying formula 17–2:

$$P = \frac{\Sigma p_t q_o}{\Sigma p_o q_o}(100) = \frac{\$3,206}{\$2,980}(100) = 107.6$$

The quantity sold in the base period, q_o, is held constant, that is, it appears both in the denominator and in the numerator. Since the quantity sold is held constant, the only factor affecting the index is price. The price of these selected hardware items increased 7.6 percent between 1986 and 1995.

Note in the previous table involving hammers, linseed oil, etc., that the quantities sold changed from 1986 to 1995. Paasche's index reflects these changes. Computing the price index using the Paasche method gives 108.3.

| | 1986 Price | 1995 Quantity | | 1995 Price | 1995 Quantity | |
	p_o	q_t	$p_o q_t$	p_t	q_t	$p_t q_t$
Hammer (each)	$ 6.00	120	$ 720.00	$ 8.00	120	$ 960.00
Linseed oil (qt.)	2.00	1,100	2,200.00	2.00	1,100	2,200.00
Sandpaper (sheet)	0.10	900	90.00	0.07	900	63.00
½ hp. motor	30.00	15	450.00	35.00	15	525.00
			$3,460.00			$3,748.00

Formula 17–4 is used and the essential calculations are:

$$P = \frac{\Sigma p_t q_t}{\Sigma p_o q_t}(100) = \frac{\$3,748}{\$3,460}(100) = 108.3$$

Thus, the price of these selected items using current quantities consumed as weights increased 8.3 percent between 1986 and 1995. The Paasche method has one serious drawback. As the time period changes from 1993 to 1994 to 1995, etc., the quantity consumed for each one of those years must be collected and all the calculations redone.

Exercise 1

Check your answers against those in the ANSWER section.

The manager of a small marine discount store believes that prices of marine products have risen dramatically since 1988. Others disagree. To investigate, he selected a few items and recorded the prices and quantities sold the first week of April, 1988 and the first week of April 1995.

| | 1988 | | 1995 | |
	Price	Quantity Sold	Price	Quantity Sold
Economy marine battery	$ 25.00	32	$ 40.00	30
Steering cable	22.00	8	30.00	8
Bimini top	325.00	2	500.00	2
Depth finder	300.00	2	450.00	2

(a) Compute a simple aggregate cost (price) index. (b) Determine the weighted price index using the Laspeyres and Paasche methods.

Problem 3

Hannah Simpson, an accountant, graduated from college in 1985 and received a starting salary of $22,000. By 1996 her salary had increased to $50,000. The consumer price index (1982–84 = 100) in 1985 was 107.6 and in 1996 it was 150.7. Convert her salary to 1985 dollars and determine her real income. What conclusion would you make?

Solution

By converting her actual yearly income of $22,000 and $50,000 to real incomes, changes in her standard of living between two time periods can be evaluated. If money income is increasing faster than the consumer price index, then a person's standard of living is higher than the base period. This would mean in Hannah's case she could buy more goods and services in 1996 than in 1985. Conversely, if consumer prices are rising at a faster rate than her money income, then her standard of living is declining. That is, she can buy less. Real income is computed using formula 17–6, which is:

$$\text{Real income} = \frac{\text{Money income}}{\text{CPI}}(100)$$

For 1985
$$\text{Real Income} = \frac{\$22,000}{107.6}(100) = \$20,446$$

For 1996
$$\text{Real Income} = \frac{\$50,000}{150.7}(100) = \$33,179$$

Thus in terms of constant 1982–84 base period dollars, Hannah's salary increased $12,733, found by $33,179 – $20,446. This is an increase in real income of 62.3%, found by ($12,733/$20,446)(100).

Problem 4

The Consumer Price Index in the base period of 1982–84 is set at 100. The CPI was 148.2 in January 1996. What is the purchasing power of the dollar for the base period and January 1996?

Solution

The purchasing power of the dollar for a particular time period is found by:

$$\text{Purchasing power of the dollar} = \frac{\$1}{\text{CPI}}(100)$$

$$\text{For the base period} = \frac{\$1}{100.0}(100) = \$1.00$$

$$\text{For January 1996} = \frac{\$1}{148.2}(100) = \$0.67$$

Assume that a hamburger and an order of french fries cost $1 in the base period of 1982–84. Thus if you had $1,000 you could buy 1,000 orders. However, in January 1996 that same $1,000 could only purchase 670 orders (because the price of burger and french fries had increased).

Exercise 2

Check you answers against those in the ANSWER section.

Carl Eger had an annual income in the base period of $40,000 and by 1996 his income had increased to $50,000. During the same period the consumer price index rose from 100 to 150.7. What was Carl's real income in 1996? Did his income keep pace with inflation? Compare the value of $1.00 in the base period with that of the year 1996.

CHAPTER ASSIGNMENT 17
Index Numbers

Name _____ Section _____ Score _____

Part I Select the correct answer and write the appropriate letter in the space provided.

___ 1. The base period is
   a. always 1982–84.
   b. usually a year such as 1990, or a group of years such as 1982–84.
   c. always reported in dollars.
   d. a number such as 104.67

___ 2. A given period refers to
   a. the period in the numerator of the fraction.
   b. the year 1967.
   c. a dollar value such as $25,000.
   d. the smaller of the two values.

___ 3. A Laspeyres Price Index uses as its weights
   a. given period quantities.
   b. base period quantities
   c. base period prices
   d. given period prices

___ 4. In an aggregate price index
   a. the prices of several commodities are added.
   b. no consideration is given to the units.
   c. it does not consider the quantities involved.
   d. all of the above.

___ 5. The Paasche Price index uses as its weights the
   a. given period quantities.
   b. base period quantities.
   c. base period prices.
   d. given period prices.

___ 6. The current base period for the Consumer Price Index is
   a. 1994.
   b. 1982–84.
   c. 1982.
   d. 1984.

___ 7. The Index of Industrial Production for 1996 is 135.4 (1982–84 = 100). This means that production
   a. increases $35.4 in 1996.
   b. production declined 35.4 percent since 1982.
   c. production increased 35.4 percent since 1982–84.
   d. decreased 35.4 percent in 1996.

___ 8. A firm sold $50,000 of a particular product in 1992 and $60,000 in 1996. Using 1992 as the base, what is the index for 1996?
   a. $10,000
   b. 20 percent.
   c. 120 percent.
   d. 83.3 percent.

___ 9. An index has 1980 as its base. The index reported in 1990 was 127.2 and in 1995 it was 186.7. The percent increase from 1990 to 1995 is
   a. 46.8 percent.
   b. 27.2 percent.
   c. 59.5 percent.
   d. none of the above.

___ 10. Which of the following price indexes uses *current* period quantities in its base?
   a. a value index.
   b. a simple index.
   c. Laspeyres Price Index.
   d. Paasche Price Index.

Part II Fill in the blank with the correct answer.

11. What is the base of most indexes? _____

12. A _____ is found by dividing the given period sales by the base period sales.

13. The _____ is found by dividing the CPI into $1.00.

14. A _____ measures the change in price quantity or value from one period to another.

15. The GNP is 3,000 billion and the current consumer price index is 140. The value of the GNP in terms of the base period is _____.

Part III Record your answer in the space provided. Show essential work.

16. The net sales for the Toro Company, a manufacturer of lawn mowers and other lawn care equipment, is given below. Develop an index showing the change in net sales for the selected years. Use 1988 as the base period.

Year	Net sales ($000)
1988	$609,205
1989	643,566
1991	711,555
1994	922,000

17. The following table shows the prices and quantities consumed by a family of four for selected food commodities for 1990 and 1995. Use 1990 as the base period.

	1990		1995	
Commodity	Price	Quantity	Price	Quantity
Ground beef (per lb.)	$1.30	500	$1.80	700
Milk (½ gallon)	.90	200	1.10	250
Cookies (dozen)	1.00	100	1.20	200
Steak (per pound)	2.10	50	3.00	40

a. Determine the simple index for steak for 1995.

b. Determine a simple aggregate price index for 1995.

c. Determine a Laspeyres price index for 1995.

d. Determine a Paasche price index for 1995.

e. Determine a value index for 1995.

18. The table below reports the net profit for Jerdoneck Tool and Die, Inc. for the years 1990 and 1995. Also reported is the tool and die index for the same years (1985 = 100).

Year	Net profit	Index
1990	$45,380	120
1995	65,035	180

a. What was the percent increase in the index from 1990 to 1995?

b. Convert the index to a 1990 base. What is the new index for 1995?

c. Determine the net profit for 1995 in terms of the 1990 base. Comment on the change.

_____

_____

_____

18

TIME SERIES AND FORECASTING

CHAPTER GOALS

After completing this chapter, you will be able to:

1. Explain the meaning of each of the components of a time series, namely the trend, cyclical, seasonal, and irregular or erratic variation.
2. Determine the linear trend equation for time series data.
3. Compute a moving average.
4. Compute the trend equation for a nonlinear trend.
5. Use the linear and nonlinear trend equations to estimate future time periods.
6. Determine a set of seasonal indexes using the ratio-to-moving-average method.
7. Deseasonalize data using seasonal indexes.
8. Determine a seasonally adjusted forecast.

Introduction

It if often necessary to analyze past sales, and/or production data, in order to estimate future events. A collection of data over a period of time is called a **time series**. The collection can be recorded yearly, quarterly, monthly, or weekly. The sales of Team Sports, a sporting goods store that opened in 1978, reported by month, is an example of a time series. Another example would be the employment in the Atlantic City, New Jersey hotels since 1990, by quarter. Analysis of historical data is useful to management in current decision making as well as intermediate and long-range estimates.

Components of a Time Series

A time series value consists of four components: trend, cyclical, seasonal, and erratic. The **trend** is the long-run direction of the time series. That direction may be upward such as the sales at Team Sports. The trend may be downward. The manager of your bookstore would attest that the sales of slide rules have declined since 1975 to virtually zero today (because calculators and home computers have replaced slide rules in business and universities).

While the long-run direction of the time series may be increasing, there may be "ups and downs" that seem to follow the business cycle. These periods of prosperity and recession are referred to as **cyclical variation**. The third component of a time series is the **seasonal variation**. Many sales, production, and other time series fluctuate with the season. Sales of toys are highest during the Christmas season, and rentals of skis at a ski resort are much higher in February than in July.

Irregular variation may be divided into two components, **episodic** and **residual**. Episodic variations are unpredictable, but they can be identified. Major floods, hurricanes, or strikes are examples of unpredictable events but it is possible to identify the time period in which they happened. Residual is the random variation that is present after the episodic fluctuations have been removed from the data.

Types of Trend Equations

If sales, employment, production, and other business series increase or decrease over a period of time and approximate a straight line, the equation for this growth is given by formula 18–1.

$$Y' = a + bt \qquad \text{18–1}$$

where
Y' is the projected value of Y for a selected value of t.
a is the Y-intercept. That is, it is the estimated value of Y when $t = 0$.
b is the slope of the line. It is the average change in Y for each unit change of t.
t is any value of t (time) that is chosen.

If the general trend of a time series does not follow a straight line when plotted on arithmetic graph paper the least squares trend equation should not be used to approximate past trends or to estimate future values. A series that appears curvilinear when plotted on arithmetic graph paper, for example, should be fitted with a **logarithmic trend equation**. It has the equation:

$$\log Y' = \log a + \log b(t)$$

There are many other types of equations that may be fitted to the data, such as second and third degree polynomials. A good first step in determining which equation to use is to plot the data with time on the horizontal axis and sales, production, or the variable of interest on the vertical axis.

Seasonal Variation

Seasonal variations recur regularly within a period of one year. As the name seasonal implies, climatic conditions are often responsible for the variation in the time series. Construction activities, sales of skis and suntan lotion, and the production of corn are examples of products whose production and consumption are related to the weather. Department store sales increase around holidays such as Easter, Christmas, and the start of the new school year. The purpose of this chapter is to develop techniques to isolate the seasonal component of a time series in order to make better estimates.

There are several reasons for measuring a seasonal pattern. The first reason is to understand the seasonal pattern and to compare other years. For example, we may want to compare the sales this March with the sales in March for previous years. A second reason for determining an index is to use it for short-term planning. Seasonal patterns are useful in short-term planning. A firm in the lawn care business in the Great Lakes region, for example, will want to begin hiring seasonal employees early in April when the weather starts to get warm. The ratio-to-moving-average method of isolating the seasonal component will be examined in the **Problem** section.

Briefly, this method eliminates the trend (T), cyclical (C), and irregular (I) components from the original data (Y).

GLOSSARY

Time series—A listing of data over a period of time. The period of time might be months, quarters, years, weeks, etc.

Trend—The long-run direction of the time series.

Cyclical—Often referred to as the "business cycle." A typical cycle has a period of prosperity, recession, depression, and recovery.

Episodic—The variation in a time series that is due to unusual causes that can be identified such as strikes, tornado damage, or fire.

Residual—The random variation in a time series.

Seasonal—The variation in a time series that occurs within a year.

Ratio-to-moving-average method—A method for determining the typical seasonal indexes.

Seasonal index—A value that identifies the effects of various seasons. The index is usually reported monthly or quarterly.

CHAPTER PROBLEMS

Problem 1

The sales (in $ millions) for the years 1991 to 1994 of Grape Juice, Inc. are shown below. The sales are also shown on the line chart.

Year	Sales ($ million)
1991	736
1992	781
1993	889
1994	942
1995	974

Determine the least squares trend equation for the sales in millions of dollars. Estimate the sales for 1997, using the trend equation.

Solution

To simplify the calculations, the years are replaced by codes. In this problem we'll let the year 1991 be 1, 1992 be 2, and so on. This will reduce the size of the terms used in computing the trend equation. The trend equation is of the form $Y' = a + bt$, where Y' is the estimated sales, a is the Y intercept, b is the slope of the trend equation, and t is the coded time value. The computations needed are shown in the following table.

Year	Sales ($ million) Y	t	Yt	t^2
1991	736	1	736	1
1992	781	2	1562	4
1993	889	3	2667	9
1994	942	4	3768	16
1995	974	5	4870	25
	4322	15	13,603	55

The values of a and b are determined using the formulas 12–4 and 12–5. To emphasize that the time is used as the independent variable t is used in place of X.

$$b = \frac{\Sigma Yt - (\Sigma Y)(\Sigma t)/n}{\Sigma t^2 - (\Sigma t)^2/n} = \frac{13,603 - 4322(15)/5}{55 - (15)^2/5} = 63.70$$

$$a = \frac{\Sigma Y}{n} - b\frac{\Sigma t}{n} = \frac{4322}{5} - (63.7)\frac{15}{5} = 673.3$$

The trend equation is $Y' = 673.3 + 63.7t$. How do we interpret this equation? The value of 673.3 is the intersection with the Y-axis. This is the estimated sales when the coded year is 0. The value 63.70 is the rate of change. That is, sales are increasing at a rate of 63.7 per year. Recall that the sales are in millions of dollars.

To estimate sales for 1997, the first step is to determine the code for that year. The code is 7 found by subtracting 1990 from 1997. Next 7 is substituted for t in the trend equation and the value of Y' determined.

$$Y' = 673.3 + 63.7t = 673.3 + 63.7(7) = 1119.2$$

The estimated sales for 1997 is 1119.2. (Remember that sales is in $ millions.)

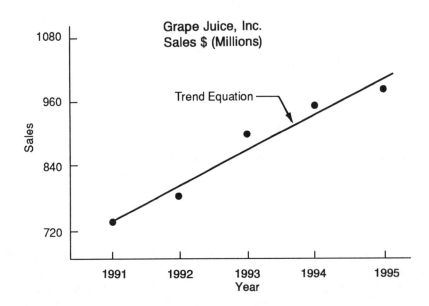

Grape Juice, Inc.
Sales $ (Millions)

Exercise 1

Check your answers against those in the ANSWER section.

The following table reports the average shareholder's equity (in billions of dollars) for the TGE Corporation from 1991 to 1995. Plot the data and develop a linear trend equation. Estimate the equity for 1996.

Year	Average Shareholder's Equity
1991	4.3
1992	4.6
1993	5.2
1994	6.1
1995	6.9

Problem 2

The number of passengers carried by Northeastern Airlines from 1988 to 1994 is shown below.

Year	Passengers (000)
1988	3.3
1989	4.1
1990	4.9
1991	6.4
1992	9.0
1993	12.8
1994	16.9

Determine a trend equation and estimate the number of passengers for 1996.

Solution

The data on the number of passengers carried by Northeastern Airlines is shown in the following chart. The number of passengers is increasing, but not in a linear fashion. In fact, the number of passengers not only increased but the amount of the increase was larger each year. This suggests that the trend is not linear, and that a logarithmic equation is appropriate.

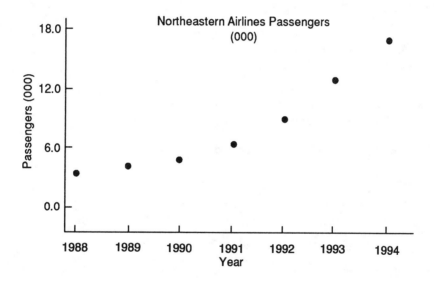

The MINITAB system is used to determine the logarithmic equation. The first step is to enter the years, next the codes for the years, and finally the number of passengers. The **LET** command is used to determine the logs of the number of passengers. Finally, the **REGRESSION** procedure is used, with the log of the number of passengers as the dependent variable and the coded years as the independent variable. This output is as follows:

```
MTB > set c1
DATA> 1988:1994
DATA> end
MTB > set c2
DATA> 1:7
DATA> end
MTB > set c3
DATA> 3.3 4.1 4.9 6.4 9 12.8 16.9
DATA> end
MTB > name c1 'Year' c2 'Code' c3 'Pass-ger' c4 'Log-pass'
MTB > logten c3 c4
MTB > print c1-c4

  Row    Year    Code   Pass-ger   Log-pass

    1    1988      1        3.3     0.51851
    2    1989      2        4.1     0.61278
    3    1990      3        4.9     0.69020
    4    1991      4        6.4     0.80618
    5    1992      5        9.0     0.95424
    6    1993      6       12.8     1.10721
    7    1994      7       16.9     1.22789

MTB > Regress 'Log-pass' 1 'Code';
SUBC>   Constant.

Regression Analysis


The regression equation is
Log-pass = 0.362 + 0.121 Code

Predictor        Coef        Stdev     t-ratio         p
Constant      0.36229      0.02678       13.53     0.000
Code         0.120751     0.005987       20.17     0.000

s = 0.03168     R-sq = 98.8%     R-sq(adj) = 98.5%

Analysis of Variance

SOURCE        DF           SS           MS         F         p
Regression     1      0.40826      0.40826    406.75     0.000
Error          5      0.00502      0.00100
Total          6      0.41328
```

The number of passengers for 1996 can be estimated using the logarithmic equation. The code for 1996 is 9, found by 1996 − 1987. Substituting $t = 9$ into the equation.

$$Y' = 0.36229 + 0.120751t = 0.36229 + 0.120751(9) = 1.449049$$

The antilog of 1.449049 is 28.122. So the estimated number of passengers in 1996 is 28.122 thousand.

```
┌─────────────────────────────────────────────────────────────────────────┐
```

Exercise 2

Check your answers against those in the ANSWER section.

The imports in millions of dollars, for the Zeta Company are shown below. Develop a logarithmic trend equation and predict imports for 1996.

Year	Imports (000)
1991	$2.0
1992	3.0
1993	4.4
1994	6.0
1995	8.5

Problem 3

The enrollment by quarter at Starbrich Tech is given below in thousands of students for the year 1992 to 1995. Compute the seasonal indexes for each quarter using the ratio-to-moving-average method.

Student Enrollment by Quarter (000)

Year	Winter	Spring	Summer	Fall
1992	3.2	2.8	0.8	3.2
1993	3.0	2.8	0.9	3.5
1994	3.5	3.4	0.9	4.1
1995	4.0	3.8	1.0	4.3

Solution

A seasonal index computed using the ratio-to-moving-average method is a 6-step procedure.

Step 1. **Calculate a four-quarter moving total**. Adding the four quarters of 3.2 + 2.8 + 0.8 + 3.2 = 10.0. The total is "moved along" by adding spring, summer, fall of 1992 and winter of 1993. That is 2.8 + 0.8 + 3.2 + 3.0 = 9.8. A convenient way to do this on a hand calculator is to subtract the winter quarter of 1992 namely 3.2, from the total 10.0 and then add the winter quarter of 1993, namely 3.0. The result is 9.8. Continuing 2.8 is subtracted from 9.8 and the Spring 1993 enrollment of 2.8 is added to obtain the next moving total. This subtraction and addition to the moving total is continued until all quarter enrollments are used.

Step 2. **Divide the moving totals by 4**. Each moving total in column 2 is divided by four to give a four-quarter average and the result reported in column 3. This value is called the moving average.

Step 3. **The moving averages are then centered.** This step is required because the four-quarter moving average does not have the same center as any of the quarterly values. To explain further, the winter quarter data is centered at 2/15/92, and the spring quarter at 5/15/92, the summer at 8/15/92 and the fall at 11/15/92. When these four periods are totaled and then averaged, the resulting value is centered at 7/1/92. Thus the value of 2.5, the first value in column 3, is centered at 7/1/92, which does not correspond to the center of any of the quarters. By averaging consecutive moving averages the average is then adjusted to the proper time. For the first two values in column 3 the 2.5, centered at 7/1/92, is averaged with 2.450, which is centered at 10/1/92, to obtain 2.475, which is centered at 8/15/92.

Step 4. **Determine the specific seasonal.** The specific seasonal index for each quarter is then computed by dividing the quarterly enrollment in column 1 by the centered four-quarter moving average in column 4 and multiplying the result by 100. The specific seasonal for the summer quarter of 1992 is 32.3 found by (0.8/2.4750)(100). The specific seasonals are in column 5.

Year	Qtr.	Col. (1) Enrollment	Col. (2) 4-Qtr. Moving Total	Col. (3) 4-Qtr. Moving Avg.	Col. (4) Centered Moving Avg.	Col. (5) Specific Seasonal
1992	Winter	3.2				
	Spring	2.8				
			10.0	2.500		
	Summer	0.8			2.4750	32.3
			9.8	2.450		
	Fall	3.2			2.4500	130.6
			9.8	2.450		
1993	Winter	3.0			2.4625	121.8
			9.9	2.475		
	Spring	2.8			2.5125	111.4
			10.2	2.550		
	Summer	0.9			2.6125	34.4
			10.7	2.675		
	Fall	3.5			2.7500	127.3
			11.3	2.825		
1994	Winter	3.5			2.8250	123.9
			11.3	2.825		
	Spring	3.4			2.9000	117.2
			11.9	2.975		
	Summer	0.9			3.0375	29.6
			12.4	3.100		
	Fall	4.1			3.1500	130.2
			12.8	3.200		
1995	Winter	4.0			3.2125	124.5
			12.9	3.225		
	Spring	3.8			3.2500	116.9
			13.1	3.275		
	Summer	1.0				
	Fall	4.3				

Step 5. **Determine the mean of the specific seasonals.** The specific seasonals are organized into a table and the mean specific seasonal for each quarter is determined. For the winter quarter the mean is 123.4.

		Quarter		
Year	Winter	Spring	Summer	Fall
1989			32.3	130.6
1990	121.8	111.4	34.4	127.3
1991	123.9	117.2	29.6	130.2
1992	124.5	116.9		
Total	370.2	345.5	96.3	388.1
Mean	123.4	115.2	32.1	129.4
Typical Index	123.37	115.17	32.09	129.37

Total:
- 400.1
- 400.0

Step 6. **Adjust the means**. The total of the four means should theoretically be 400.0 because the average of the four quarters is designated as 100.0. However, the total may not be equal to 400.0 due to rounding. A correction factor, therefore, is applied to each mean to arrive at the typical seasonal indexes. It is computed by:

$$\text{Correction factor} = \frac{400.0}{\text{Total of means}}$$

$$\text{For this problem} = \frac{400.0}{400.1} = 0.99975$$

Multiplying each of the means by the correction factor gives the four typical seasonal indexes

Winter	123.37
Spring	115.17
Summer	32.09
Fall	129.37

Note that enrollment is traditionally high in the fall and winter, and drops off sharply in the summer. The summer enrollment is typically only 32.09 percent of the mean enrollment, or nearly 70 percent below the mean enrollment for the year.

Exercise 3

Check your answers against those in the ANSWER section.

The quarterly sales for the Norton Company are given in millions of dollars for four years. Compute the quarterly seasonal index using the ratio-to-moving-average method.

		Quarter		
Year	I	II	III	IV
1992	2	8	10	2
1993	4	10	10	4
1994	4	12	14	4
1995	6	16	20	4

Problem 4

The Kinzua Boat Rental Company estimates that 24,000 boat rentals will be made this coming year. The seasonal index for the month of July is 130. What are the estimated rentals for July?

Solution

If there were no seasonal variation, 2,000 boats would be rented each month, found by 24,000/12. However, the index of 130 for July indicates that rentals are 30 percent above average for that month. To determine the projected rentals for July, we increase the average rental by 30 percent. This is computed by 2,000 (1.30) [or 2,000 (130/100)] which equals 2,600 rentals.

Exercise 4

Check your answers against those in the ANSWER section.

Refer to Problem 4. Suppose the seasonal index for June was computed to be 120 and 47 for November. Determine the seasonally adjusted sales for June and November.

Problem 5

The Director Admissions at Starbrick Tech needs an estimate of enrollment for each quarter of 1996. Use the enrollment data for the year 1992 to 1995 and the seasonal indexes determined in **Problem 3** to find a trend equation for enrollment. Use the trend equation and the seasonal values to estimate enrollment for each quarter of 1996.

Solution

First we need to determine the seasonally adjusted trend equation. In the following table the actual enrollment for each quarter is shown in the "Students" column and the seasonal index is shown in the "Index" column. To determine the deseasonalized trend value, the actual enrollment is divided by the seasonal index. For example, the actual enrollment in the winter quarter of 1992 was 3.2 students (in thousands) and the seasonal index is 123.37 for the winter quarter. The deseasonalized enrollment is 2.5938, found by 3.2/1.2337.

Year	Quarter	Code	Students	Index	Deseasonalized
1992	Winter	1	3.2	1.2337	2.59382
	Spring	2	2.8	1.1517	2.43119
	Summer	3	0.8	0.3209	2.49299
	Fall	4	3.2	1.2937	2.47353
1993	Winter	5	3.0	1.2337	2.43171
	Spring	6	2.8	1.1517	2.43119
	Summer	7	0.9	0.3209	2.80461
	Fall	8	3.5	1.2937	2.70542
1994	Winter	9	3.5	1.2337	2.83699
	Spring	10	3.4	1.1517	2.95216
	Summer	11	0.9	0.3209	2.80461
	Fall	12	4.1	1.2937	3.16920
1995	Winter	13	4.0	1.2337	3.24228
	Spring	14	3.8	1.1517	3.29947
	Summer	15	1.0	0.3209	3.11624
	Fall	16	4.3	1.2937	3.32380

The MINITAB system is used to determine the trend equation with the seasonal effect removed. From the MINITAB output, which follows, the deseasonalized trend equation is $Y' = 2.2787 + .0636t$. This trend equation indicates that over the 16 quarters the deseasonalized growth rate was about 64 students per quarter. (Recall that the enrollment data was reported in thousands.)

```
MTB >  regr c4 1 c1

The regression equation is
Deseason = 2.28 + 0.0636 Code

Predictor        Coef       Stdev     t-ratio        p
Constant      2.27871     0.07132      31.95      0.000
Code         0.063602    0.007376       8.62      0.000
```

Assuming that the 16 periods of historical data are reasonably good predictors of future enrollment at Starbrick Tech, we can use the trend equation to project 1996 enrollment. The winter quarter of 1996 is period 17, so $t = 17$ is substituted in the trend equation.

$$Y' = 2.2787 + .0636t = 2.2787 + .0636(17) = 3.3599$$

The estimated enrollment for the winter quarter is 3.3599, or 3,360 students, without considering the seasonal effect. The index for winter is 123.37, which indicates that winter is 23.37 percent above the typical quarter, so the actual enrollment for the winter quarter is estimated at 4.145, or 4,145 students, found by 3.3599(1.2337). The estimates for the other quarters are determined in a similar fashion and this information is summarized in the following table.

Year	Quarter	Code	Deseasonalized Enrollment	Seasonal Index	Forecast
1996	Winter	17	3.3599	123.37	4,145
	Spring	18	3.4235	115.17	3,943
	Summer	19	3.4871	32.09	1,119
	Fall	20	3.5507	129.37	4,594

The enrollment for the fall quarter is normally the highest, and the smallest for the summer. This is also true for the estimates in 1996.

Exercise 5

Check your answers against those in the ANSWER section.

The quarterly sales for the Norton Company were reported in Exercise 3 and a seasonal index was computed for each quarter. Deseasonalize the data and determine the trend equation. Estimate the seasonally adjusted sales for the four quarters of 1996.

CHAPTER ASSIGNMENT 18

Times Series and Forecasting

Name _____ Section _____ Score _____

Part I Select the correct answer and write the appropriate letter in the space provided.

___ 1. A listing of values over a period of time is called a
   a. trend.
   b. time series.
   c. seasonal index.
   d. residual.

___ 2. The long-term behavior of a variable over an extended period of time is called
   a. the seasonal index.
   b. the cyclical variation.
   c. the trend.
   d. episodic variation.

___ 3. A period of prosperity followed by recession is called a
   a. cyclical variation.
   b. trend.
   c. seasonal variation.
   d. irregular variation.

___ 4. When we plot a trend equation, the variable plotted along the horizontal axis is
   a. the dependent variables.
   b. sales.
   c. time.
   d. log of time.

___ 5. The variation within a year, such as retail sales during the Christmas holidays, is called the
   a. trend.
   b. seasonal variation.
   c. irregular variation.
   d. cyclical variation.

___ 6. In June of 1995 the Youngsville TrueValue Hardware store suffered severe damage to its contents during a flood. This is an example of
   a. residual variation.
   b. cyclical variation.
   c. seasonal variation because it happened during the summer.
   d. episodic variation.

___ 7. The purpose of determining the ratio-to-moving average when computing a seasonal index is to eliminate the
   a. random variation.
   b. trend.
   c. episodic variation.
   d. none of the above.

___ 8. The reason for centering a moving average is to
   a. convert the average to an index.
   b. remove the random variation.
   c. find the correction factor.
   d. align the time periods.

___ 9. A monthly index is being developed for the company sales. The moving total will consist of
   a. four quarterly sales values.
   b. logs of sales.
   c. logs of quarters.
   d. twelve monthly sales values.

___ 10. The index for October for imports by Wines, Inc. is 90. The actual imports for October were $450,000. The seasonally adjusted imports are
   a. $405,000
   b. $450,000
   c. $500,000
   d. none of the above.

Part II Fill in the blank with the correct answer.

11. Irregular variation may be divided into two components. These components are _____ and _____.

12. A _____ is determined by dividing the actual time series value by the centered moving average and multiplying the result by 100.

13. If a seasonal index is less than 100, this indicates that the value for the quarter is _____ than the typical quarter.

14. The ratio-to-moving average is a component in finding the _____.

15. The long-run direction of a time series is called the _____.

Part III Record your answer in the space provided. Show essential calculations.

16. The earnings per share for Anderson & Co. from 1990 to 1995 are as shown below.

Year	Earning per share
1990	$0.94
1991	1.81
1992	4.05
1993	3.92
1994	4.18
1995	5.20

   a. Develop a least squares trend equation. Code the year 1990 as 1.

   b. Estimate the earnings per share for 1998.

17. The following table shows the number of homes built by Custom Builders, Inc. in the last four years by quarter. Develop a seasonal index for each quarter using the ratio-to-moving average method.

Year	I	II	III	IV
1992	5	9	8	8
1993	6	9	9	8
1994	6	10	10	7
1995	6	10	9	8

Year	Qtr.	Passengers	4-Qtr. Moving Total	4-Qtr. Moving Avg.	Centered Moving Avg.	Specific Seasonal
1992	I					
	II					
	III					
	IV					
1993	I					
	II					
	III					
	IV					
1994	I					
	II					
	III					
	IV					
1995	I					
	II					
	III					
	IV					

Year	Quarter				
	I	II	III	IV	
1992					
1993					
1994					
1995					
Total					Total
Mean					
Typical Index					

CHAPTER GOALS

After completing this chapter, you will be able to:

1. Define the terms event, act, state of nature and payoff.
2. Develop a payoff table and an opportunity loss table.
3. Compute the expected payoff for a particular act.
4. Compute the expected opportunity loss for a particular act.
5. Determine the expected value of perfect information.

Introduction

The approach to decision making in the previous chapters was to set up a null hypothesis and an alternate hypothesis, formulate a decision rule, take a sample from the population, and then on the basis of the sample information make a decision about the null hypothesis. This is the **classical** approach to decision making. This chapter considers a slightly different approach to decision making called decision theory. In **decision theory** various alternative courses of action are considered. However, the monetary values of these courses of action are taken into account for the purpose of determining the optimum course of action.

Terms in Decision Making

Under conditions of certainty there are several courses of action available to the decision maker, and the decision maker knows the result of each course of action. The purchasing agent at a hospital may need to purchase 1,000 new bed sheets. He will check with several supplies and obtain prices for sheets of comparable quality and then make the purchase from the supplier offering the best price. Note that no uncertainty regarding future events exists.

Decision making under conditions of *uncertainty* also entails several courses of action, but in addition there is uncertainty regarding future events. For example, a businessman has $100,000 to invest and he is considering investing it in drilling oil wells.

If he strikes oil he makes a profit ten times his original investment. If it is a dry well he loses his money. Note, therefore, there is a condition of uncertainty. The unknown future outcomes are called the **states of nature**. In the oil drilling problem there are two states of nature; either the well will produce oil or it will not. The investor has two courses of action, or alternatives, either to invest or not to invest. Thus the **acts** are the courses of action available to the decision maker. For each combination of a state of nature and a course of action there is a **payoff** or **outcome**. These terms are summarized in the following payoff table showing the problems facing the investor.

Payoff Table

| | State of Nature | |
| | | |
Act	Strike Oil	Does Not Strike Oil
Invest in oil well	$1,000,000	−$100,000
Do not invest in oil well	0	0

The payoff from the act "Investing in the oil well" and the state of nature "strike oil" is $1,000,000.

Opportunity Loss Table

The difference between what a decision maker could have made had he known the state of nature and what he actually made is referred to as **regret** or **opportunity loss**. A payoff table is easily converted to an opportunity loss table by finding the *maximum* payoff for each state of nature and subtracting all other entries in the column from the maximum value. In the oil drilling problem if the state of nature is to strike oil the opportunity loss for selecting the event "do not invest" is $1,000,000, found by $1,000,000 (the optimum event) minus 0 (the payoff for selecting the course of action "do not invest").

The following table is an opportunity loss table for the oil well problem

Opportunity Loss Table

| Event | State of Nature | |
	Strike Oil	Does Not Strike Oil
Invest in oil well	0	$100,000
Do not invest in oil well	$1,000,000	0

In an opportunity loss table values cannot be negative.

Evaluating Courses of Action

Under conditions of uncertainty the various courses of action can be compared if the probability of the various states of nature can be estimated. These estimates may be obtained from an analysis of historical data, or on the basis of subjective estimates. Suppose geological studies indicated the probability of striking oil was .05, and the probability of not striking oil was .95. That is $P(S_1) = .05$ and $P(S_2) = .95$. The **expected payoff** called the EMV for the act of investing can be obtained as follows:

State of Nature	Payoff	Probabilty of State of Nature	Expected Value
Strike oil S_1	$1,000,000	.05	$50,000
Do not strike oil S_2	$-$ $100,000	.95	$-$$95,000
			$-$$45,000

The expected payoff is the probability of each state of nature times the payoff for the particular combination of act and state of nature. In the previous examples the expected payoff is a $-$$45,000, a loss of $45,000 for the act of investing.

The expected payoff for the act of investing is compared with that of not investing.

State of Nature	Payoff	Probability of State of Nature	Expected Value
Strike oil S_1	0	.05	$0
Do not strike oil S_2	0	.95	0
			$0

The expected payoff for not investing is 0. Using the expected value of the various outcomes as the decision criterion, the decision rule would be to select the largest expected value. If you were the investor would you rather lose $45,000 or lose $0? Undoubtedly you would select to lose $0.

The Value of Perfect Information

The concept of perfect information refers to the value of knowing with certainty, which state of nature will occur. In the oil well problem, the investor would know beforehand which state of nature would happen, that is whether the oil well is dry or not. The **value of perfect information** is calculated by determining the difference between the maximum payoff under conditions of certainty and the maximum payoff under uncertainty. It may be thought of as the cost of uncertainty.

GLOSSARY

State of nature—The unknown future event. The state of nature is not under the control of the decision maker.

Acts—Two or more possible actions available to the decision maker.

Payoff—The result of a particular combination of an act and a state of nature.

Opportunity loss—The difference between the payoff a decision maker receives for a chosen action and the maximum that the decision maker could have received for choosing the action yielding the highest payoff for the state of nature that occurred.

CHAPTER PROBLEMS

Problem 1

Jan's Cake Shop is a small bakery that specializes in decorating cakes. These cakes are baked early each morning for sale that day. Any cakes not sold the same day they are baked must be discarded. Jan knows, from her records, that she can always sell between 11 and 14 cakes, but she would like to know how many to bake each day to maximize her profit. From the last 50 business days she is able to develop the following probability distribution. Interpreting, 12 cakes were sold on 25 days, or 50% of the days.

Number of Cakes Sold	Days	Probability
11	10	.20
12	25	.50
13	10	.20
14	5	.10
	50	1.00

Suppose each cake is sold for $10.00, and the cost to bake plus the ingredients and labor is $6.00. (a) Develop a payoff table. (b) Using the expected value criterion make a recommendation as to the number of cakes to bake. (c) What is the value of perfect information?

Solution

(a) The first step is to develop a payoff table. There are four acts, or alternative decisions, open to Jan. She can bake 11, 12, 13 or 14 cakes each day. There are also four states of nature, and one of these will happen each day. The four states of nature are that 11, 12, 13, or 14 cakes are demanded. The payoff for the act of baking 11 cakes and the state of nature of 11 cakes being demanded is a payoff of $44, found by (number sold)(selling price) − (number baked)(cost) = (11)($10) − (11)($6). So the entry in the first row and the first column is $44. What is the profit if the demand is 14 cakes but only 11 are baked? Only 11 cakes were baked and hence only 11 can be sold. So the profit (payoff) is $44 found by 11 × $4. How about the payoff for baking 14 cakes and a demand of 11? Note that in this case Jan has 3 unsold cakes at a value of 3 × $6 = $18, which must be deducted from the total amount sold. The same equation is used to determine the payoff— (number sold)(selling price) − (number baked)(cost) = (11)($10) − (14)($6) = $26. The other entries in the payoff table are developed similarly.

		State of Nature (Demand)			
Act Cakes Baked		S_1 11	S_2 12	S_3 13	S_4 14
11	A_1	$44	$44	$44	$44
12	A_2	38	48	48	48
13	A_3	32	42	52	52
14	A_4	26	36	46	56

269

The **expected payoff** or expected monetary value, written EMV (A$_i$) for each act (alternative course of action) is computed using the historical sales. For the act of baking 14 cakes, the expected payoff is $38, as shown below.

Expected Payoff for Baking 14 Cakes (EMV (A$_4$))

State of Nature (Demand)	Payoff V(A$_4$,S$_j$)	Probability P(S$_j$)	V(A$_4$,S$_j$)·P(S$_j$)
11 Cakes S$_1$	$26	.20	$ 5.20
12 Cakes S$_2$	36	.50	18.00
13 Cakes S$_3$	46	.20	9.20
14 Cakes S$_4$	56	.10	5.60
			$38.00 ← EMV(A$_4$)

These calculations are summarized as follows:

$$EMV(A_i) = \Sigma P(S_j) \cdot V(A_i, S_j) \qquad \text{19–1}$$

where

$EMV(A_i)$ refers to the expected value of the various decision alternatives. There may be several decision possibilities. We will let 1 stand for the first alternative, 2 for the second, and so on. The lowercase letter i represents the range of decision alternatives.

$P(S_j)$ refers to the probability of the various states of nature. There can be an unlimited number, so we'll let j represent the various possible outcomes.

$V(A_i, S_j)$ refers to the value of the various payoffs. Note that each payoff is the result of a combination of a decision alternative and a state of nature.

The EMV(A$_4$), the expected monetary value for the decision alternative of baking 14 cakes is computed using formula 19–1.

$$EMV(A_4) = P(S_1) \cdot V(A_4,S_1) + P(S_2) \cdot V(A_4,S_2) + P(S_3) \cdot V(A_4,S_3) + P(S_4) \cdot V(A_4,S_4)$$
$$= .20(\$26.00) + .50(\$36.00) + .20(\$46.00) + .10(\$56.00)$$
$$= \$38.00$$

The expected payoffs for all four acts are shown below.

EMV(A$_i$)	Number of Cakes	Expected Payoff
1	11	$44.00
2	12	46.00
3	13	43.00
4	14	38.00

(b) The act of baking 12 cakes has the largest expected profit—$46.00. In the long run if Jan baked 12 cakes each day her profit would be the largest. We recommend that Jan bake 12 cakes.

Suppose an old prospector came by the bakery and said he could predict, without error, the demand (state of nature) for the day. This information would be available before she started to bake the cakes. How much should Jan be willing to pay him for the information? In essence, the old prospector is removing the uncertainty from the decision making process. The expected payoff under conditions of certainty, written in *EVPI*, is computed as follows:

Column 1 State of Nature (Demand)	Column 2 Payoff $V(A^*,S_j)$	Column 3 Probability $P(S_j)$	Column 4 Payoff $P(S_j)V(A^*,S_j)$
11 Cakes	44	.20	$ 8.80
12 Cakes	48	.50	24.00
13 Cakes	52	.20	10.40
14 Cakes	56	.10	5.60
			$48.80

The symbol $V(A^*,S_j)$ refers to the best alternative for a given state of nature.

If the prospector said the demand today will be 12, Jan would bake 12 cakes because that will maximize her profit. This will occur 50 percent of the time, which is obtained from Column 3 of the probability distribution. If Jan always knew her demand she could make $48.80 per day. Using the expected value criterion she can make $46 per day.

(c) The value of perfect information EVPI is $2.80, found by $48.80 − $46.00. Jan should be willing to pay up to $2.80 to remove the uncertainty from her decision making process.

Exercise 1

Check your answers against those in the ANSWER section.

A bank is trying to decide whether to make a one-year loan of $100,000 to Sharkey Chevy. Past experiences has shown that one of three outcomes will occur if the loan is made:

1. The loan is repaid plus the 10 percent interest without a problem.
2. The customer, Sharkey Chevy in this case, has difficulty paying the loan. However, the bank is finally repaid with 10 percent interest, but collection fees cost the bank $2,000.
3. The customer goes bankrupt and the bank only collects 70 percent of the amount loaned.

If the bank does not make the loan it can make eight percent interest for the year elsewhere. Historical records reveal the following probabilities for the various states of nature.

States of Nature	Probability
Repaid	.85
Repaid with difficulty	.10
Bankrupt	.05
	1.00

Develop a payoff table, determine the optimum act using the expected value criterion, and compute the value of perfect information.

Problem 2

Using the data from Jan's Cake Shop in Problem 1, develop an opportunity loss table and compute the expected opportunity loss.

Solution

A loss table is generated from a payoff table. Recall the payoff table for this problem was part of Problem 1. The opportunity loss is the difference between what could have been made had the decision maker known the state of nature and thus selected the maximum payoff, the payoff for the other acts. For Jan's Cake Shop, had she known the state of nature was that 11 cakes would be sold, designated S_1, she would have obviously selected to bake 11 cakes. Hence, $44 − $44 = $0, so the opportunity loss would have been $0. Had the state of nature been 11 and Jan decided to bake 12 cakes, the opportunity loss wold be $6, found by $44 − $38.

Had the demand been 13, but Jan decided to bake 11 cakes, the opportunity loss would be $8, found by $52 − $44. The full table is shown below.

Opportunity Loss Table
State of Nature
(Demand)

Act	11	12	13	14
11	$ 0	$ 4	$ 8	$12
12	6	0	4	8
13	12	6	0	4
14	18	12	6	0

The expected opportunity loss is determined in the same way as expected payoff. For example, the expected opportunity loss for the act of baking 13 cakes is computed as follows:

Opportunity Loss
For Baking 13 Cakes

State of Nature	Opportunity Loss	Probability of State of Nature	Expected Opportunity Loss
11 Cakes baked	$12	.20	$2.40
12 Cakes baked	6	.50	3.00
13 Cakes baked	0	.20	0
14 Cakes baked	4	.10	0.40
			$5.80

The calculations are summarized as follows:

$$EOL(A_j) = \Sigma (P(S_j) \cdot (R(A_j, S_j) \qquad \text{19–2}$$

where

$EOL(A_j)$ refers to the expected opportunity loss for a particular decision alternative.
$P(S_j)$ refers to the probability associated with the various states of nature.
$R(A_j, S_j)$ refers to the regret or loss for a particular combination of a state of nature and a decision alternative.

The $EOL(A_3)$, the regret or opportunity loss for selecting the alternative of baking 13 cakes, is computed as follows using formula 19–2.

$$
\begin{aligned}
EOL(A_3) &= P(S_1) \cdot R(A_2,S_1) + P(S_2) \cdot R(A_2,S_2) + P(S_3) \cdot R(A_2, S_3) + P(S_4) \cdot R(A_2,S_4) \\
&= .20(\$12.00) + .50(\$6) + .20(\$0) + .10(\$4) \\
&= \$5.80
\end{aligned}
$$

The expected opportunity loss is the smallest for the act of baking 12 cakes. In fact, it is exactly the same as the value of perfect information. The expected opportunity loss measures the uncertainty in the decision-making process.

Expected Opportunity Loss

	Expected Opportunity
Act	*Loss*
11 Cakes baked	$ 4.80
12 Cakes baked	2.80
13 Cakes baked	5.80
14 Cakes baked	10.80

Exercise 2

Check your answers against those in the ANSWER section.

Using the bank loan problem in Exercise 1, develop an opportunity loss table and compute the expected opportunity loss for each decision alternative.

CHAPTER ASSIGNMENT 19
An Introduction to Decision Making Under Uncertainty

Name _____ Section _____ Score _____

Part I Select the correct answer and write the appropriate letter in the space provided.

___ 1. In decision theory there is uncertainty regarding
    a. course of action.
    b. payoffs.
    c. states of nature.
    d. the value of perfect information.

___ 2. The term ''decision theory'' refers to
    a. classical hypothesis testing.
    b. subjective probability.
    c. the alternate hypothesis.
    d. two or more decision alternatives.

___ 3. The unknown future outcomes are called.
    a. courses of action.
    b. states of nature.
    c. the opportunity loss.
    d. the value of perfect information.

___ 4. For each combination of course of action and state of nature there is
    a. a payoff.
    b. an expected value of perfect information.
    c. an expected value.
    d. none of the above.

___ 5. the expected value of perfect information and the expected opportunity loss
    a. are always equal.
    b. have no relationship with each other.
    c. have the same standard deviation.
    d. equal the particular state of nature.

___ 6. Two or more courses of action available to the decision maker are called
    a. states of nature.
    b. decision alternatives or acts.
    c. the expected value.
    d. none of the above.

___ 7. The difference between the optimum decision and any other decision is called
    a. an expected value.
    b. a payoff.
    c. an opportunity loss.
    d. the expected value of perfect information.

___ 8. A decision maker does not have control over
    a. the payoff table.
    b. the decision alternatives.
    c. the states of nature.
    d. the opportunity loss table.

___ 9. An opportunity loss table reports the amount of opportunity loss for each state of nature and
   a. course of action.
   b. payoff.
   c. expected value.
   d. expected value of perfect information.

___ 10. When all the facts are known in a decision situation, it can be said that the decision was made under
   a. uncertainty.
   b. certainty.
   c. opportunity.
   d. subjectivity.

Part II Fill in the blank with the correct answer.

11. In statistical decision making, the act that results in the maximum payoff also yields the minimum _____.

12. An uncertain condition in decision making is also called _____.

13. The cost of uncertainty is also called the _____.

14. Each combination of decision alternative and state of nature results in a _____.

15. The expected monetary value is also called the _____.

Part III Record your answer in the space provided. Show all essential work.

16. The owner of the Spaghetti Warehouse is considering expansion. The owner owns the land nearby and could build his own building on that land. If he decides to build the new building and the economy improves, he estimates that his first year profits will be $100,000. If he builds his own building and there is a recession, he will lose $40,000. He could expand the current restaurant. If he selects this alternative, he estimates he will make an additional $25,000 if the economy improves, and lose $5,000 if there is a recession. He could also do nothing, in which case there is no additional profit or loss. The probability the economy will improve is .25, and the probability of a recession is .75.

a. Develop a payoff table for the various acts and states of nature.

	States of Nature	
Acts	Economy improves	Recession
Build new		
Expand		
Do nothing		

b. compute the expected payoff for each alternative.

c. Determine the expected value of perfect information.

d. Convert the payoff to an opportunity loss table.

	States of Nature	
Acts	Economy improves	Recession
Build new		
Expand		
Do nothing		

e. What course of action would you recommend?

_____

_____

_____

_____

_____

Answer Section

Solutions to Exercises

Chapter 2

1.

Class limits	f	Midpoint
15 up to 25	6	20
25 up to 35	11	30
35 up to 45	3	40
	20	

2.

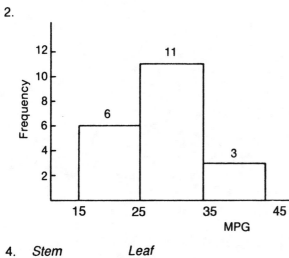

3.

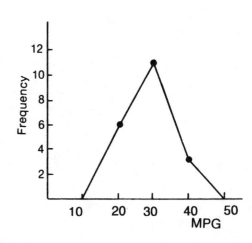

4.

Stem	Leaf
1	899
2	013577899
3	0002267
4	0

5.

True Class Limits	Class Frequency	Cum. Frequency	Percent Cum. Freq.
15 up to 25	6	6	30
25 up to 35	11	17	85
35 up to 45	3	20	100

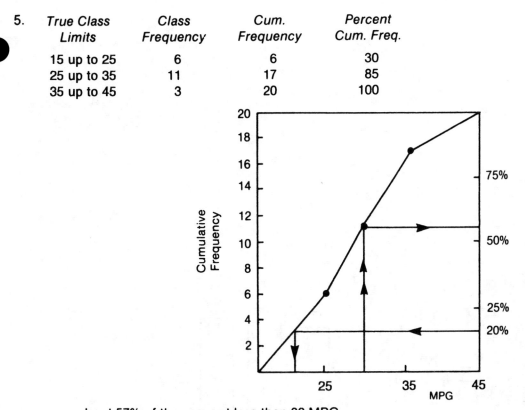

a. about 57% of the cars get less than 30 MPG
b. 20% of the cars obtain about 20 MPG or less

6.

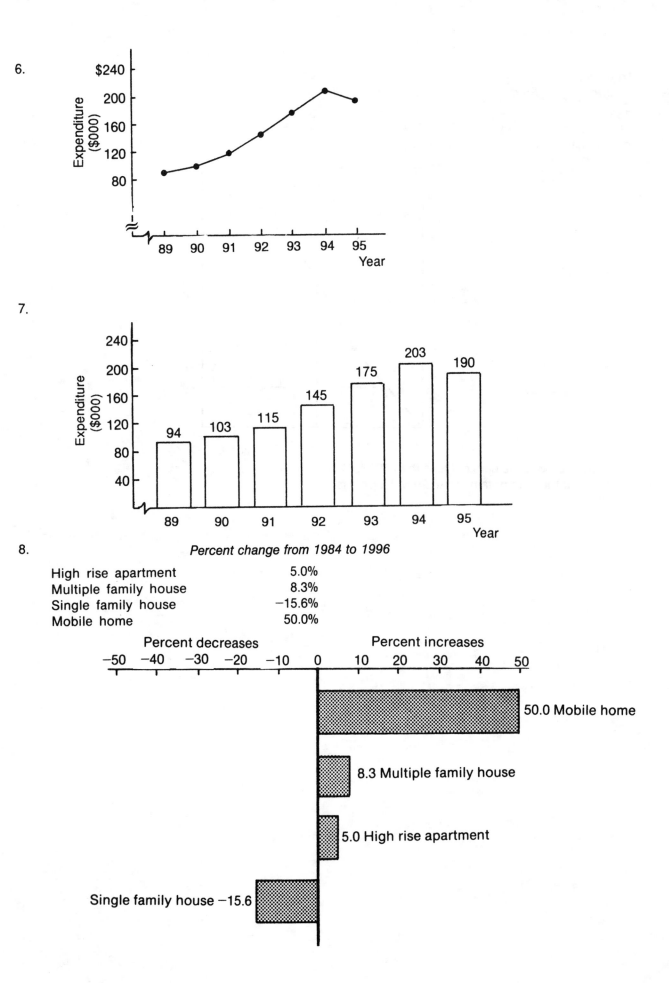

7.

8. *Percent change from 1984 to 1996*

High rise apartment   5.0%
Multiple family house   8.3%
Single family house   −15.6%
Mobile home   50.0%

282

9.

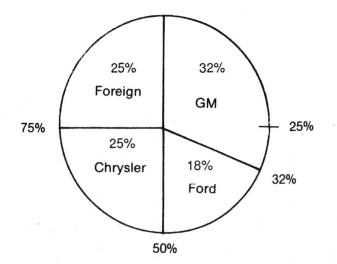

Chapter 3

1. $\overline{X} = 6$, median = 5, modes = 4 and 8

2.
Limits	f	X	fx	CF
$ 6 up to $ 9	2	7.5	15.0	2
9 up to 12	8	10.5	84.0	10
12 up to 15	20	13.5	270.0	30
15 up to 18	14	16.5	231.0	44
18 up to 21	6	19.5	117.0	50
	50		717.0	

a. $\overline{X} = \dfrac{717}{50} = 14.34$

b. Median $= 12 + \dfrac{25 - 10}{20}(3) = 14.25$

c. Mode $= 13.5$

3. $GM = \sqrt[45]{\dfrac{159}{51}} - 1 = \sqrt[45]{3.117647} - 1$

$$= 1.02559 - 1.0$$
$$= .02559$$

Chapter 4

1. a. range = $30 − $10 = 20

   b. $MD = \dfrac{26.8}{5} = 5.36$

   c. $s^2 = \dfrac{1625 - \dfrac{(83)^2}{5}}{5-1} = 61.8$

   d. $s = \sqrt{61.8} = 7.861$

2.

Weekly income	f	X	fx	fx^2	CF
$100 up to $150	5	125	625	78,125	5
150 up to 200	9	175	1575	275,625	14
200 up to 250	20	225	4,500	1,012,500	34
250 up to 300	18	275	4,950	1,361,250	52
300 up to 350	5	325	1,625	528,125	57
350 up to 400	3	375	1,125	421,875	60
	60		14,400	3,677,500	

$$s = \sqrt{\dfrac{3,677,500 - \dfrac{(14,400)^2}{60}}{59}} = 61.27$$

$$Q_1 = 200 + \dfrac{15 - 14}{20}(50) = \$202.50$$

$$Q_3 = 250 + \dfrac{45 - 34}{18}(50) = \$280.56$$

$$QD = \dfrac{280.56 - 202.50}{2} = 39.03$$

3. $sk = \dfrac{3(990 - 950)}{70} = 1.71$

Chapter 5

1. a. $\dfrac{90}{300} = .30$

   b. $\dfrac{270}{300} = .90$

2. .68, found by $.60 + .20 - .12$

3. a. $P(3) = (.10)(.10)(.10) = .001$
   b. $P(\text{None}) = (.90)(.90)(.90) = .729$
   c. $P(\text{At least one}) = 1 - P(\text{None}) = 1 - .729 = .271$

4. a. $P(\text{Both female}) = \left(\dfrac{6}{10}\right)\left(\dfrac{5}{9}\right) = .33$

   b. $P(\text{At least one male}) = \left(\dfrac{4}{10}\right)\left(\dfrac{3}{9}\right) + \left(\dfrac{4}{10}\right)\left(\dfrac{6}{9}\right) + \left(\dfrac{6}{10}\right)\left(\dfrac{4}{9}\right) = .67$

5. a. $P(\text{Heart attack or heavy smoker}) = \dfrac{180}{500} + \dfrac{125}{500} - \dfrac{90}{500} = .43$

   b. $P(\text{Heavy smoker no heart attack}) = \dfrac{35}{500} = .07$

6.

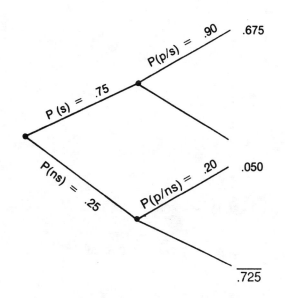

$$P(s/p) = \frac{(.75)\,(.90)}{(.75)\,(.90) + (.25)(.20)} = \frac{.675}{.725} = .931$$

7. $(5)\,(10) = 50$

8. $\dfrac{8!}{4!} = 8 \cdot 7 \cdot 6 \cdot 5 = 1{,}680$

9. $\dfrac{8!}{5!3!} = \dfrac{8 \cdot 7 \cdot 6}{3 \cdot 2} = 56$

Chapter 6

1. $\mu \doteq \Sigma X \cdot P(X) = 0(60) + 1.(.30) + 2(.10) = 0.50$

    $\sigma^2 = \Sigma (X - \mu)^2\ P(X) = (0 - .5)^2(.6) + (1 - .5)^2(.3) + (2 - .5)^2(.10)$
    $$= .45$$

2. | | Probability | |
    |---|---|---|
    | R,R,NR | (.60) (.60) (.40) = | .144 |
    | R,NR,R | (.60) (.40) (.60) = | .144 |
    | NR,R,R | (.40) (.60) (.60) = | .144 |
    | | | .432 |

    $P(2) = \dfrac{3!}{2!\ (3 - 2)!}\ (.60)^2\ (.40)^1 = .432$

3. a. $P(0) = .014$
    b. $P(r \geq 5) = P(5) + P(6) + \cdots = .158 + .079 + .029 + .008 + .001$
        $$= .275$$
    c. $P(2 \leq r \leq 4) = .168 + .240 + .231 = .39$

4. $\mu = (1{,}000) (.002) = 2.00$

    a. $P(0) = 0.1353$
    b. $P(X \geq 2) = 1 - [P(0) + P(1)] = 1 - [0.1353 + 0.2707] = 0.594$

5. $N = 30,\ s = 5,\ n = 4,\ r = 2$

    $$P(2) = \frac{\binom{5}{2} \binom{30 - 5}{4 - 2}}{\binom{30}{4}} = 0.109$$

Chapter 7

1. a. $z = \dfrac{2.00 - 2.02}{0.015} = -1.33$ $\qquad$ $0.5000 - 0.4082 = 0.0918$

    b. $z = \dfrac{2.03 - 2.02}{0.015} = 0.67$ $\qquad$ $0.4082 + 0.2486 = 0.6568$

    c. $2.05 = \dfrac{X - 2.02}{0.015}$ $\qquad$ $X = 2.02 + 0.03 = 2.05$

2. $\mu = (300) (0.90) = 270$

    $\sigma = \sqrt{300 (0.90) (0.10)} = 5.20$

    $z = \dfrac{265.5 - 270}{5.20} = -0.87$ $\qquad$ $P(X > 265.5) = .3078 + .5000 = .8078$

Chapter 8

1. a. $_5C_3 = \dfrac{5!}{3!2!} = 10$

   b.
Sample Number	Homes Sold	Total Homes Sold	Mean Number of Homes Sold
1	ABC	13	4.33
2	ABD	17	5.67
3	ABE	11	3.67
4	BCD	16	5.33
5	BCE	10	3.33
6	CDE	17	5.67
7	CDA	20	6.67
8	DEA	18	6.00
9	DEB	14	4.67
10	ACE	14	4.67

   c.
Mean Preparation Time	Frequency	Probability
3.33	1	0.1
3.67	1	0.1
4.33	1	0.1
4.67	2	0.2
5.33	1	0.1
5.67	2	0.2
6.00	1	0.1
6.67	1	0.1
	10	1.0

   d.

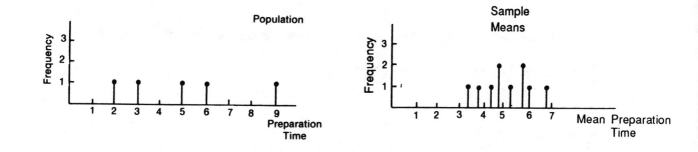

2. $\$150 \pm 2.33 \left(\dfrac{\$20}{\sqrt{36}}\right) = \$150 \pm \$7.77 = \$142.23$ to $\$157.77$

3. $\$150 \pm 2.33 \left(\dfrac{\$20}{\sqrt{36}}\right)\left(\sqrt{\dfrac{200-36}{200-1}}\right) = \$150 \pm \$7.05 = \$142.95$ to $\$157.05$

4. $0.60 \pm 1.645 \sqrt{\dfrac{(0.60)(1-0.60)}{100}} = .60 \pm .08 = .52$ and $.68$

5. $n = \left[\dfrac{(2.58)(0.25)}{0.20}\right]^2 = 10.4 = 11$

6. $n = (.33)(1-.33)\left(\dfrac{2.33}{0.04}\right)^2 = 751$

287

Chapter 9

1. $H_0: \mu \le \$30$
   $H_1: \mu > \$30$
   H_0 is rejected if z is greater than 1.645.

   $$z = \frac{\$33 - \$30}{\$12/\sqrt{40}} = 1.58$$

   H_0 is not rejected. No increase in the mean amount spent.

   $p\text{-value} = P(z > 1.58) = .5000 - .4429 = .0571$

2. Let Youngsville be population 1.
   $H_0: \mu_1 \le \mu_2$
   $H_1: \mu_1 > \mu_2$
   H_0 is rejected if z is greater than 1.645.

   $$z = \frac{6.9 - 4.9}{\sqrt{\dfrac{(3.8)^2}{60} + \dfrac{(3.0)^2}{70}}} = 3.29$$

   H_0 is rejected. It takes Youngsville longer to respond to fires.

3. $H_0: p \ge .40$
   $H_1: p < .40$
   H_0 is rejected if z is less than -1.28

   $$z = \frac{\dfrac{60}{200} - .40}{\sqrt{\dfrac{(.40)\,(.60)}{200}}} = -2.89$$

   H_0 is rejected. Less than 40 percent of the viewing audience watched the concert.

   $p\text{-value} = P(z < -2.89) = .5000 - .4981 = .0019$

4. Let population 1 be women

   $H_0: p_1 \le p_2$
   $H_1: p_1 > p_2$

   H_0 is rejected if z is greater than 1.645.

   $$\bar{p}_c = \frac{45 + 25}{150 + 100} = .28$$

   $$z = \frac{.30 - .25}{\sqrt{\dfrac{(.28)(.72)}{150} + \dfrac{(.28)(.72)}{100}}} = .86$$

   H_0 is not rejected. The proportion of smokers is the same.

   $p\text{-value} = P(z > 0.86) = .5000 - .3051 = .1949$

Chapter 10

● H_0: $\mu \leqslant 10$
H_1: $\mu > 10$

H_0 is rejected if t is greater than 3.365.

X	X²
9	81
12	144
14	196
15	225
10	100
12	144
72	890

$$\bar{X} = \frac{72}{6} = 12$$

$$s = \sqrt{\frac{890 - \frac{(72)^2}{6}}{5}} = 2.28$$

$$t = \frac{12 - 10}{2.28/\sqrt{6}} = 2.15$$

H_0 is not rejected. Employee breaks are not longer than ten minutes.

The p-value is between .050 and .025.

2. Let population 1 refer to the mall.
H_0: $\mu_1 \leqslant \mu_2$
H_1: $\mu_1 > \mu_2$
● H_0 is rejected if z is greater than 2.552.

$$s_p^2 = \frac{(10-1)(12)^2 + (10-1)(10)^2}{10 + 10 - 2} = 122$$

$$t = \frac{40 - 36}{\sqrt{122\left(\frac{1}{10} + \frac{1}{10}\right)}} = 0.81$$

H_0 is not rejected. There is no difference in mean amount spent at the mall and downtown.

p-value is greater than .10.

3. H_0: $\mu_d = 0$
H_1: $\mu_d \neq 0$

Reject H_0 if t is less than -2.365 or greater than 2.365

Electric	Gas	d	d²
265	260	5	25
271	270	1	1
260	250	10	100
250	255	−5	25
248	250	−2	4
280	275	5	25
257	260	−3	9
262	260	2	4
		13	193

$$\bar{d} = \frac{13}{8} = 1.625$$

$$s_d = \sqrt{\frac{193 - \frac{(13)^2}{8}}{7}} = 4.96$$

$$t = \frac{1.625}{\frac{4.96}{\sqrt{8}}} = 0.93$$

H_0 is not rejected. There is no difference in the heating cost.

Chapter 11

1. H_0: $\mu_1 = \mu_2 = \mu_3$
H_1: Not all means are equal.

H_0 is rejected if F is greater than 3.59.

$$\text{SS Total} = 681 - \frac{(111)^2}{20} = 64.95$$

$$\text{SST} = \frac{(19)^2}{5} + \frac{(52)^2}{7} + \frac{(40)^2}{8} - \frac{(111)^2}{20} = 42.4357$$

$$\text{SSE} = 64.95 - 42.4357 = 22.5143$$

$$F = \frac{\frac{42.4357}{2}}{\frac{22.5143}{17}} = 16.02$$

H_0 is rejected. There is a difference in the mean number correct.

2. a. 4

    b. 5

    c. 20

    d. H_0: $\mu_1 = \mu_2 = \mu_3 = \mu_4$
        H_1: Not all means are equal
        H_0 is rejected if $F > 3.49$

    $$F = \frac{15}{12} = 1.25$$

    H_0 is not rejected. No difference in the treatment means.

    e. H_0: $\mu_1 = \mu_2 = \mu_3 = \mu_4 = \mu_5$
        H_1: Not all means are equal
        H_0 is rejected if $F > 3.26$

    $$F = \frac{50}{12} = 4.17$$

    H_0 is rejected. The block means differ.

3. H_0: $\sigma_H^2 \leq \sigma_T^2$; H_1: $\sigma_H^2 > \sigma_T^2$

    H_0 is rejected if $F > 3.18$

    $$F = \frac{(60)^2}{(30)^2} = 4.00$$

    H_0 is rejected. There is more variation in the Harmon forecast.

Chapter 12

1. a.

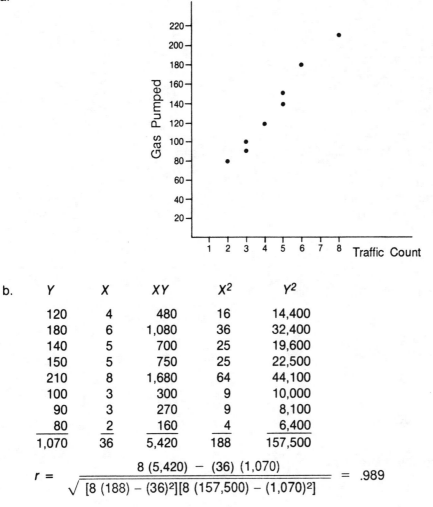

b.

Y	X	XY	X²	Y²
120	4	480	16	14,400
180	6	1,080	36	32,400
140	5	700	25	19,600
150	5	750	25	22,500
210	8	1,680	64	44,100
100	3	300	9	10,000
90	3	270	9	8,100
80	2	160	4	6,400
1,070	36	5,420	188	157,500

$$r = \frac{8\,(5,420) - (36)\,(1,070)}{\sqrt{[8\,(188) - (36)^2][8\,(157,500) - (1,070)^2]}} = .989$$

c. $r^2 = (.989)^2 = 9.78$ About 97.8 percent of the variation in gasoline pumped is explained by the traffic count.

d. $H_0: \rho \leq 0$
    $H_1: \rho > 0$

    H_0 is rejected if t is greater than 1.943.

$$t = \frac{0.989\ \sqrt{6}}{\sqrt{1 - (.989)^2}} = 16.38$$

H_0 is rejected. There is positive correlation in the population.

2.   a. $b = \dfrac{8\,(5{,}420) - (36)\,(1{,}070)}{8\,(188) - (36)^2} = 23.269$

$a = \dfrac{1{,}070}{8} - 23.269\left(\dfrac{36}{8}\right) = 29.040$

$s_{y,\,x} = \sqrt{\dfrac{157{,}500 - 29.040\,(1{,}070) - 23.269\,(5{,}420)}{8 - 2}} = 7.179$

   b. $Y' = 29.040 + 23.269\,(4) = 122.116$

$$\Sigma X^2 - \dfrac{(\Sigma X)^2}{n} = 188 - \dfrac{(36)^2}{8} = 26,\ \bar{X} = \dfrac{36}{8} = 4.5$$

$122.116 \pm 2.447\,(7.179)\sqrt{\dfrac{1}{8} + \dfrac{(4 - 4.5)^2}{26}}$

122.116 ± 6.445

   c. $122.116 \pm 2.447\,(7.179)\sqrt{1 + \dfrac{1}{8} + \dfrac{(4.0 - 4.5)^2}{26}}$

122.116 ± 18.712

3. $R^2 = \dfrac{14{,}078}{14{,}388} = .9785$

$r = \sqrt{.9785} = .9892$

$s_{y.x} = \sqrt{51.67} = 7.1880$

Chapter 13

1. No problem with multicollinearity

    H_o: $\beta_1 = \beta_2 = 0$
    H_1: Not all β's are zero

    H_o is rejected if $F > 4.74$

    $F = 8.534/1.004 = 8.5$

H_o is rejected. At least one regression coefficient is not equal to zero.

2. H_o: $\beta_1 = 0$ H_o: $\beta_2 = 0$
    H_1: $\beta_1 \neq 0$ H_1: $\beta_2 \neq 0$

    Reject H_0 if $t < -2.365$ or $t > 2.365$

    H_o for β_1 is rejected but H_o is not rejected for β_2. It appears temperature is related to usage but output is not.

3. The conditions of homoscedesticity and normality are satisfied.

Chapter 14

1. H_0: Distribution is uniform.
    H_1: Distribution is not uniform.

    Reject H_0 if the computed value of χ^2 is greater than 7.815.

Location	f_o	f_e	$\dfrac{(f_o - f_e)^2}{f_e}$
Left front	28	25	0.36
Left rear	20	25	1.00
Right front	29	25	0.64
Right rear	23	25	0.16
	100		2.16

H_o is not rejected. There is no difference in the failure rates.

2. H_0: There has been no change in the distribution
    H_1: There has been a change in the distribution

    H_o is rejected if $\chi^2 > 7.815$.

Company	f_o	f_e	$\dfrac{(f_o - f_e)^2}{f_e}$
GM	330	336	.107
Ford	275	264	.458
Chysler	174	176	.023
Other	21	24	.375
Total	800	800	0.963

H_o is not rejected. There has been no change in the distribution.

3. H_0: There is no relationship between gender and amount of time spent watching TV.
      H_1: There is a relationship between gender and amount of time spent watching TV.
      H_0 is rejected if $\chi^2 > 5.991$

f_o	f_e	$\dfrac{(f_o - f_e)^2}{f_e}$
70	75	0.333
90	85	0.294
100	75	8.333
60	85	7.353
55	75	5.333
105	85	4.706
		26.352

H_0 is rejected because χ^2 is greater than 5.991. There is a relationship between gender and the amount of time spent watching TV.

Chapter 15

1.

Student	Recent Score	Original Score	Sign of Difference
John Barr	119	112	+
Bill Sedwick	103	108	−
Marcia Elmquist	115	115	0
Ginger Thealine	109	100	+
Larry Clark	131	120	+
Jim Redding	110	108	+
Carol Papalia	109	113	−
Victor Suppa	113	126	−
Dallas Paul	94	95	−
Carol Kozoloski	119	110	+
Joe Sass	118	117	+
P.S. Sundar	112	102	+

H_0: There is no change in IQ scores ($p \leq 0.50$)
H_1: Recent IQ scores have increased over the scores in the 1960's ($p > 0.50$)

There are 12 observations, but there is one case where the difference is 0 (Marcia Elmquist), so n = 11. Because $P(X \geq 9) = .032$ and $P(X > 8) = .102$. H_0 is rejected if there are 9 or more plus signs. Since there are only 7, H_0 cannot be rejected. IQ's have not increased.

2. $H_0: p \leqslant 0.50$
$H_1: p > 0.50$

H_o is rejected if $z > 1.645$

$$z = \frac{(30 - .50) - 25.0}{.5\sqrt{50}} = 1.27$$

H_o cannot be rejected. IQ scores have not increased.

3. H_0: There is no difference in the IQ scores.
H_1: The IQ scores have increased.

H_0 is rejected if the smaller of R^+ and R^- is 13 or less.

Student	Recent	Original	Diff.	Rank	R^+	R^-
Barr	119	112	7	6	6.0	
Sidwick	103	108	−5	5		5.0
Elmquist	115	115	0			
Thesleine	109	100	9	7.5	7.5	
Clark	131	120	11	10	10.0	
Redding	110	108	2	3	3.0	
Papalia	109	113	−4	4		4.0
Suppa	113	126	−13	11		11.0
Paul	94	95	−1	1.5		1.5
Kozoloski	119	110	9	7.5	7.5	
Sass	118	117	1	1.5	1.5	
Boggs	112	102	10	9	9.0	
					44.5	21.5

Since 21.5 is not less than or equal to 13, H_o is not rejected. There has been no change in IQ scores.

4. H_0: The two populations are the same
H_1: The two populations are not the same
Reject H_0 if $z < -1.96$ or $z > 1.96$

Tough		Long Last		
Miles	Rank	Miles	Rank	
24	2	35	9	
31	7	46	15	
37	11	49	16	
44	14	52	17	
36	10	41	13	
30	6	40	12	
28	4	32	8	
21	1	29	5	
	55	27	3	
			98	

$$z = \frac{55 - \dfrac{8(8 + 9 + 1)}{2}}{\sqrt{\dfrac{8(9)\,(8 + 9 + 1)}{12}}}$$

$$= -1.636$$

H_0 is not rejected. The distributions of miles driven are the same.

5. H_0: The distributions of occupancy rates are the same.
   H_1: The distributions of occupancy rates are not the same.

   H_0 is rejected if χ^2 is greater than 5.991.

   $$H = \frac{12}{16(17)} \left(\frac{(24.5)^2}{6} + \frac{(42.5)^2}{5} + \frac{(69.0)^2}{5} \right) - 3(17) = 11.36$$

   H_0 is rejected. The occupancy rates are not the same.

6.

Team	News	Free Press	d	d^2
Penn State	1	2	-1	1
Ohio State	2	1	1	1
Michigan	3	5	-2	4
Iowa	4	6	-2	4
Wisconsin	5	3	2	4
Michigan State	6	7	-1	1
Indiana	7	8	-1	1
Minnesota	8	9	-1	1
Purdue	9	10	-1	1
Illinois	10	4	6	36
Northwestern	11	11	0	0
				54

$$r_s = 1 - \frac{6(54)}{11(121-1)} = 0.754$$

There is a strong positive correlation between the ratings.

Chapter 16

1. $P(x \leq 2 \mid p = .30 \text{ and } n = 25) = .008$
   from Appendix A where
   $c = 2, n = 25$ and $p = .30$.

Chapter 17

1. Simple aggregate index: $\dfrac{\$1,020}{\$672}(100) = 151.79$

   Laspeyres Index: $P = \dfrac{\$3,420}{\$2,226}(100) = 153.64$

   Paasche's Index: $P = \dfrac{\$3,340}{\$2,176}(100) = 153.49$

2. 1996 real income: $\dfrac{\$50,000}{150.7}(100) = \$33,179$

   His salary decreased $6,821 in real dollars.

   1990 purchasing power $\dfrac{\$1}{150.7}(100) = \$0.66$

Chapter 18

1.

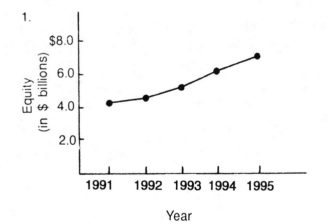

Year	Equity Y	t	Yt	t^2
91	4.3	1	4.3	1
92	4.6	2	9.2	4
93	5.2	3	15.6	9
94	6.1	4	24.4	16
95	6.9	5	34.5	25
	27.1	15	88.0	55

$$b = \frac{88.0 - (27.1)(15)/5}{55 - (15)^2/5} = \frac{6.7}{10} = 0.67$$

$$a = \frac{27.1}{5} - 0.67\left(\frac{15}{5}\right) = 3.41$$

$$Y' = 3.41 + 0.67(t) = 3.41 + 0.67(6) = 5.6947$$

2.

```
MTB >    Print c1-c4

Row    Year    Code   Imports    Log-Impt

  1    1991     1       2.0      0.301030
  2    1992     2       3.0      0.477121
  3    1993     3       4.4      0.643453
  4    1994     4       6.0      0.778151
  5    1995     5       8.5      0.929419


MTB > Regress 'Log-Impt' 1 'Code';
SUBC>   Constant.

Regression Analysis


The regression equation is
Log-Impt = 0.158 + 0.156 Code

Predictor       Coef        Stdev     t-ratio        p
Constant      0.15849      0.01497      10.59      0.002
Code          0.155781     0.004514     34.51      0.000
```

The prediction for 1996 is:

$$Y' = 0.15849 + 0.155781(6) = 1.093176$$

The antilog of 1.093176 is 12.393, so the prediction for 1996 is 12.393 million.

3. The output is:

Period	Quarter	S–I	Period	Quarter	S–I
1	1	–	3	1	0.5000
	2	–		2	1.4118
	3	1.7391		3	1.6000
	4	0.3200			
2	1	0.6154	4	4	0.4211
	2	14815		1	0.5581
	3	1.4286		2	1.3913
	4	0.5517		3	–
				4	–

↓   ↓   ↓   ↓

Seasonal Index by Quarter

Quarter	Seasonal Index
1	0.5578
2	1.4282
3	1.5892
4	0.4309

4. June = 2,000 (1.20) = 2,400
    November = 2,000 (0.47) = 940

5. $Y' = 4.0434 + 0.46079(t)$, First quarter of 1992 = 1.

Qtr	Trend	Seasonal	Forecast
17	11.87683	0.5578	6.6248
18	12.33762	1.4282	17.6206
19	12.79841	1.5892	20.3392
20	13.2592	0.4309	5.7134

Chapter 19

1.

	Repaid	Difficulty	Bankrupt
Loan	$110,000	$108,000	$ 70,000
No Loan	108,000	108,000	108,000

(Loan)   EMV(A_1) = 0.85 ($110,000) + 0.10 ($108,000) + 0.05 ($70,000) = $107,800
(No Loan) EMV(A_2) = $108,000

Since $108,000 is greater than $107,800 the banker should not make the loan.

EMV = 0.85 ($110,000) + 0.10 ($108,000) + 0.05 ($108,000) = $109,700
EVPI = $109,700 − $108,000 = $1,700

2.

	Repaid	Difficulty	Bankrupt
Loan	0	0	$38,000
No Loan	$2,000	0	0

EOL(A_1) (Loan)   = 0.05 ($38,000) = $1,900

EOL(A_2) (No Loan) = 0.85 ($ 2,000) = $1,700

Appendixes

TABLES

Appendix A

BINOMIAL PROBABILITY DISTRIBUTION

n = 1
PROBABILITY

r	0.05	0.10	0.20	0.30	0.40	0.50	0.60	0.70	0.80	0.90	0.95
0	0.950	0.900	0.800	0.700	0.600	0.500	0.400	0.300	0.200	0.100	0.050
1	0.050	0.100	0.200	0.300	0.400	0.500	0.600	0.700	0.800	0.900	0.950

n = 2
PROBABILITY

r	0.05	0.10	0.20	0.30	0.40	0.50	0.60	0.70	0.80	0.90	0.95
0	0.903	0.810	0.640	0.490	0.360	0.250	0.160	0.090	0.040	0.010	0.003
1	0.095	0.180	0.320	0.420	0.480	0.500	0.480	0.420	0.320	0.180	0.095
2	0.003	0.010	0.040	0.090	0.160	0.250	0.360	0.490	0.640	0.810	0.903

n = 3
PROBABILITY

r	0.05	0.10	0.20	0.30	0.40	0.50	0.60	0.70	0.80	0.90	0.95
0	0.857	0.729	0.512	0.343	0.216	0.125	0.064	0.027	0.008	0.001	0.000
1	0.135	0.243	0.384	0.441	0.432	0.375	0.288	0.189	0.096	0.027	0.007
2	0.007	0.027	0.096	0.189	0.288	0.375	0.432	0.441	0.384	0.243	0.135
3	0.000	0.001	0.008	0.027	0.064	0.125	0.216	0.343	0.512	0.729	0.857

n = 4
PROBABILITY

r	0.05	0.10	0.20	0.30	0.40	0.50	0.60	0.70	0.80	0.90	0.95
0	0.815	0.656	0.410	0.240	0.130	0.063	0.026	0.008	0.002	0.000	0.000
1	0.171	0.292	0.410	0.412	0.346	0.250	0.154	0.076	0.026	0.004	0.000
2	0.014	0.049	0.154	0.265	0.346	0.375	0.346	0.265	0.154	0.049	0.014
3	0.000	0.004	0.026	0.076	0.154	0.250	0.346	0.412	0.410	0.292	0.171
4	0.000	0.000	0.002	0.008	0.026	0.063	0.130	0.240	0.410	0.656	0.815

n = 5
PROBABILITY

r	0.05	0.10	0.20	0.30	0.40	0.50	0.60	0.70	0.80	0.90	0.95
0	0.774	0.590	0.328	0.168	0.078	0.031	0.010	0.002	0.000	0.000	0.000
1	0.204	0.328	0.410	0.360	0.259	0.156	0.077	0.028	0.006	0.000	0.000
2	0.021	0.073	0.205	0.309	0.346	0.313	0.230	0.132	0.051	0.008	0.001
3	0.001	0.008	0.051	0.132	0.230	0.313	0.346	0.309	0.205	0.073	0.021
4	0.000	0.000	0.006	0.028	0.077	0.156	0.259	0.360	0.410	0.328	0.204
5	0.000	0.000	0.000	0.002	0.010	0.031	0.078	0.168	0.328	0.590	0.774

n = 6
PROBABILITY

r	0.05	0.10	0.20	0.30	0.40	0.50	0.60	0.70	0.80	0.90	0.95
0	0.735	0.531	0.262	0.118	0.047	0.016	0.004	0.001	0.000	0.000	0.000
1	0.232	0.354	0.393	0.303	0.187	0.094	0.037	0.010	0.002	0.000	0.000
2	0.031	0.098	0.246	0.324	0.311	0.234	0.138	0.060	0.015	0.001	0.000
3	0.002	0.015	0.082	0.185	0.276	0.313	0.276	0.185	0.082	0.015	0.002
4	0.000	0.001	0.015	0.060	0.138	0.234	0.311	0.324	0.246	0.098	0.031
5	0.000	0.000	0.002	0.010	0.037	0.094	0.187	0.303	0.393	0.354	0.232
6	0.000	0.000	0.000	0.001	0.004	0.016	0.047	0.118	0.262	0.531	0.735

BINOMIAL PROBABILITY DISTRIBUTION (*continued*)

n = 7
PROBABILITY

r	0.05	0.10	0.20	0.30	0.40	0.50	0.60	0.70	0.80	0.90	0.95
0	0.698	0.478	0.210	0.082	0.028	0.008	0.002	0.000	0.000	0.000	0.000
1	0.257	0.372	0.367	0.247	0.131	0.055	0.017	0.004	0.000	0.000	0.000
2	0.041	0.124	0.275	0.318	0.261	0.164	0.077	0.025	0.004	0.000	0.000
3	0.004	0.023	0.115	0.227	0.290	0.273	0.194	0.097	0.029	0.003	0.000
4	0.000	0.003	0.029	0.097	0.194	0.273	0.290	0.227	0.115	0.023	0.004
5	0.000	0.000	0.004	0.025	0.077	0.164	0.261	0.318	0.275	0.124	0.041
6	0.000	0.000	0.000	0.004	0.017	0.055	0.131	0.247	0.367	0.372	0.257
7	0.000	0.000	0.000	0.000	0.002	0.008	0.028	0.082	0.210	0.478	0.698

n = 8
PROBABILITY

r	0.05	0.10	0.20	0.30	0.40	0.50	0.60	0.70	0.80	0.90	0.95
0	0.663	0.430	0.168	0.058	0.017	0.004	0.001	0.000	0.000	0.000	0.000
1	0.279	0.383	0.336	0.198	0.090	0.031	0.008	0.001	0.000	0.000	0.000
2	0.051	0.149	0.294	0.296	0.209	0.109	0.041	0.010	0.001	0.000	0.000
3	0.005	0.033	0.147	0.254	0.279	0.219	0.124	0.047	0.009	0.000	0.000
4	0.000	0.005	0.046	0.136	0.232	0.273	0.232	0.136	0.046	0.005	0.000
5	0.000	0.000	0.009	0.047	0.124	0.219	0.279	0.254	0.147	0.033	0.005
6	0.000	0.000	0.001	0.010	0.041	0.109	0.209	0.296	0.294	0.149	0.051
7	0.000	0.000	0.000	0.001	0.008	0.031	0.090	0.198	0.336	0.383	0.279
8	0.000	0.000	0.000	0.000	0.001	0.004	0.017	0.058	0.168	0.430	0.663

n = 9
PROBABILITY

r	0.05	0.10	0.20	0.30	0.40	0.50	0.60	0.70	0.80	0.90	0.95
0	0.630	0.387	0.134	0.040	0.010	0.002	0.000	0.000	0.000	0.000	0.000
1	0.299	0.387	0.302	0.156	0.060	0.018	0.004	0.000	0.000	0.000	0.000
2	0.063	0.172	0.302	0.267	0.161	0.070	0.021	0.004	0.000	0.000	0.000
3	0.008	0.045	0.176	0.267	0.251	0.164	0.074	0.021	0.003	0.000	0.000
4	0.001	0.007	0.066	0.172	0.251	0.246	0.167	0.074	0.017	0.001	0.000
5	0.000	0.001	0.017	0.074	0.167	0.246	0.251	0.172	0.066	0.007	0.001
6	0.000	0.000	0.003	0.021	0.074	0.164	0.251	0.267	0.176	0.045	0.008
7	0.000	0.000	0.000	0.004	0.021	0.070	0.161	0.267	0.302	0.172	0.063
8	0.000	0.000	0.000	0.000	0.004	0.018	0.060	0.156	0.302	0.387	0.299
9	0.000	0.000	0.000	0.000	0.000	0.002	0.010	0.040	0.134	0.387	0.630

BINOMIAL PROBABILITY DISTRIBUTION (*continued*)

n = 10
PROBABILITY

r	0.05	0.10	0.20	0.30	0.40	0.50	0.60	0.70	0.80	0.90	0.95
0	0.599	0.349	0.107	0.028	0.006	0.001	0.000	0.000	0.000	0.000	0.000
1	0.315	0.387	0.268	0.121	0.040	0.010	0.002	0.000	0.000	0.000	0.000
2	0.075	0.194	0.302	0.233	0.121	0.044	0.011	0.001	0.000	0.000	0.000
3	0.010	0.057	0.201	0.267	0.215	0.117	0.042	0.009	0.001	0.000	0.000
4	0.001	0.011	0.088	0.200	0.251	0.205	0.111	0.037	0.006	0.000	0.000
5	0.000	0.001	0.026	0.103	0.201	0.246	0.201	0.103	0.026	0.001	0.000
6	0.000	0.000	0.006	0.037	0.111	0.205	0.251	0.200	0.088	0.011	0.001
7	0.000	0.000	0.001	0.009	0.042	0.117	0.215	0.267	0.201	0.057	0.010
8	0.000	0.000	0.000	0.001	0.011	0.044	0.121	0.233	0.302	0.194	0.075
9	0.000	0.000	0.000	0.000	0.002	0.010	0.040	0.121	0.268	0.387	0.315
10	0.000	0.000	0.000	0.000	0.000	0.001	0.006	0.028	0.107	0.349	0.599

n = 11
PROBABILITY

r	0.05	0.10	0.20	0.30	0.40	0.50	0.60	0.70	0.80	0.90	0.95
0	0.569	0.314	0.086	0.020	0.004	0.000	0.000	0.000	0.000	0.000	0.000
1	0.329	0.384	0.236	0.093	0.027	0.005	0.001	0.000	0.000	0.000	0.000
2	0.087	0.213	0.295	0.200	0.089	0.027	0.005	0.001	0.000	0.000	0.000
3	0.014	0.071	0.221	0.257	0.177	0.081	0.023	0.004	0.000	0.000	0.000
4	0.001	0.016	0.111	0.220	0.236	0.161	0.070	0.017	0.002	0.000	0.000
5	0.000	0.002	0.039	0.132	0.221	0.226	0.147	0.057	0.010	0.000	0.000
6	0.000	0.000	0.010	0.057	0.147	0.226	0.221	0.132	0.039	0.002	0.000
7	0.000	0.000	0.002	0.017	0.070	0.161	0.236	0.220	0.111	0.016	0.001
8	0.000	0.000	0.000	0.004	0.023	0.081	0.177	0.257	0.221	0.071	0.014
9	0.000	0.000	0.000	0.001	0.005	0.027	0.089	0.200	0.295	0.213	0.087
10	0.000	0.000	0.000	0.000	0.001	0.005	0.027	0.093	0.236	0.384	0.329
11	0.000	0.000	0.000	0.000	0.000	0.000	0.004	0.020	0.086	0.314	0.569

n = 12
PROBABILITY

r	0.05	0.10	0.20	0.30	0.40	0.50	0.60	0.70	0.80	0.90	0.95
0	0.540	0.282	0.069	0.014	0.002	0.000	0.000	0.000	0.000	0.000	0.000
1	0.341	0.377	0.206	0.071	0.017	0.003	0.000	0.000	0.000	0.000	0.000
2	0.099	0.230	0.283	0.168	0.064	0.016	0.002	0.000	0.000	0.000	0.000
3	0.017	0.085	0.236	0.240	0.142	0.054	0.012	0.001	0.000	0.000	0.000
4	0.002	0.021	0.133	0.231	0.213	0.121	0.042	0.008	0.001	0.000	0.000
5	0.000	0.004	0.053	0.158	0.227	0.193	0.101	0.029	0.003	0.000	0.000
6	0.000	0.000	0.016	0.079	0.177	0.226	0.177	0.079	0.016	0.000	0.000
7	0.000	0.000	0.003	0.029	0.101	0.193	0.227	0.158	0.053	0.004	0.000
8	0.000	0.000	0.001	0.008	0.042	0.121	0.213	0.231	0.133	0.021	0.002
9	0.000	0.000	0.000	0.001	0.012	0.054	0.142	0.240	0.236	0.085	0.017
10	0.000	0.000	0.000	0.000	0.002	0.016	0.064	0.168	0.283	0.230	0.099
11	0.000	0.000	0.000	0.000	0.000	0.003	0.017	0.071	0.206	0.377	0.341
12	0.000	0.000	0.000	0.000	0.000	0.000	0.002	0.014	0.069	0.282	0.540

BINOMIAL PROBABILITY DISTRIBUTION (*continued*)

$n = 13$
PROBABILITY

r	0.05	0.10	0.20	0.30	0.40	0.50	0.60	0.70	0.80	0.90	0.95
0	0.513	0.254	0.055	0.010	0.001	0.000	0.000	0.000	0.000	0.000	0.000
1	0.351	0.367	0.179	0.054	0.011	0.002	0.000	0.000	0.000	0.000	0.000
2	0.111	0.245	0.268	0.139	0.045	0.010	0.001	0.000	0.000	0.000	0.000
3	0.021	0.100	0.246	0.218	0.111	0.035	0.006	0.001	0.000	0.000	0.000
4	0.003	0.028	0.154	0.234	0.184	0.087	0.024	0.003	0.000	0.000	0.000
5	0.000	0.006	0.069	0.180	0.221	0.157	0.066	0.014	0.001	0.000	0.000
6	0.000	0.001	0.023	0.103	0.197	0.209	0.131	0.044	0.006	0.000	0.000
7	0.000	0.000	0.006	0.044	0.131	0.209	0.197	0.103	0.023	0.001	0.000
8	0.000	0.000	0.001	0.014	0.066	0.157	0.221	0.180	0.069	0.006	0.000
9	0.000	0.000	0.000	0.003	0.024	0.087	0.184	0.234	0.154	0.028	0.003
10	0.000	0.000	0.000	0.001	0.006	0.035	0.111	0.218	0.246	0.100	0.021
11	0.000	0.000	0.000	0.000	0.001	0.010	0.045	0.139	0.268	0.245	0.111
12	0.000	0.000	0.000	0.000	0.000	0.002	0.011	0.054	0.179	0.367	0.351
13	0.000	0.000	0.000	0.000	0.000	0.000	0.001	0.010	0.055	0.254	0.513

$n = 14$
PROBABILITY

r	0.05	0.10	0.20	0.30	0.40	0.50	0.60	0.70	0.80	0.90	0.95
0	0.488	0.229	0.044	0.007	0.001	0.000	0.000	0.000	0.000	0.000	0.000
1	0.359	0.356	0.154	0.041	0.007	0.001	0.000	0.000	0.000	0.000	0.000
2	0.123	0.257	0.250	0.113	0.032	0.006	0.001	0.000	0.000	0.000	0.000
3	0.026	0.114	0.250	0.194	0.085	0.022	0.003	0.000	0.000	0.000	0.000
4	0.004	0.035	0.172	0.229	0.155	0.061	0.014	0.001	0.000	0.000	0.000
5	0.000	0.008	0.086	0.196	0.207	0.122	0.041	0.007	0.000	0.000	0.000
6	0.000	0.001	0.032	0.126	0.207	0.183	0.092	0.023	0.002	0.000	0.000
7	0.000	0.000	0.009	0.062	0.157	0.209	0.157	0.062	0.009	0.000	0.000
8	0.000	0.000	0.002	0.023	0.092	0.183	0.207	0.126	0.032	0.001	0.000
9	0.000	0.000	0.000	0.007	0.041	0.122	0.207	0.196	0.086	0.008	0.000
10	0.000	0.000	0.000	0.001	0.014	0.061	0.155	0.229	0.172	0.035	0.004
11	0.000	0.000	0.000	0.000	0.003	0.022	0.085	0.194	0.250	0.114	0.026
12	0.000	0.000	0.000	0.000	0.001	0.006	0.032	0.113	0.250	0.257	0.123
13	0.000	0.000	0.000	0.000	0.000	0.001	0.007	0.041	0.154	0.356	0.359
14	0.000	0.000	0.000	0.000	0.000	0.000	0.001	0.007	0.044	0.229	0.488

BINOMIAL PROBABILITY DISTRIBUTION (continued)

n = 15
PROBABILITY

r	0.05	0.10	0.20	0.30	0.40	0.50	0.60	0.70	0.80	0.90	0.95
0	0.463	0.206	0.035	0.005	0.000	0.000	0.000	0.000	0.000	0.000	0.000
1	0.366	0.343	0.132	0.031	0.005	0.000	0.000	0.000	0.000	0.000	0.000
2	0.135	0.267	0.231	0.092	0.022	0.003	0.000	0.000	0.000	0.000	0.000
3	0.031	0.129	0.250	0.170	0.063	0.014	0.002	0.000	0.000	0.000	0.000
4	0.005	0.043	0.188	0.219	0.127	0.042	0.007	0.001	0.000	0.000	0.000
5	0.001	0.010	0.103	0.206	0.186	0.092	0.024	0.003	0.000	0.000	0.000
6	0.000	0.002	0.043	0.147	0.207	0.153	0.061	0.012	0.001	0.000	0.000
7	0.000	0.000	0.014	0.081	0.177	0.196	0.118	0.035	0.003	0.000	0.000
8	0.000	0.000	0.003	0.035	0.118	0.196	0.177	0.081	0.014	0.000	0.000
9	0.000	0.000	0.001	0.012	0.061	0.153	0.207	0.147	0.043	0.002	0.000
10	0.000	0.000	0.000	0.003	0.024	0.092	0.186	0.206	0.103	0.010	0.001
11	0.000	0.000	0.000	0.001	0.007	0.042	0.127	0.219	0.188	0.043	0.005
12	0.000	0.000	0.000	0.000	0.002	0.014	0.063	0.170	0.250	0.129	0.031
13	0.000	0.000	0.000	0.000	0.000	0.003	0.022	0.092	0.231	0.267	0.135
14	0.000	0.000	0.000	0.000	0.000	0.000	0.005	0.031	0.132	0.343	0.366
15	0.000	0.000	0.000	0.000	0.000	0.000	0.000	0.005	0.035	0.206	0.463

n = 16
PROBABILITY

r	0.05	0.10	0.20	0.30	0.40	0.50	0.60	0.70	0.80	0.90	0.95
0	0.440	0.185	0.028	0.003	0.000	0.000	0.000	0.000	0.000	0.000	0.000
1	0.371	0.329	0.113	0.023	0.003	0.000	0.000	0.000	0.000	0.000	0.000
2	0.146	0.275	0.211	0.073	0.015	0.002	0.000	0.000	0.000	0.000	0.000
3	0.036	0.142	0.246	0.146	0.047	0.009	0.001	0.000	0.000	0.000	0.000
4	0.006	0.051	0.200	0.204	0.101	0.028	0.004	0.000	0.000	0.000	0.000
5	0.001	0.014	0.120	0.210	0.162	0.067	0.014	0.001	0.000	0.000	0.000
6	0.000	0.003	0.055	0.165	0.198	0.122	0.039	0.006	0.000	0.000	0.000
7	0.000	0.000	0.020	0.101	0.189	0.175	0.084	0.019	0.001	0.000	0.000
8	0.000	0.000	0.006	0.049	0.142	0.196	0.142	0.049	0.006	0.000	0.000
9	0.000	0.000	0.001	0.019	0.084	0.175	0.189	0.101	0.020	0.000	0.000
10	0.000	0.000	0.000	0.006	0.039	0.122	0.198	0.165	0.055	0.003	0.000
11	0.000	0.000	0.000	0.001	0.014	0.067	0.162	0.210	0.120	0.014	0.001
12	0.000	0.000	0.000	0.000	0.004	0.028	0.101	0.204	0.200	0.051	0.006
13	0.000	0.000	0.000	0.000	0.001	0.009	0.047	0.146	0.246	0.142	0.036
14	0.000	0.000	0.000	0.000	0.000	0.002	0.015	0.073	0.211	0.275	0.146
15	0.000	0.000	0.000	0.000	0.000	0.000	0.003	0.023	0.113	0.329	0.371
16	0.000	0.000	0.000	0.000	0.000	0.000	0.000	0.003	0.028	0.185	0.440

BINOMIAL PROBABILITY DISTRIBUTION (*continued*)

$n = 17$
PROBABILITY

r	0.05	0.10	0.20	0.30	0.40	0.50	0.60	0.70	0.80	0.90	0.95
0	0.418	0.167	0.023	0.002	0.000	0.000	0.000	0.000	0.000	0.000	0.000
1	0.374	0.315	0.096	0.017	0.002	0.000	0.000	0.000	0.000	0.000	0.000
2	0.158	0.280	0.191	0.058	0.010	0.001	0.000	0.000	0.000	0.000	0.000
3	0.041	0.156	0.239	0.125	0.034	0.005	0.000	0.000	0.000	0.000	0.000
4	0.008	0.060	0.209	0.187	0.080	0.018	0.002	0.000	0.000	0.000	0.000
5	0.001	0.017	0.136	0.208	0.138	0.047	0.008	0.001	0.000	0.000	0.000
6	0.000	0.004	0.068	0.178	0.184	0.094	0.024	0.003	0.000	0.000	0.000
7	0.000	0.001	0.027	0.120	0.193	0.148	0.057	0.009	0.000	0.000	0.000
8	0.000	0.000	0.008	0.064	0.161	0.185	0.107	0.028	0.002	0.000	0.000
9	0.000	0.000	0.002	0.028	0.107	0.185	0.161	0.064	0.008	0.000	0.000
10	0.000	0.000	0.000	0.009	0.057	0.148	0.193	0.120	0.027	0.001	0.000
11	0.000	0.000	0.000	0.003	0.024	0.094	0.184	0.178	0.068	0.004	0.000
12	0.000	0.000	0.000	0.001	0.008	0.047	0.138	0.208	0.136	0.017	0.001
13	0.000	0.000	0.000	0.000	0.002	0.018	0.080	0.187	0.209	0.060	0.008
14	0.000	0.000	0.000	0.000	0.000	0.005	0.034	0.125	0.239	0.156	0.041
15	0.000	0.000	0.000	0.000	0.000	0.001	0.010	0.058	0.191	0.280	0.158
16	0.000	0.000	0.000	0.000	0.000	0.000	0.002	0.017	0.096	0.315	0.374
17	0.000	0.000	0.000	0.000	0.000	0.000	0.000	0.002	0.023	0.167	0.418

$n = 18$
PROBABILITY

r	0.05	0.10	0.20	0.30	0.40	0.50	0.60	0.70	0.80	0.90	0.95
0	0.397	0.150	0.018	0.002	0.000	0.000	0.000	0.000	0.000	0.000	0.000
1	0.376	0.300	0.081	0.013	0.001	0.000	0.000	0.000	0.000	0.000	0.000
2	0.168	0.284	0.172	0.046	0.007	0.001	0.000	0.000	0.000	0.000	0.000
3	0.047	0.168	0.230	0.105	0.025	0.003	0.000	0.000	0.000	0.000	0.000
4	0.009	0.070	0.215	0.168	0.061	0.012	0.001	0.000	0.000	0.000	0.000
5	0.001	0.022	0.151	0.202	0.115	0.033	0.004	0.000	0.000	0.000	0.000
6	0.000	0.005	0.082	0.187	0.166	0.071	0.015	0.001	0.000	0.000	0.000
7	0.000	0.001	0.035	0.138	0.189	0.121	0.037	0.005	0.000	0.000	0.000
8	0.000	0.000	0.012	0.081	0.173	0.167	0.077	0.015	0.001	0.000	0.000
9	0.000	0.000	0.003	0.039	0.128	0.185	0.128	0.039	0.003	0.000	0.000
10	0.000	0.000	0.001	0.015	0.077	0.167	0.173	0.081	0.012	0.000	0.000
11	0.000	0.000	0.000	0.005	0.037	0.121	0.189	0.138	0.035	0.001	0.000
12	0.000	0.000	0.000	0.001	0.015	0.071	0.166	0.187	0.082	0.005	0.000
13	0.000	0.000	0.000	0.000	0.004	0.033	0.115	0.202	0.151	0.022	0.001
14	0.000	0.000	0.000	0.000	0.001	0.012	0.061	0.168	0.215	0.070	0.009
15	0.000	0.000	0.000	0.000	0.000	0.003	0.025	0.105	0.230	0.168	0.047
16	0.000	0.000	0.000	0.000	0.000	0.001	0.007	0.046	0.172	0.284	0.168
17	0.000	0.000	0.000	0.000	0.000	0.000	0.001	0.013	0.081	0.300	0.376
18	0.000	0.000	0.000	0.000	0.000	0.000	0.000	0.002	0.018	0.150	0.397

BINOMIAL PROBABILITY DISTRIBUTION (*continued*)

n = 19
PROBABILITY

r	0.05	0.10	0.20	0.30	0.40	0.50	0.60	0.70	0.80	0.90	0.95
0	0.377	0.135	0.014	0.001	0.000	0.000	0.000	0.000	0.000	0.000	0.000
1	0.377	0.285	0.068	0.009	0.001	0.000	0.000	0.000	0.000	0.000	0.000
2	0.179	0.285	0.154	0.036	0.005	0.000	0.000	0.000	0.000	0.000	0.000
3	0.053	0.180	0.218	0.087	0.017	0.002	0.000	0.000	0.000	0.000	0.000
4	0.011	0.080	0.218	0.149	0.047	0.007	0.001	0.000	0.000	0.000	0.000
5	0.002	0.027	0.164	0.192	0.093	0.022	0.002	0.000	0.000	0.000	0.000
6	0.000	0.007	0.095	0.192	0.145	0.052	0.008	0.001	0.000	0.000	0.000
7	0.000	0.001	0.044	0.153	0.180	0.096	0.024	0.002	0.000	0.000	0.000
8	0.000	0.000	0.017	0.098	0.180	0.144	0.053	0.008	0.000	0.000	0.000
9	0.000	0.000	0.005	0.051	0.146	0.176	0.098	0.022	0.001	0.000	0.000
10	0.000	0.000	0.001	0.022	0.098	0.176	0.146	0.051	0.005	0.000	0.000
11	0.000	0.000	0.000	0.008	0.053	0.144	0.180	0.098	0.017	0.000	0.000
12	0.000	0.000	0.000	0.002	0.024	0.096	0.180	0.153	0.044	0.001	0.000
13	0.000	0.000	0.000	0.001	0.008	0.052	0.145	0.192	0.095	0.007	0.000
14	0.000	0.000	0.000	0.000	0.002	0.022	0.093	0.192	0.164	0.027	0.002
15	0.000	0.000	0.000	0.000	0.001	0.007	0.047	0.149	0.218	0.080	0.011
16	0.000	0.000	0.000	0.000	0.000	0.002	0.017	0.087	0.218	0.180	0.053
17	0.000	0.000	0.000	0.000	0.000	0.000	0.005	0.036	0.154	0.285	0.179
18	0.000	0.000	0.000	0.000	0.000	0.000	0.001	0.009	0.068	0.285	0.377
19	0.000	0.000	0.000	0.000	0.000	0.000	0.000	0.001	0.014	0.135	0.377

n = 20
PROBABILITY

r	0.05	0.10	0.20	0.30	0.40	0.50	0.60	0.70	0.80	0.90	0.95
0	0.358	0.122	0.012	0.001	0.000	0.000	0.000	0.000	0.000	0.000	0.000
1	0.377	0.270	0.058	0.007	0.000	0.000	0.000	0.000	0.000	0.000	0.000
2	0.189	0.285	0.137	0.028	0.003	0.000	0.000	0.000	0.000	0.000	0.000
3	0.060	0.190	0.205	0.072	0.012	0.001	0.000	0.000	0.000	0.000	0.000
4	0.013	0.090	0.218	0.130	0.035	0.005	0.000	0.000	0.000	0.000	0.000
5	0.002	0.032	0.175	0.179	0.075	0.015	0.001	0.000	0.000	0.000	0.000
6	0.000	0.009	0.109	0.192	0.124	0.037	0.005	0.000	0.000	0.000	0.000
7	0.000	0.002	0.055	0.164	0.166	0.074	0.015	0.001	0.000	0.000	0.000
8	0.000	0.000	0.022	0.114	0.180	0.120	0.035	0.004	0.000	0.000	0.000
9	0.000	0.000	0.007	0.065	0.160	0.160	0.071	0.012	0.000	0.000	0.000
10	0.000	0.000	0.002	0.031	0.117	0.176	0.117	0.031	0.002	0.000	0.000
11	0.000	0.000	0.000	0.012	0.071	0.160	0.160	0.065	0.007	0.000	0.000
12	0.000	0.000	0.000	0.004	0.035	0.120	0.180	0.114	0.022	0.000	0.000
13	0.000	0.000	0.000	0.001	0.015	0.074	0.166	0.164	0.055	0.002	0.000
14	0.000	0.000	0.000	0.000	0.005	0.037	0.124	0.192	0.109	0.009	0.000
15	0.000	0.000	0.000	0.000	0.001	0.015	0.075	0.179	0.175	0.032	0.002
16	0.000	0.000	0.000	0.000	0.000	0.005	0.035	0.130	0.218	0.090	0.013
17	0.000	0.000	0.000	0.000	0.000	0.001	0.012	0.072	0.205	0.190	0.060
18	0.000	0.000	0.000	0.000	0.000	0.000	0.003	0.028	0.137	0.285	0.189
19	0.000	0.000	0.000	0.000	0.000	0.000	0.000	0.007	0.058	0.270	0.377
20	0.000	0.000	0.000	0.000	0.000	0.000	0.000	0.001	0.012	0.122	0.358

BINOMIAL PROBABILITY DISTRIBUTION (*concluded*)

$n = 25$
PROBABILITY

r	0.05	0.10	0.20	0.30	0.40	0.50	0.60	0.70	0.80	0.90	0.95
0	0.277	0.072	0.004	0.000	0.000	0.000	0.000	0.000	0.000	0.000	0.000
1	0.365	0.199	0.024	0.001	0.000	0.000	0.000	0.000	0.000	0.000	0.000
2	0.231	0.266	0.071	0.007	0.000	0.000	0.000	0.000	0.000	0.000	0.000
3	0.093	0.226	0.136	0.024	0.002	0.000	0.000	0.000	0.000	0.000	0.000
4	0.027	0.138	0.187	0.057	0.007	0.000	0.000	0.000	0.000	0.000	0.000
5	0.006	0.065	0.196	0.103	0.020	0.002	0.000	0.000	0.000	0.000	0.000
6	0.001	0.024	0.163	0.147	0.044	0.005	0.000	0.000	0.000	0.000	0.000
7	0.000	0.007	0.111	0.171	0.080	0.014	0.001	0.000	0.000	0.000	0.000
8	0.000	0.002	0.062	0.165	0.120	0.032	0.003	0.000	0.000	0.000	0.000
9	0.000	0.000	0.029	0.134	0.151	0.061	0.009	0.000	0.000	0.000	0.000
10	0.000	0.000	0.012	0.092	0.161	0.097	0.021	0.001	0.000	0.000	0.000
11	0.000	0.000	0.004	0.054	0.147	0.133	0.043	0.004	0.000	0.000	0.000
12	0.000	0.000	0.001	0.027	0.114	0.155	0.076	0.011	0.000	0.000	0.000
13	0.000	0.000	0.000	0.011	0.076	0.155	0.114	0.027	0.001	0.000	0.000
14	0.000	0.000	0.000	0.004	0.043	0.133	0.147	0.054	0.004	0.000	0.000
15	0.000	0.000	0.000	0.001	0.021	0.097	0.161	0.092	0.012	0.000	0.000
16	0.000	0.000	0.000	0.000	0.009	0.061	0.151	0.134	0.029	0.000	0.000
17	0.000	0.000	0.000	0.000	0.003	0.032	0.120	0.165	0.062	0.002	0.000
18	0.000	0.000	0.000	0.000	0.001	0.014	0.080	0.171	0.111	0.007	0.000
19	0.000	0.000	0.000	0.000	0.000	0.005	0.044	0.147	0.163	0.024	0.001
20	0.000	0.000	0.000	0.000	0.000	0.002	0.020	0.103	0.196	0.065	0.006
21	0.000	0.000	0.000	0.000	0.000	0.000	0.007	0.057	0.187	0.138	0.027
22	0.000	0.000	0.000	0.000	0.000	0.000	0.002	0.024	0.136	0.226	0.093
23	0.000	0.000	0.000	0.000	0.000	0.000	0.000	0.007	0.071	0.266	0.231
24	0.000	0.000	0.000	0.000	0.000	0.000	0.000	0.001	0.024	0.199	0.365
25	0.000	0.000	0.000	0.000	0.000	0.000	0.000	0.000	0.004	0.072	0.277

Appendix B

FACTORS FOR CONTROL CHARTS

Number of Items in Sample, n	Chart for Averages	Chart for Ranges		
	Factors for Control Limits	Factors for Central Line	Factors for Control Limits	
	A_2	d_2	D_3	D_4
2	1.880	1.128	0	3.267
3	1.023	1.693	0	2.575
4	.729	2.059	0	2.282
5	.577	2.326	0	2.115
6	.483	2.534	0	2.004
7	.419	2.704	.076	1.924
8	.373	2.847	.136	1.864
9	.337	2.970	.184	1.816
10	.308	3.078	.223	1.777
11	.285	3.173	.256	1.744
12	.266	3.258	.284	1.716
13	.249	3.336	.308	1.692
14	.235	3.407	.329	1.671
15	.223	3.472	.348	1.652

Source: Adapted from American Society for Testing and Materials. *Manual on Quality Control of Materials*, 1951, Table B2, p. 115. For detailed table and explanation, see Acheson J. Duncan. *Quality Control and Industrial Statistics*, 3d ed. (Homewood, III.: Richard 1974), Table M. p. 927.

POISSON DISTRIBUTION: PROBABILITY OF EXACTLY X OCCURRENCES

					μ				
X	0.1	0.2	0.3	0.4	0.5	0.6	0.7	0.8	0.9
0	0.9048	0.8187	0.7408	0.6703	0.6065	0.5488	0.4966	0.4493	0.4066
1	0.0905	0.1637	0.2222	0.2681	0.3033	0.3293	0.3476	0.3595	0.3659
2	0.0045	0.0164	0.0333	0.0536	0.0758	0.0988	0.1217	0.1438	0.1647
3	0.0002	0.0011	0.0033	0.0072	0.0126	0.0198	0.0284	0.0383	0.0494
4	0.0000	0.0001	0.0003	0.0007	0.0016	0.0030	0.0050	0.0077	0.0111
5	0.0000	0.0000	0.0000	0.0001	0.0002	0.0004	0.0007	0.0012	0.0020
6	0.0000	0.0000	0.0000	0.0000	0.0000	0.0000	0.0001	0.0002	0.0003
7	0.0000	0.0000	0.0000	0.0000	0.0000	0.0000	0.0000	0.0000	0.0000

					μ				
X	1.0	2.0	3.0	4.0	5.0	6.0	7.0	8.0	9.0
0	0.3679	0.1353	0.0498	0.0183	0.0067	0.0025	0.0009	0.0003	0.0001
1	0.3679	0.2707	0.1494	0.0733	0.0337	0.0149	0.0064	0.0027	0.0011
2	0.1839	0.2707	0.2240	0.1465	0.0842	0.0446	0.0223	0.0107	0.0050
3	0.0613	0.1804	0.2240	0.1954	0.1404	0.0892	0.0521	0.0286	0.0150
4	0.0153	0.0902	0.1680	0.1954	0.1755	0.1339	0.0912	0.0573	0.0337
5	0.0031	0.0361	0.1008	0.1563	0.1755	0.1606	0.1277	0.0916	0.0607
6	0.0005	0.0120	0.0504	0.1042	0.1462	0.1606	0.1490	0.1221	0.0911
7	0.0001	0.0034	0.0216	0.0595	0.1044	0.1377	0.1490	0.1396	0.1171
8	0.0000	0.0009	0.0081	0.0298	0.0653	0.1033	0.1304	0.1396	0.1318
9	0.0000	0.0002	0.0027	0.0132	0.0363	0.0688	0.1014	0.1241	0.1318
10	0.0000	0.0000	0.0008	0.0053	0.0181	0.0413	0.0710	0.0993	0.1186
11	0.0000	0.0000	0.0002	0.0019	0.0082	0.0225	0.0452	0.0722	0.0970
12	0.0000	0.0000	0.0001	0.0006	0.0034	0.0113	0.0263	0.0481	0.0728
13	0.0000	0.0000	0.0000	0.0002	0.0013	0.0052	0.0142	0.0296	0.0504
14	0.0000	0.0000	0.0000	0.0001	0.0005	0.0022	0.0071	0.0169	0.0324
15	0.0000	0.0000	0.0000	0.0000	0.0002	0.0009	0.0033	0.0090	0.0194
16	0.0000	0.0000	0.0000	0.0000	0.0000	0.0003	0.0014	0.0045	0.0109
17	0.0000	0.0000	0.0000	0.0000	0.0000	0.0001	0.0006	0.0021	0.0058
18	0.0000	0.0000	0.0000	0.0000	0.0000	0.0000	0.0002	0.0009	0.0029
19	0.0000	0.0000	0.0000	0.0000	0.0000	0.0000	0.0001	0.0004	0.0014
20	0.0000	0.0000	0.0000	0.0000	0.0000	0.0000	0.0000	0.0002	0.0006
21	0.0000	0.0000	0.0000	0.0000	0.0000	0.0000	0.0000	0.0001	0.0003
22	0.0000	0.0000	0.0000	0.0000	0.0000	0.0000	0.0000	0.0000	0.0001

AREAS UNDER THE NORMAL CURVE

Example:
If z = 1.96, then
0.4750 of the area is
between 0 and 1.96.

Z	0.00	0.01	0.02	0.03	0.04	0.05	0.06	0.07	0.08	0.09
0.0	0.0000	0.0040	0.0080	0.0120	0.0160	0.0199	0.0239	0.0279	0.0319	0.0359
0.1	0.0398	0.0438	0.0478	0.0517	0.0557	0.0596	0.0636	0.0675	0.0714	0.0753
0.2	0.0793	0.0832	0.0871	0.0910	0.0948	0.0987	0.1026	0.1064	0.1103	0.1141
0.3	0.1179	0.1217	0.1255	0.1293	0.1331	0.1368	0.1406	0.1443	0.1480	0.1517
0.4	0.1554	0.1591	0.1628	0.1664	0.1700	0.1736	0.1772	0.1808	0.1844	0.1879
0.5	0.1915	0.1950	0.1985	0.2019	0.2054	0.2088	0.2123	0.2157	0.2190	0.2224
0.6	0.2257	0.2291	0.2324	0.2357	0.2389	0.2422	0.2454	0.2486	0.2517	0.2549
0.7	0.2580	0.2611	0.2642	0.2673	0.2704	0.2734	0.2764	0.2794	0.2823	0.2852
0.8	0.2881	0.2910	0.2939	0.2967	0.2995	0.3023	0.3051	0.3078	0.3106	0.3133
0.9	0.3159	0.3186	0.3212	0.3238	0.3264	0.3289	0.3315	0.3340	0.3365	0.3389
1.0	0.3413	0.3438	0.3461	0.3485	0.3508	0.3531	0.3554	0.3577	0.3599	0.3621
1.1	0.3643	0.3665	0.3686	0.3708	0.3729	0.3749	0.3770	0.3790	0.3810	0.3830
1.2	0.3849	0.3869	0.3888	0.3907	0.3925	0.3944	0.3962	0.3980	0.3997	0.4015
1.3	0.4032	0.4049	0.4066	0.4082	0.4099	0.4115	0.4131	0.4147	0.4162	0.4177
1.4	0.4192	0.4207	0.4222	0.4236	0.4251	0.4265	0.4279	0.4292	0.4306	0.4319
1.5	0.4332	0.4345	0.4357	0.4370	0.4382	0.4394	0.4406	0.4418	0.4429	0.4441
1.6	0.4452	0.4463	0.4474	0.4484	0.4495	0.4505	0.4515	0.4525	0.4535	0.4545
1.7	0.4554	0.4564	0.4573	0.4582	0.4591	0.4599	0.4608	0.4616	0.4625	0.4633
1.8	0.4641	0.4649	0.4656	0.4664	0.4671	0.4678	0.4686	0.4693	0.4699	0.4706
1.9	0.4713	0.4719	0.4726	0.4732	0.4738	0.4744	0.4750	0.4756	0.4761	0.4767
2.0	0.4772	0.4778	0.4783	0.4788	0.4793	0.4798	0.4803	0.4808	0.4812	0.4817
2.1	0.4821	0.4826	0.4830	0.4834	0.4838	0.4842	0.4846	0.4850	0.4854	0.4857
2.2	0.4861	0.4864	0.4868	0.4871	0.4875	0.4878	0.4881	0.4884	0.4887	0.4890
2.3	0.4893	0.4896	0.4898	0.4901	0.4904	0.4906	0.4909	0.4911	0.4913	0.4916
2.4	0.4918	0.4920	0.4922	0.4925	0.4927	0.4929	0.4931	0.4932	0.4934	0.4936
2.5	0.4938	0.4940	0.4941	0.4943	0.4945	0.4946	0.4948	0.4949	0.4951	0.4952
2.6	0.4953	0.4955	0.4956	0.4957	0.4959	0.4960	0.4961	0.4962	0.4963	0.4964
2.7	0.4965	0.4966	0.4967	0.4968	0.4969	0.4970	0.4971	0.4972	0.4973	0.4974
2.8	0.4974	0.4975	0.4976	0.4977	0.4977	0.4978	0.4979	0.4979	0.4980	0.4981
2.9	0.4981	0.4982	0.4982	0.4983	0.4984	0.4984	0.4985	0.4985	0.4986	0.4986
3.0	0.4987	0.4987	0.4987	0.4988	0.4988	0.4989	0.4989	0.4989	0.4990	0.4990

TABLE OF RANDOM NUMBERS

02711	08182	75997	79866	58095	83319	80295	79741	74599	84379
94873	90935	31684	63952	09865	14491	99518	93394	34691	14985
54921	78680	06635	98689	17306	25170	65928	87709	30533	89736
77640	97636	37397	93379	56454	59818	45827	74164	71666	46977
61545	00835	93251	87203	36759	49197	85967	01704	19634	21898
17147	19519	22497	16857	42426	84822	92598	49186	88247	39967
13748	04742	92460	85801	53444	65626	58710	55406	17173	69776
87455	14813	50373	28037	91182	32786	65261	11173	34376	36408
08999	57409	91185	10200	61411	23392	47797	56377	71635	08601
78804	81333	53809	32471	46034	36306	22498	19239	85428	55721
82173	26921	28472	98958	07960	66124	89731	95069	18625	92405
97594	25168	89178	68190	05043	17407	48201	83917	11413	72920
73881	67176	93504	42636	38233	16154	96451	57925	29667	30859
46071	22912	90326	42453	88108	72064	58601	32357	90610	32921
44492	19686	12495	93135	95185	77799	52441	88272	22024	80631
31864	72170	37722	55794	14636	05148	54505	50113	21119	25228
51574	90692	43339	65689	76539	27909	05467	21727	51141	72949
35350	76132	92925	92124	92634	35681	43690	89136	35599	84138
46943	36502	01172	46045	46991	33804	80006	35542	61056	75666
22665	87226	33304	57975	03985	21566	65796	72915	81466	89205
39437	97957	11838	10433	21564	51570	73558	27495	34533	57808
77082	47784	40098	97962	89845	28392	78187	06112	08169	11261
24544	25649	43370	28007	06779	72402	62632	53956	24709	06978
27503	15558	37738	24849	70722	71859	83736	06016	94397	12529
24590	24545	06435	52758	45685	90151	46516	49644	92686	84870
48155	86226	40359	28723	15364	69125	12609	57171	86857	31702
20226	53752	90648	24362	83314	00014	19207	69413	97016	86290
70178	73444	38790	53626	93780	18629	68766	24371	74639	30782
10169	41465	51935	05711	09799	79077	88159	33437	68519	03040
81084	03701	28598	70013	63794	53169	97054	60303	23259	96196
69202	20777	21727	81511	51887	16175	53746	46516	70339	62727
80561	95787	89426	93325	86412	57479	54194	52153	19197	81877
08199	26703	95128	48599	09333	12584	24374	31232	61782	44032
98883	28220	39358	53720	80161	83371	15181	11131	12219	55920
84568	69286	76054	21615	80883	36797	82845	39139	90900	18172
04269	35173	95745	53893	86022	77722	52498	84193	22448	22571
10538	13124	36099	13140	37706	44562	57179	44693	67877	01549
77843	24955	25900	63843	95029	93859	93634	20205	66294	41218
12034	94636	49455	76362	83532	31062	69903	91186	65768	55949
10524	72829	47641	93315	80875	28090	97728	52560	34937	79548
68935	76632	46984	61772	92786	22651	07086	89754	44143	97687
89450	65665	29190	43709	11172	34481	95977	47535	25658	73898
90696	20451	24211	97310	60446	73530	62865	96574	13829	72226
49006	32047	93086	00112	20470	17136	28255	86328	07293	38809
74591	87025	52368	59416	34417	70557	86746	55809	53628	12000
06315	17012	77103	00968	07235	10728	42189	33292	51487	64443
62386	09184	62092	46617	99419	64230	95034	85481	07857	42510
86848	82122	04028	36959	87827	12813	08627	80699	13345	51695
65643	69480	46598	04501	40403	91408	32343	48130	49303	90689
11084	46534	78957	77353	39578	77868	22970	84349	09184	70603

STUDENT *t* DISTRIBUTION

df	Level of significance for one-tailed test					
	.10	.05	.025	.01	.005	.0005
	Level of significance for two-tailed test					
	.20	.10	.05	.02	.01	.001
1	3.078	6.314	12.706	31.821	63.657	636.619
2	1.886	2.920	4.303	6.965	9.925	31.599
3	1.638	2.353	3.182	4.541	5.841	12.924
4	1.533	2.132	2.776	3.747	4.604	8.610
5	1.476	2.015	2.571	3.365	4.032	6.869
6	1.440	1.943	2.447	3.143	3.707	5.959
7	1.415	1.895	2.365	2.998	3.499	5.408
8	1.397	1.860	2.306	2.896	3.355	5.041
9	1.383	1.833	2.262	2.821	3.250	4.781
10	1.372	1.812	2.228	2.764	3.169	4.587
11	1.363	1.796	2.201	2.718	3.106	4.437
12	1.356	1.782	2.179	2.681	3.055	4.318
13	1.350	1.771	2.160	2.650	3.012	4.221
14	1.345	1.761	2.145	2.624	2.977	4.140
15	1.341	1.753	2.131	2.602	2.947	4.073
16	1.337	1.746	2.120	2.583	2.921	4.015
17	1.333	1.740	2.110	2.567	2.898	3.965
18	1.330	1.734	2.101	2.552	2.878	3.922
19	1.328	1.729	2.093	2.539	2.861	3.883
20	1.325	1.725	2.086	2.528	2.845	3.850
21	1.323	1.721	2.080	2.518	2.831	3.819
22	1.321	1.717	2.074	2.508	2.819	3.792
23	1.319	1.714	2.069	2.500	2.807	3.768
24	1.318	1.711	2.064	2.492	2.797	3.745
25	1.316	1.708	2.060	2.485	2.787	3.725
26	1.315	1.706	2.056	2.479	2.779	3.707
27	1.314	1.703	2.052	2.473	2.771	3.690
28	1.313	1.701	2.048	2.467	2.763	3.674
29	1.311	1.699	2.045	2.462	2.756	3.659
30	1.310	1.697	2.042	2.457	2.750	3.646
40	1.303	1.684	2.021	2.423	2.704	3.551
60	1.296	1.671	2.000	2.390	2.660	3.460
120	1.289	1.658	1.980	2.358	2.617	3.373
∞	1.282	1.645	1.960	2.326	2.576	3.291